# Magical Energy Healing:

# The Ruach Healing Method

By

Robert Zink & Rachael Haas

# MAGICAL ENERGY HEALING:
## THE RUACH HEALING METHOD

ROBERT ZINK & RACHAEL HAAS

ILLUSTRATED BY JOHN ASHTON GOLDEN

Published by
Law of Attraction Solutions, LLC
3439 NE Sandy Blvd #124
Portland, OR 97232

www.lawofattractionsolutions.com

ISBN: 978-0-9908250-3-6

*Dedicated to Judith Evelyn Reib,*

*for the healing she brought to an entire community*

*and the Light she gave to the World.*

## ACKNOWLEDGMENTS

Over the last 20 years, in the process of refining the information contained in this book, many people provided contributions for which without them this book would never have been completed. The acknowledgment you are reading does not even scratch the surface of how deeply thankful and grateful I am to these individuals.

The Healing Circle is a Sacred Space and the Community of Healers are a Sacred Family. There are so many people in my Healing Circle and Community that influenced and mentored me who deserve an acknowledgment. These people brought true healing into the world. I am forever indebted to S.L. MacGregor Mathers, who codified an entire system of magic from which my studies have drawn upon. Others who poured their healing energy into my Sacred Circle are the late John Gold and Don C. Squire, Sr. These two individuals nurtured me at a very young time in my life after losing my mother. I must also send my gratitude to the late Donald Michael Kraig who inspired my magical studies and gave me several ideas on blending the idea of the chakras with the Tree of Life.

Another that influenced me from a very young age, in fact from my birth, was my mother Dorthye L. Zink, R.N. From the time I can remember, I was blessed with a curiosity of healing and how it works. It was my dear mother who fed this curiosity by allowing me to spend countless hours exploring her medical and nursing books. She even helped teach me how to draw the human skeleton.

As I continue to look around my healing circle there are countless others who encouraged me and helped me to perfect the Ruach Healing Method. I cannot forget to mention my Reiki Master, Victoria Lanakila Generao. She initiated me into Usui Teate Reiki, teaching me to be a conduit of Divine Light. Her openness to Light and Love is a healing inspiration to all who know her. I must also thank Reiki Master Steve A. Sarlaí for all the encouragement through the years and his active creation in Ruach Healing Workshops.

I would also like to take a moment to give special thanks to a few more people. Thank you to John Golden for all the incredible art work and illustrations he created. I pushed him hard and he did not disappoint me. Thanks to Angela Vennum and Chad Thursby for all their spelling and editing help; I know it was not easy. I must extend my deepest thanks and gratitude to my partner and co-author Rachael Haas who inspired and kicked me at the same time, to get this book done so that others may benefit. She is an incredible natural healer, who has a wonderful sixth sense for the healing process.

Finally words cannot convey my appreciation to all the students, brothers and sisters who helped evolve and develop this incredible system of healing. One of these healing brothers that helped the Ruach Healing Method evolve is Ramses Arce. He is one of the most gifted healers in the world. His techniques and ideas are incredible but more importantly they are loving and spiritual. Another that played an important role in the evolution of Ruach Healing is Lisa (Harris) Rosillo, who allowed me countless hours to heal her migraines and other conditions. She is a true inspiration to me and others; I wish I could have done more for her. It was all those hours working with her that taught me how to deal more effectively with stubborn illnesses. I must also thank my very first patient, Jim. His memory continues to inspire me to this day. You will read of Jim's story throughout this book.

My gratitude goes out to all those who have attended a Ruach Healing Workshop. As well as, all those that have shared with me their time, energy and enthusiasm for this book.

Finally, the spiritual information and knowledge that is contained within this book does not come from one person. It comes from a Healing Community, a family of healers. There are so many people, some I have not heard from in years, that played a role in influencing my healing journey. I cannot think of all their names as some of them have long passed in and out of my life. However, I do truly remember their energy. I am grateful that they are a part of my healing family. My deepest thanks goes out to all of you.

Light in Extension,

Robert Zink

Grand Master and Founder of the Ruach Healing Method

# Table of Contents

## Table Index

## Illustration Index

# FORWARD

Aloha e komo mai oukou … Greetings and Welcome to All!

I am a Reiki practitioner of Mikao Usui's System of Natural Healing as propagated from Japan through Sensei Chris Marsh, Sensei Steve Taggert and Sensei Hiroshi Doi as Usui Teate Reiki. I run the THE HALAU Sanctuarium Ordinis Melchisedech. The Halau is also a Sanctuarium of the Alpha et Omega Order of Melchizedek. This school teaches many healing modalities. One of which is Usui Shiki Ryoho Reiki. This is the system most practitioners in mainland America know, as it was taught by Sensei Hawayo Tanaka in Hawai'i. I always encourage my students to enlarge their energy-working knowledge and experience by training in advanced Reiki techniques, as well as, non-Reiki "energy-working" systems; like the Ruach Healing Method.

Many cultures have known since ancient times that an unseen energy flows through all living things. This energy is directly connected to the quality of health we experience. This energy is the basis for the Ruach Healing Method. In recent scientific experiments, this "life force" energy has been verified as measurable and definable. Medical physicians now consider the role that life force energy plays in the functioning of the immune system and the body's healing processes.

Reiki is a healing practice that taps into life force energy. Because this energy has intelligence, it has the ability to improve health in mind, body and spirit. Learning about healing and learning to heal are journeys that require a conscious partnership between your physical/emotional body and your spiritual self. This partnership is an important expression of an individual's multidimensional perception of the surrounding multi-verse. The Ruach Healing Method does all this and MORE! While Reiki works with energy, Ruach Healing works with energy, colors, Planets, Elements, and the Tree of Life.

The *"goal"* of the Ruach Healing Method is the activation of your spiritual energy field. In Reiki the spiritual energy field, and development into a spiritual Merkaba allows your consciousness to expand and experience the higher dimensions of this universe. The Ruach Healing Method further activates of the higher dimensional levels of spiritual energy fields allowing your consciousness to expand even further. Learning the Magical Ruach Healing Method is an important path to include on your journey. I recommend every serious healing practitioner study and consider incorporating the methodologies described here. The Ruach Healing Method allows you to enjoy an expansive multidimensional healing experiences. The sacred techniques described within these pages will open you to the actual, personal experience of "walking between worlds."

The *"path"* of the Ruach Healing Method is a non-linear process, yet it has an overall structure or pattern. It is not a measurement of your personal spiritual achievement. The trans-mutational stages can take years, months, or a few minutes to move through depending on the will of spirit and karmic influences. Each person has a unique vibrational pattern or light signature, the LOVE that you are as originally sparked by Ke Akua: your Aloha Spirit. The Ruach Healing process activates different patterns in accordance with the particular level or levels that you are consciously and unconsciously processing in your present life experience. Your soul and divine blueprint determines where you are in any given moment of your evolution and what is needed to best serve your own purpose as a Healer.

The *"way"* of the Ruach Healing Method is a union of different aspects of ceremonial magic, the Emerald Tablet, the Tree of Life and associated teachings in Kabbalah. The ancient teachings of Tree of Life illustrate divine emanations of creation of everything in the universe. Metaphorically, these teachings are alchemical references for further perfection of the soul. These wonderful teachings frame the healing concepts of the Ruach Healing Method and we invite you to enjoy them within these pages. Understanding how Light emanates is essential to competency as an energy worker, but the way is not easily discernible. The Tree of Life provides that very road map for the Ruach Healer.

The *"reward"* of the Ruach Healing Method is experiencing another level of energy sensitivity that you can heal the world with. The amount of energy received and integrated will be exactly that which will best serve your highest intent at that particular moment in time. All this energy empowers your healing abilities; as you grow you will see amazing rewards in your patients. The greatest way to serve God, serve all mankind, serve the planet, and serve ourselves is to create lives, moment by moment, as masterpieces of "Healing Joy". This is Aloha.

Each of us must first create in our own lives what we desire in our families, communities, societies and countries to be able to shift the entire global collective. As you proceed on this new aspect of your healing journey, you will begin living a new life pattern of change... from being numb to violence, polarity and disease, to being receptive and reflective of a world of peace, compassion and equality in being One with each other and the environment. Your new reality, perceptions alchemically gleaned between the lines while studying the Ruach Healing Method, will positively attract clarity through acceptance, forgiveness and love manifesting in your own life. Your healing abilities and capabilities expand by studying the techniques of the Ruach Healing Method and adding that proficiency to your metaphysical tool bag makes you a co-creator of Heaven on Earth.

I have had the honor and pleasure of learning lessons of invaluable knowledge and understanding from my mentor in ceremonial magic and the Ruach Healing Method, Robert Zink. I remember seeing Robert in the lobby of a temple gathering and he excitedly told me, "Hey Lana, I've got something for you: it's Reiki on steroids!", and he wasn't kidding. The man knows his stuff! For several years now, my students have learned the Ruach Healing Method alongside our advanced Reiki kotodama. The two systems are complementary blended, and yield consistently positive healing results when competently applied. Carpe diem. "Seek to learn that you may serve" is the call you answered when you picked up this book … well done! Run towards this emanation of Light because ***all knowledge is not contained in only one school.***

In Love, Unity and Peace … Aloha Ke Akua.

Rev. Dr. Victoria Lanakila Generao, JD, PhD

Reiki Grandmaster, 18th Dan

HPS, A&O Order of Melchizedek

# INTRODUCTION

*Before you read this book, understand that at times you will read the word "I" and at other times you will read the word "we". When the word "I" is used, it is speaking of Robert Zink and generally his experience over the last 2 ½ decades as a healer. When the word "we" is used, it is speaking of Robert Zink and Rachael Haas. The instances of "we" are generally related to both of their teachings, healing concepts, and philosophy.*

*Another thing to keep in mind is the use of "energy field" and "aura". The "energy field" includes everything from the electricity in the brain, heart, and aura, while the "aura" is only the vibrational current around the body. While there is a technical difference between energy field and aura, for the purposes of this book at times they are interchanged and used synonymously.*

The goal of the Ruach Healing Method is to empower you as a healer and discover your continuous life-giving connection to Divine Source, so that you might use this connection for healing yourself, others, and the world at large. This book contains many tools and techniques for developing a unique magical healer's relationship to the Divine. As your connection to Divine Source grows, you will learn how to focus and share your connection so that others may receive extraordinary and astonishing healing. Your hands are your sacred tools for magical healing and the Ruach Healing Method. The force that flows through your hands and carries with it healing power is called **"Ruach"**. Ruach is the source of all life, healing and miracles. Prepare yourself to move into a world where your intentions, focus, visualization and actions do incredible things.

Magical healing, no matter what the system or modality, is about the healer's unique synergy and profound understanding that s/he is both *in* the Divine Source and the Divine Source is *within.* The true magical healer becomes a conduit for amazing healing and restoration of the spiritual, emotional and physical body. As you begin to learn and train in the Ruach Healing Method, you will awaken forces and powers within yourself that you may have never realized existed. We believe you have the ability to change lives, so let's begin.

We will start at the beginning with a simple question; "What is Ruach?". The word Ruach itself finds its source in Hebrew. Ruach is the life force that we all emerge from. Ruach is the creative energy that originates from Divine Source. Ruach is a concept taught in the Kabbalah. Kabbalah is the foundation for much of the information in this book. There are thousands of books on the Kabbalah, but for the purposes of Ruach Healing, our study will be kept basic, focusing mostly on the Tree of Life and how to practically apply Ruach or Life Force for healing.

As you can imagine, the subject of Kabbalah can become quite detailed and fascinating. There are many possible levels of understanding Kabbalah. For our purposes, however, it is *only* necessary to understand how to apply these concepts to regenerate healthy cells and optimize healing. We want to make it clear up front that this is *not* a book about Kabbalah, although Kabbalah provides us with a deeper understanding of the energies we will use in the Ruach Healing Method.

The Ruach Healing Method is more than Kabbalistic. It draws from Hermeticism, Healing Touch, Energy Therapy, and Reiki, as well as, other forms of healing that have developed out of various magical healing techniques. However, there is no denying the large Kabbalistic influence on the Ruach Healing Method.

Along with the Kabbalistic information, the Ruach Healing Method draws upon the knowledge of the Esoteric Order of the Golden Dawn. While we will apply some Golden Dawn concepts, this is not another "notorious" Golden Dawn book. This book is for serious healers who genuinely want to learn how to apply esoteric wisdom to practical healing. The Ruach Healing Method is in a category all its own.

You will notice that this book is divided into two sections. The first section is "Theory" and the second is "Healing". As with learning any new skill, there must be some background knowledge that creates the foundation for the practical application. If you have never studied the Kabbalah, don't feel frustrated or overwhelmed with all the information in the Theory section. It is okay and recommended to read and reread anything you need, until you grasp the concepts.

As you study the Theory of Ruach Healing, you will understand the nature of the "Deity" and the Three Veils of Negative-Existence as they pertain to healing. The veils are: Ain, Ain Soph and Ain Soph Aur. We will briefly discuss what they are, what they mean, and why using Kabbalah to develop a relationship with the Divine Source is a powerful modality that will greatly aid you to be an effective healer. So, while the basics of the Three Veils of Negative-Existence are discussed for healing purposes, an in-depth study can be done which falls outside the scope of this book.

Advanced healing techniques are taught using the Three Veils to Master Ruach Healers in workshops.

You may ask why learning all this theory is important. It's important because it is what differentiates the Ruach Practitioner from medical practitioners and purely intuitive healers, with absolutely no training. Medical Practitioners spend years in medical school learning to understand the mechanics of the body and its functions. Their focus is on surgical techniques and the use of pharmaceuticals to relieve conditions. In contrast, a Ruach Healer is awakening various life giving energies that originate from Divine Source. That being said, it is absolutely necessary to create and maintain a relationship with the Divine; be it God, Divine Source, the gods, the Universe, Buddha or however you define the creative force of the universe.

In the process of connecting with the Divine, you will come to understand the Tree of Life as a powerful mandala for healing. The concept of the Tree of Life goes back to the book of Genesis. From it we have taken a description of ten numbers and twenty-two letters. According to Rabbi Aryeh Kaplan in his wonderful book titled, *"Sefer Yetzirah: The Book of Creation"*, "the ten numbers are the Sephirot which are the most basic concepts of existence, and the twenty-two letters represent different levels of consciousness which interconnect the Sephirot". We will also discuss the Sephirot and how they fit into the

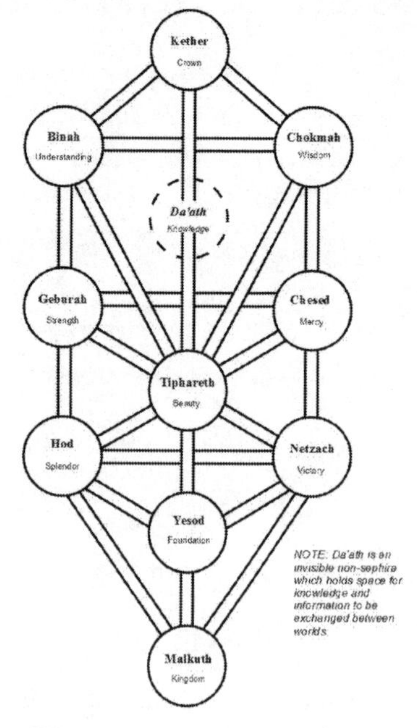


*Illustration 1: Tree of Life*

healing process. At this level, we will not cover the paths within the Tree of Life. This is more advanced work and will be covered in another book or at a weekend Ruach Healing workshop.

Your magical healing abilities will continue to grow as you learn to utilize the Divine names of God, Archangels, Angels, and Choir of Angels in relation to the Sephirot, Elements, and Planets. You will be invoking these Divine and Angelic names in the healing process. If this sounds like a lot of work, it is not, but it will require your attention. When you invoke the color, the Divine Name, the Angel etc. you have effectively created a lens by which to focus the Divine White Brilliance (D.W.B.).

One of the more curious things we will cover is the "Vitality Gates". They are similar to the chakras, with the exception that in our studies and experiences with thousands of patients, it is evident that these Vitality Gates work in a paddle wheel fashion, bringing in life force energy into the energy field of the human body, and taking out waste. The Vitality Gates accomplish all of the things chakras do, but with the added benefit of spiritual waste removal.

*Illustration 2: Emerald Tablet of Hermes*

The Ruach Healing Method provided a study of the astral body. The interaction between the subtle body, or the energy field, and the physical body is extremely intimate. It is in this unique connection, between the energy field and the physical body that we see perhaps the greatest expression of the Emerald Tablet of Hermes. **"As above, so below, and as below, so above."** In general, the whole of spiritual healing, works on the premise, that if we can affect the subtle body, we can also affect the physical body.

The study of the Ruach Healing Theory will include exercises for you to use to protect yourself as a healer. It is extremely important for the Ruach Healer to maintain his or her energy in the Divine, so as not to absorb anything that is being removed from the patient. Many of the exercises used for protection are borrowed and/or modified from the Golden Dawn tradition. Once again we will remind you that this is not a book on the Golden Dawn; it is a book of manifesting yourself as a healer.

As you can see, there is much to comprehend from the theory of Ruach Healing. The second section of this book on healing is very practical with hands on exercises. You will learn how to start the healing process by fact-finding. It is extremely important to talk with your patients to uncover the knowledge of what is going on in their body. Questioning and kinesiology (muscle testing) will allow you to directly heal any issue the patient might be suffering from.

Fact-finding leads to scanning the patient. You will learn how to scan for congestion and depletion in the patient's energy field. You will learn how to create and use an "Astral Fire Container" for all that you cleanse out of the patient. This book will then describe how to charge the aura of the patient and untangle the "Vitality Rays" for maximum healing effect. Your work on the patient will conclude with the sealing of the aura, using the power of the mystical symbol of the Rose and Cross. This book will then empower your scanning, cleansing, charging, and sealing of the patient with details on how to utilize Elemental and Planetary healing techniques.

These techniques become the foundation for a full understanding of what we refer to as "Long Distance Healing." As the name implies, this is the process of performing healing work on someone who is in a different physical location than the healer. The patient could live on the other side of the city, across the state, or even on the other side of the world. The best part about it, is that you use the same basic healing techniques whether the patient is in the same room with you or located remotely.

As you practice the Ruach Healing Method, you will find that it is possible to perform healing on two people who have identical illnesses with each experiencing varying degrees of results. If this happens do not be discouraged. Healing is an art; the subject of healing is as complex as human beings themselves. There is no way to know in advance if someone will be healed or helped in any way. It may be that the patient will be healed at a later time, or in a deeper and more profound way than you as a healer can imagine. Trust in the Universe and Divine Source is essential. As the saying goes, "Man proposes and God disposes."

# NOTES:

# PART I: THEORY

## NOTES:

# CHAPTER 1: The Big Breakthrough: How the Ruach Healing Method Came to Life

Jim hadn't been around for 3 - 4 months. He was a student of mine in our local Golden Dawn Lodge. At this point in my life, I had been studying and teaching Kabbalah for about fifteen years. My studies also included ceremonial magic through the Esoteric Order of the Golden Dawn, Hermetics, Hypnosis and a profound curiosity about how life works on this planet. It was about 10 o'clock at night, class had just let out, and for the most part, everyone had departed. I heard a knock on the door and thought somebody must have forgotten something. It was Jim.

Now, I remembered Jim as about 6'2" and weighed in at about 200 pounds. I recalled that Jim was fairly muscular and glowed with a healthy tan, but when I answered the door that night, I was shocked. There stood an emaciated human being that looked but a few beats away from the grave. His mother was out in the car with the engine running. Jim delivered the grim news to me...he was dying of AIDS and he asked for my healing help. He was hoping that I knew some sort of ceremonial rite I could perform that might give him a fighting chance. I may repeat several times throughout this book that I am not the creator of the Ruach Healing Method; I merely took the **Awakenings** given to me through mentors and Masters of Esoteric Magic and codified it into an easy-to-use, workable system. I received the Awakenings and now, through this book and workshops, seek to pass the Awakenings and knowledge of the Ruach Healing Method on to others.

That night something amazing happened. I asked Jim to take a seat in the chair that I purposely placed in the center of the room. I could feel the sickness sucking the life-force out of him. I began to get in touch with those feelings...What exactly was this energy? Was I feeling the eternal spirit that lives within all of us, including Jim? Or, was I feeling the subtle body, the etheric body, that some would call the energy field or the astral self? Like a ton of bricks falling on me, I realized for certain that I felt the subtle waves of Jim's energy field. Suddenly, my hands were reaching out inches away from his withering energy field. I began to feel holes and gaps; somewhat similar to the holes you would see in Swiss cheese. Other areas of the energy surrounding Jim felt hard or congested. My heart was jumping out of my chest! I realized that I was in touch with Jim's energy field on a deeper level than I had ever felt before.

Over the years I have refined my methods for scanning the energy field, which you will learn as you read on in future chapters. Jim had a profound effect on me because he was totally and completely open to anything I wanted to try. In reflection, I recall waiting for the bi-weekly T-cell and viral count, so I could immediately adjust my techniques to further improve the results of these tests. I believe that it is important to note that this was before there were many medications available to treat HIV or AIDS. In the three months that I performed healing on Jim, I discovered how the Kabbalistic Tree of Life interacted with the energy field. I learned that what the Eastern traditions call chakras really acted quite differently in relation to the human energy field on the body then what most traditions taught. This was a big revelation at the time, and will be expanded upon later in this book. I not only developed the ability to feel Jim's energy field, but also how to see and test it as well.

Jim kept improving. Each week color was creeping back into his cheeks, weight was increasing, and vitality was returning into his being. Everyone who knew of Jim, including his physicians, was *astonished.* I had worked together with Jim for several months adding new energies to his body. Then, as quickly as he had come into my life, Jim was gone. I called his home, but no one answered. I even drove over to his house on numerous occasions, but still no Jim.

Three months later, that familiar late night knock on the door happened. Before answering the door, I already knew it was Jim. He had gained sixty-five pounds, his T-cell count was normal, showed no signs of AIDS whatsoever and he had just returned from a long vacation in Hawaii. Jim looked great, appeared healthy, and more importantly....he felt great! He thanked me for the work I had done, and I thanked him for trusting me and all the mystics and masters that I had culled this information from. Jim was a happy man and so was I. His life would never be the same and neither would mine. From that moment on, I devoted a significant amount of my time to reading literally any book I could find on spiritual, mystical and magical healing. I know that as you continue to read this book, you will develop skills that will thrill you to the core as you see miracles manifest themselves right before your eyes!

Shortly after working with Jim, I began to develop a positive obsession with scanning nearly everyone's energy field. I wanted to know as much as I could, so in a sense, each patient became a teacher as I would scan their energy field and learn to magically charge it. I began to apply various sounds and symbols to my healing work. While I had some unbelievable victories, I also discovered some startling facts about myself and the healing process in general. You must have a clean energy field in order to clean your patient's energy field.

The universe has an interesting way of connecting people for the purpose of teaching us great things. Susan was a friend of mine who introduced me to a dear friend of hers that was a construction worker who had suffered a tragic accident. His name was Pete. When I first met Pete, I found it hard to believe that this scrawny little guy was indeed a construction worker. Pete had a Spirit, as tough as the nails he pounded into the wood. He had three vertebrae knocked out of place, and you could literally see them protruding from his back, somewhat similar to that of a reptile. Surgery was out of the question, as the risk of full paralysis was extremely high. Pete was in constant pain; the only relief he received came from his weekly visit to the chiropractor and a constant flow of Vicodin. When I first met him, he was walking with the support of two canes.

I will never forget the first time I used the Ruach Healing Method on Pete. We were sitting out in our backyard, on a nice, warm, sunny California day. I believe the Sun to be a vital energy source, so working outdoors provided a very positive environment to perform healing. After a thorough scanning of Pete, especially in his spinal region, I quickly discovered that I was able to move energy up and down his spine. The next thing I knew, Pete was vomiting all over my lawn. I didn't realize it at the time, but I soon discovered that anyone who was a non-smoker got either a queasy stomach, felt dizzy, or vomited when I did Ruach on their spinal area. The reason was quite simple... My energy field was not clean! It was permeated with the filth that comes from being a cigarette smoker. I apologize if I am offending any smokers reading this book and I am certainly not suggesting that you totally abstain from healing work. Just know that you run the risk of making a lot of people sick if you continue to contaminate your body and energy field with cigarettes.

There are chemical processes in the body that are dynamic and affect every aspect of our being, especially our ability to acquire, control, and direct energy. Finding a balanced diet that works for you is very important as well. I am not pushing any one diet. It is up to you to find it. You must find one that optimizes how you feel. Putting toxins in your body is going to automatically mitigate health and vital energy over a period of time. Eventually, those toxins will show up in your energy field. Does that mean you can't do Ruach Healing on people if you smoke or drink regularly? No, that's not the case. No one is expecting you to be perfect, but eventually you find that living a healthy lifestyle and eating a proper diet will improve your abilities and effectiveness as a healer. What is important is that if you have addictions, such as nicotine, that you focus on eliminating the addiction to achieve your maximum healing potential. *You are less effective as a healer when you need healing yourself.* An unhealed healer can create problems for those that come to them for help.

## Simple Methods for Cleaning Your Own Aura

Later in the book, we will share more formal methods of cleaning, protecting, and energizing your own or other people's auras. During the time I worked with Pete, I made some simple yet remarkable discoveries. The following are some of my discoveries. You might be familiar with some of these through modern research and scientific studies that were not available at the time I discovered them.

- **Drinking fresh spring water beforehand helps to invigorate the energy field; cleanses and clears it of negative energies and lower vibrations that cause sickness.**

- **Bicycle riding or exercising of some sort provides the vitality necessary for the healer to work on an individual with a severe injury.**

- **Decreasing meat intake, down to a couple times per week, while increasing your fish intake and/or adding nuts to your diet. Reducing meat intake helps to optimize your physical condition and aura. Some people find drinking milk makes it easier to maintain a vegetarian diet, if one is able to handle dairy protein.**

- **Performing the Four-Fold Breath meditation; for ten to fifteen minutes before healing work increases the stability and vitality of the healers own energy field (Detailed directions in Chapter 2).**

I confess that I didn't quit smoking at the time, but I did cut back. This resulted in Pete no longer having instances of nausea during the healing work I did for him. I worked on Pete for approximately ten days before he threw away his canes for good. Three weeks later, he was springing from the diving board at his apartment swimming pool. I still don't fully know how it happened; it seemed impossible even to his chiropractor that his vertebrae could be readjusting on its own. Shortly thereafter, Pete threw away the Vicodin, and he and Susan moved to the southern part of the USA. I received regular reports for some time from Susan, every report being positive. He went back to work and is healthy, happy, and thankful. I like Miracles!

## My Simple Philosophy of Ruach Healing

The goals of the spiritual healer are to relieve physical maladies, reduce the severity of major illnesses, and increase the rate of healing when used in combination with conventional medicine and medication. From my beginning, and the healing experiences with Jim, my healing philosophy began to evolve. My healing evolution developed as I read hundreds of books on the subject, and with each one come a philosophy. Mine is rather simple:

> ***"I believe that spiritual healing from the Ruach Healing Method can relieve chronic disease conditions by harmonizing the subtle body or energy field to the Divine Source using the Tree of Life as a guideline."***

One benefit of Ruach Healing is referred to as "compressed morbidity." This idea of *compressed morbidity* is key in our philosophy of the Ruach Healing Method. The concept is simple: a long, high quality life with a short dying time at the end is what compressed morbidity is. In reality, we all have a terminal disease called "*life*". Eventually we all die, but what will our quality of life be while we live? People want to live as long as possible. They want to live lives that are pain free and disease free, in order to remain independent, to think independently, and to act independently. At the end of our lives, we can drift off to sleep, later discovering that we have died and gone to the next life. Compressed morbidity is a shortened time of suffering at the very end of our existence. No one wants to go through the extended morbidity that many people have today, going in and out of nursing homes and/or hospitals, suffering from chronic disease.

All the techniques needed to accomplish this are found in this book. For a complete well rounded healing experience, please read this entire book before applying the techniques.

**Please note:** We recommend that all recipients continue seeing their doctors, and following their doctor's advice for surgery or medications. We are not trying to replace Western medicine or any medical system that the recipient is currently using. Our goal is to synergize our healing work with other medical modalities.

**The Ruach Healing Creed**

***To provide a greater opportunity of having a wonderful, long life of eighty, ninety, or even one hundred years or more, and then pass on simply and easily. We want people to live a quality lifestyle for as long as they possibly can.***

# CHAPTER TWO: What is the Ruach Healing Method & How Does It Work?

In the quest for true healing we seek Divine Source. Divine Source is the most potent of spiritual forces for healing. In truth it is the *ONLY* source of healing. It is the very life force that animates the universe and everything in it. The sacred force that emanates from Divine Source is called by many names, but in the tradition of the Kabbalah it is called **"Ruach"**.

Everything we do in the Ruach Healing Method is about using or molding this powerful force for healing. When there is a lack of Ruach in the energy field, weakness or even illness is highly likely. Fortunately, we as healers can invoke this powerful force and correct the imbalance in the energy field, ultimately creating healing in the physical body.

## What is Ruach?

What exactly is this powerful force called "Ruach" that the Ruach Healer uses to change the energy field of a patient and bring healing to the body. Ruach is the life force, also called ***"Chi", "Prana", "Universal Life Force", or "Orgone".*** In Hebrew, Ruach is another word for "air" or "breath". Although the Hebrew word has various meanings, including the name of the human personality in the Kabbalah, Ruach is a primal energy from which all mental and physical energy evolved. Ruach is the creative energy that originates from Divine Source.

The Latin root of the word virtue is *virtus*. The word Virtus in Latin means, strength, or energy, or force. This force or energy is referred to in the Bible as well. Simply substitute the word virtue for Ruach and it all begins to makes sense, because that is exactly what Ruach *is*. Ruach is life force, or power, strength, or energy, virtue. The entire New Testament is about the invocation of virtue for the purposes of healing. In the example of the bleeding women, Mark 5:30 (KJV) says *"And Jesus, immediately knowing in himself that virtue had gone out of him, turned him about in the press, and said, Who touched my clothes?"*. Another example of healing virtue is found in Luke 6:19 (KJV), *"And the whole multitude sought to touch him: for there went virtue out of him, and healed them all."* An example in the book of Acts shows the powerful Ruach Peter held. *"Insomuch that they brought forth the sick into the streets, and laid them on beds and couches, that at the least the shadow of Peter passing by might overshadow some of them. There came also a multitude out of the cities round about unto Jerusalem, bringing sick folks, and them which were vexed with unclean spirits: and they were healed every one."* Acts 5:15,16 (KJV). Peter must have had an astonishing energy field. Directly, Peter had power, energy, and strength. Or, another word would simply be, he was filled with virtue or Ruach.

## Origins of Ruach

The Ruach Healing Method differs from some other healing systems in that Kabbalist believe all Ruach originates from one singularity or Divine Source. Ruach can be tinctured through various filters, such as the Elements, Planets and Sephirot (levels of consciousness on the Tree of Life) but ultimately its origin is the Divine Singularity. Since antiquity, Jews depicted this unity or oneness in perhaps their most sacred verse of the Torah called the "**Shema**". It reads, *"Here oh Israel the Lord our God the Lord is one"* (Deuteronomy 6:4). Rosicrucian adepts in the Golden Dawn also symbolize this unity with the mystical formula of the notarikon or acronym called A.R.A.R.I.T.A. The word is formed from the first letters of the sentence: Achad Rosh Achdotho Rosh Ichudo Temurahzo Achad, which means, **"One is His beginning, One is His individuality, His permutation is One."** It affirms the ultimate divinity is unitary in nature. All things come from and return back to the singularity of Source.

## Where is Ruach?

Ruach is the Divine energy which permeates everything in the universe. Although there can be other interpretations for the word Ruach, we are focusing on one. Ruach is essentially "breath" or Spirit. It is the life force which comes from a Source we refer to as **"Divine White Brilliance"**. This Divine Energy or Ruach divides itself into a variety of forms and these forms correspond to various Sephirot on the Tree of Life. The flow of energy on the Tree of Life shows how the universe was created. This same concept may be overlaid on the human form. When this is done, we see how different varieties of Ruach and universal energies relate to specific areas of the human body. More importantly, from a healing perspective the Sephirot relate to levels of consciousness.

If you still have trouble grasping an understanding of Ruach, you may also think of it as the fifth element of the universe, namely, Spirit. Regardless of which term you use, the Spirit or Ruach energies are constantly flowing through every part of the universe. Spirit or Ruach is what activates the basic elements of Earth, Air, Fire and Water. Those basic elements are represented by the four lower points of a pentagram. The upper point is Spirit, or Ruach. The human body, composed of all five elements, can be seen in all points of the pentagram. With a little imagination you can imagine a human body with arms and legs outstretched forming a human pentagram.

The Pentagram is a simple geometric figure that represents the power of Ruach presiding over the lower four elements. These elements are given life through Ruach. Unfortunately, Hollywood has given the pentagram a bad name. When displayed "upside down," it is a symbol of matter ruling over Spirit. In this way it is a symbol of ignorance. The Ruach Healing Method only employs the "right side up" pentagram as a symbol. Please refer to the illustration above.

*Illustration 3: Pentagram*

The Ruach Healing Method is timeless because Ruach energy itself is timeless. It is always everywhere. Ruach force manifests in the form of motion, gravitation, and magnetism that sustains physical life, thought force and bodily action. Ruach is the primordial, absolute cosmic energy found everywhere. It exists outside the electromagnetic spectrum, away from all other forces and energies known by science. When we breathe we are inhaling life force, energizing ourselves with concentrated Ruach. When we exhale, we are exhaling the energy that we have used, energy that is no longer necessary. Our bodies are constantly in a state of receiving energy or expelling unwanted or unnecessary energy. In this way, the human body is similar to a circuit. Energy comes in from the cosmos then is used in the body and is expelled back into the cosmos.

Some of the ways of receiving energy are sleep, exercise, food, sunlight and breathing. There are also various ways of getting rid of used or unnecessary energy. Examples of these are excrement, urine, perspiration and exhalation. Removing used energy is highly important because if it remained in our bodies it will become toxic. The same danger exists in relation to the thoughts we have. How do we remove thoughts which can become toxic to our thinking? Toxic thoughts can affect our bodies as well as our minds because of the mind-body connection. In order to bring about permanent healing, whether it is caused by physical, mental or emotional problems, we must correct the cause. This means that sometimes we must deal with negative thoughts. Negative thoughts, like negative energy, must be expelled in order to have any lasting effects. If we ignore negative thoughts we risk the possibility that the physical problem will return in the future.

## Connecting to Ruach by Breathing

Breathing has a vital role in connecting the Ruach Healer to the receiving of Ruach that is everywhere all the time. Calming the breath is the first step in making the connection with Divine White Brilliance. When your breath is calm and flowing your energy is also calm and flowing. The breath exercise called the Four Fold Breath creates a clean environment for the Divine White Brilliance to be channeled through.

The Four Fold Breath will help you prepare for healing work. Learning to control one's breathing in a deep, regular, harmonic rhythm helps to increase and energize the sphere of sensation of the body. This exercise is a powerful tool for increasing the amount of healthy Ruach flowing through your energy field, while putting you in a higher yet deeper state of mental consciousness. Learning to control your breathing is the foundation to much of the healing work that flows in this book. Our suggestion is that you practice this exercise once a day. Start with maybe 4-5 minutes and slowly increase your time doing the Four Fold Breath work to 15-20 minutes. You will be amazed at how good your body begins to feel within a few short days.

## Exercise : The Four Fold Breath

*"Breath is evidence of Life." – Golden Dawn Neophyte Initiation*

**Step 1:**

Empty the lungs and remain thus while counting to four.

**Step 2:**

Inhale, counting to four, so that you feel filled with breath from the bottom of your lungs up to your neck or throat area.

**Step 3:**

Hold this breath while counting to four.

**Step 4:**

Exhale counting to four until your lungs are empty.

This should be practiced counting slowly and quietly until you find a rhythm that suits you and helps you feel comfortable and still. Having attained this, count the breath for 2-3 minutes or until you are completely quieted and relaxed. You may then proceed with a meditation or healing work.

**How Ruach Flows; Invoking Divine White Brilliance**

We now understand that Ruach is the life force that originates from Divine Source and is everywhere and always present. We have also connected to Ruach through the Four Fold Breath. So how does the Ruach Healer make the Ruach energy we have just connected to flow through themselves to the patient? The ancient sage, Hermes Trismegistus gives us the understanding of the flow of Ruach in the *"Emerald Tablet"*.

The Ruach Healing Method is based on the time-tested principles taught to humankind through the *"Emerald Tablet of Hermes"*. The Secret of Hermes, as it is sometimes called, dates back to antiquity. The oldest copy of the Emerald Tablet dates back to the 6th Century. Nobody knows how old it is and who actually wrote it. The claim is that this astonishing tablet was written by Hermes Trismegistus. He was considered the wisest of sages by the ancients. Some actually believed he was the Egyptian God of Magic called "Thoth".

The Emerald Tablet was highly regarded by European Alchemists. There are various Interpretations of the Emerald Tablet, however, there is one sentence found in all interpretations of the Emerald Tablet that acts as a corner stone for Hermetic Science, Western Occultism, Magic, Initiation, and the Ruach Healing Method.

This sentence reads as follows: ***"That which is below is like that which is above and that which is above is like that which is below."*** - Sir Isaac Newton's Translation

As a healer we must always be at work in the higher planes. We must focus our attention on the energy field of the individual. This is the higher plane in the microcosm and is an expression of the body. What we affect in the patients energy field, we eventually affect in the body. In other words, as we affect change in the energetic world we automatically bring about change in the physical world.

The physical body is an expression of the total energy field of the patient being healed and the total energy fields of the patient is an expression of the physical body. This means that when a doctor is placing a bandage on your knee because of a cut, s/he is ultimately healing your energy field at the same time. In other words, the energy field is also leaking energy or has a cut on it. This the same as what is experienced in the Four Fold Breath. Your breath becomes like that which is above; a source of flowing energy.

This is just the beginning. The Four Fold Breath is the start of invoking Divine White Brilliance. Remember, Divine White Brilliance is the source of Ruach used for all healing. Breathing connects you to Ruach and Divine White Brilliance is the tool for invoking and making Ruach energy flow.

## Exercise: Invoking Divine White Brilliance

This is a simple exercise that will help you to condition your mind and energy field, so that you can absorb and give more Life-Giving Light of Ruach to those you bring healing to. Note: We often have soft music playing in the background and incense burning. The choice is yours.

### Step 1:

Sit or stand relaxed and comfortably, with your eyes closed.

### Step 2:

Complete the Four Fold Breath exercise.

### Step 3:

Visualize the Infinite Light above your head; oftentimes referred to this as Divine White Brilliance (D.W.B.)

### Step 4:

State a magical intention in your mind, such as: "I am a healer." "I am in the healing light and the healing light is within me." "I am one with the healing light."

**Step 5:**

Visualize the "Divine White Brilliance" surrounding you and flowing within you, beginning from the Fountain Gate at the top of your head...infusing your entire being with Divine White Brilliance into your body on a cellular level to the perimeter of your aura.

**Step 6:**

Be at peace in the Infinite Light. Sit and bask in the presence of the "Divine White Brilliance".

**Step 7:**

Open yourself to a blissful state of gratitude that Divine Source is filling you with Healing Light and Knowledge.

**Step 8:**

End with these words, or words of your choosing, ***"Not unto my name but unto thy name be the Praise, Power and Glory, Forever and Ever. Amen."***

*Illustration 4: Divine White Brilliance (D.W.B.)*

In the beginning of the healing process, we are raising ourselves up to Divine Source and invoking God's healing energy down to the astral plane and subsequently down to the earthly plane. This is why we say that it is the energy of Divine Source providing the healing, not the human being who is invoking the light. We as healers are spiritual conduits for the Divine White Brilliance and the magical healing force. This concept of being a conduit is seen in the healing technique know as Reiki. I have spent many years extensively studying and mastering this healing method.

Reiki healing is a Japanese healing technique inspired by the teachings of Mikao Usui. When first introduced, Reiki was pivotal in creating a massive change in consciousness throughout the healing community. Since that revolution, healers in many fields channel pure Divine energy to heal their recipients/patients using a variety of methods, including the Ruach Healing Method. This energy channeling is used on a standard basis regardless of the other techniques employed in order to facilitate healing and maintenance of energetic health.

The exciting thing about where we're at now in human history is that with the Ruach Healing Method we can heal each other using even more advanced and thorough methods. We can even incorporate powerful Divine magic to further elevate the effectiveness of the process. Personally, as a healer and not the founder of the Ruach Healing Method, when I'm alone in a room with a patient I allow my training in a number of modalities to provide me with the most effective and appropriate methods. When you're trained in a variety of schools of thought the Divine influx now has more options to use through you. When it comes to Golden Dawn magic, then yes I am mostly a purist, but when it comes to healing I'm strictly about allowing Source to work through me to create results.

### Understanding the Duality of Gender in Healing

One concept to discuss here, is the concept of gender. We usually think of ourselves as masculine or feminine depending on our physical make-up. In all actuality, the ideas of masculine and feminine have a variety of other meanings. For example, when a man and woman engage in sexual intercourse and the woman conceives, we view the man's actions as active or masculine and the woman's as receptive or feminine. Nine months later the woman goes into labor and the baby is born. From the woman's point of view, giving birth is active or masculine. The doctors, nurses and the husband who embrace the new life of the baby are in a receiving mode so their actions are feminine. When the woman breast feeds the baby, she is again giving milk to the baby. This is considered a masculine act. In other words, a masculine act is *giving* and a feminine act is *receiving*.

The point is that giving and receiving, masculine and feminine acts, are not dictated by our gender. Within our lives, our actions sometimes take on masculine features or feminine features, regardless of whether we are male or female. It will help to keep this in mind when we enter the healing process. This is because at different times the healer and patient each play both roles. In healing, we first take or receive the patient's excess or unused energy and we remove it by giving it back to the cosmic Source. The patient is giving or releasing their energy to us. Then, later, the healer receives "Divine White Brilliance" from above and gives it to the patient who receives it into his or her body. This concept of masculine and feminine energies works constantly through the entire healing process. If it doesn't happen this way then healing usually doesn't take place.

In some traditions, notably the Eastern traditions, we learn about the masculine and feminine energy of the kundalini and its movement. The goal is to raise it from the lower chakra at the base of the spine up to the top of the head, and then back down the spine again. The purpose of this circulation is to raise vibrations and bring about spiritual illumination. In the Eastern tradition the lower area of the spine is considered to be feminine energy. So the flow of kundalini up to the top merges it with masculine energy. When it descends again it is now in balance.

Let's examine another example, in the nature of Solar and Lunar energies. We have both Solar (masculine) and Lunar (feminine) energies within us. Kabbalistic Healing balances masculine and feminine forces differently than the kundalini exercises, but is just as effective. Whereas the kundalini force starts from the bottom and rises upward; Kabbalistic Healing works in the opposite direction. The "D.W.B." is light brought from Kether above. (The "h" is silent. Pronounced, Ket-er; refer to the Tree of Life) Kether is represented by the top circle, or First Sephira, on the Tree of Life. This light is considered masculine or Solar. In order to heal, we bring it down to Yesod, which is the Ninth Sephira, right above Malkuth. Yesod, which is associated with the symbolic attributes of the

*Illustration 5: Marriage of Sun and Moon*

Moon and is therefore considered feminine. This is also where the astral world resides and where our healing efforts take place. The movement of light into Yesod from Kether is like the celestial body of the moon so poetically receiving solar light. Thus, the end result is a balancing of Solar and Lunar energies that produces the healing process.

### Using Divine White Brilliance

What happens if we bring "D.W.B." down to someone who is healthy? First of all, we always scan the patient's Vitality Gates in order to determine where there is excess energy or a lack of energy. This will be covered later in detail. Also, the truth is that no one is perfectly healthy, we are all in a state of mortality. Whenever you scan someone you will find one or more areas that need fresh energy or need to have excess energy removed. From the moment we are born, our bodies are losing and regenerating cells and energy. When we are young it is easier for healthy bodies to keep a balance between losses and gains. As we age, we may find we are fighting a losing battle. Someday we will have lost too much energy or too much of the needed cells and that is when our lives will come to an end. In the meantime, we have a valuable opportunity to use Divine White Brilliance through the Ruach Healing Method to keep our bodies in balance. We can offset the negative effects of illness and maintain our balance to extend the time we have to live healthy lives.

One word of caution here is needed! The energy we invoke passes through our bodies on the way to the patient's body. We must be careful not to accidentally pollute the "Divine White Brilliance" with energies that have been negatively affected by our own ill health, the use of cigarettes, the use of alcohol, or the use of drugs. Remember the story of Pete from Chapter 1. If you are a heavy drinker, an alcoholic, or a user of recreational drugs, you are better off not performing Ruach Healing. You certainly would be advised not to heal while you're intoxicated or ill. If you ignore this warning you could make the patient worse instead of better.

Use of marijuana is somewhat different from other recreational drugs. Extensive research shows that marijuana, used correctly, is beneficial for many medical issues. Legitimate muscle testing often shows that marijuana use can be positive to a patient. This indicates that marijuana has the potential to be a genuinely healing herb. Again, it is in your intention and use that matters. Use your best judgment if you are a patient. On the other hand if you are a healer, please wait to heal others until you are well and able to work without requiring the assistance of mind-altering medicines.

Let's expand a bit on "Ruach" or "Breath," which we have already mentioned that it is also known as "Chi" or "Life-force." To better explain this concept, we'd like to use an analogy. Let's say that hot water is the pure "Ruach Force" and that various teas "tinct" the water. The teas are the Sephirot, Elements, and Planets. Ruach exists in everything and everywhere. There is "nowhere" it is not. It ultimately comes from "Divine Source" or "God." We absorb or pull this into our bodies and energy fields, through eating, drinking and breathing and through the energy centers on the body called the "Vitality Gates" or more commonly known as the "Chakras."

The "Vitality Gates", while essentially similar should, not be confused with "Chakras". This will be explained in greater depth later on in this healing manual. For now, it is necessary to understand that the Gates collect Ruach to deliver vital energy to the energy field then unto the body. Remember, the energy body is integrated with the physical body. When the Vitality Gates on the body are working and healthy, the body is ultimately the recipient of this life force.

## Ruach Life-Force in Your Home

Now that you understand that Ruach is everywhere and that it can be collected and magnified, it makes sense to place objects around your home or office that naturally collect and magnify Ruach. In addition, it makes sense to try to remove anything that creates lower vibrational energies.

Oftentimes, people don't understand the importance of creating a special and holistic healing environment. Without a doubt the human energy field is the largest consumer of Ruach energy. However, everything has some ability to absorb energy. If, for example, vegetables did not maintain a certain amount of life force after harvesting them, then there would be no value in consuming them. The result would be devastating. Some things naturally absorb and expel pure and natural energy in our environment more than others. Plants are certainly at the top of the list. Crystals or semi-precious stones can absorb great amounts of Ruach life force, as well as, release it. Some mystics claim that building a mutual rapport with your plants and crystals allow them to attune to your vibration and particular signature. At times when you are not feeling well, these crystals and plants begin to radiate more Ruach in an effort to bring you healing and positive attunement. Running water is certainly another powerful Ruach generator to have in your home. Nowadays you can purchase fountains almost everywhere. Make sure you keep the water clean.

Candles are also positive Ruach generators too. Make sure you use clean new candles or candles that were carefully stored. If you like aged beeswax, be sure to give the candles you burn a positive intention before you light them. Different colors awaken a different spectrum of the Ruach life force. It is safe to use very vibrant colors if you charge the candles with Divine light from your hands before lighting them. Some candles such as a black one are excellent for absorbing unwanted or negative energy. We have healers who work with us that often light a black candle in the room if someone is suffering from high fever. The concept is the black candle helps to absorb the fever.

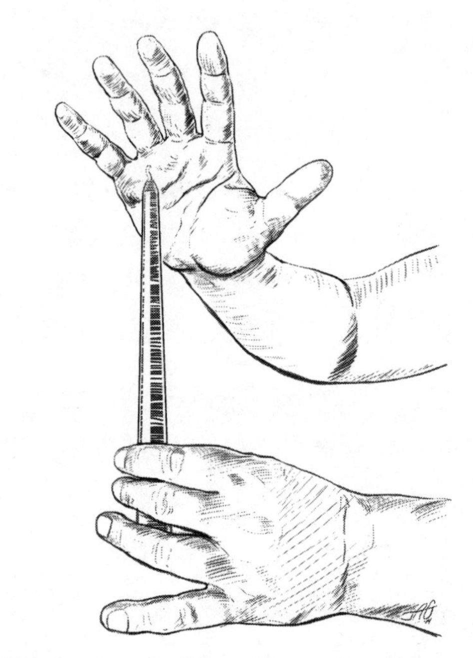

*Illustration 6: Charging a Candle*

The art of spring cleaning is not as valued as it was years ago. Skipping spring cleaning is detrimental to Ruach in your home. When was the last time all your windows were clean? If you hate cleaning I am sure that there is a teenager in the neighborhood that wants to earn some spending cash. What about your mirrors? Do you have a clear reflection that shows the Ruach in you? When was the last time you took a good look at your curtains? Fabrics are great at absorbing Ruach. Even if your curtains are not washable you will notice a huge difference if you just let them hang out on the clothes line in the sun. Your floors can tell stories. You will feel more grounded when your floors are clean and not cluttered. Don't forget to keep your refrigerator and washroom spotless. Also do not bring used items in your home without cleaning them and clearing the old energy from them. Ruach is everywhere in your home. On the next page are a few things to help you increase the higher vibrational Ruach in your home.

## The Incredible Power of Ruach

Ruach has incredible power! Ruach is the essential life force throughout the universe, therefore the power of Ruach can easily do the following: relieve pain and nervous conditions, including depression; the common cold can be cured in a fraction of the time; eyes can be restored resulting in better vision; major illness such as cancer can be destroyed, vitality can be increased; and the aging process can be slowed down. There is nothing beyond the incredible power of Ruach! The power of life force is available to you, it is literally within the palms of your hands!

***"You already have the precious mixture that will make you well. Use it."*** **-Jalal al-Din Rumi**

**10 Things That Help Generate Positive Ruach In The Home**

1. **Plants** – must be healthy
2. **Crystals** – the natural angles of uncut crystals amplify energy and have not been weakened by human handling and processing; polished stones can be great sun catchers
3. **Running Water** – must be clean
4. **Cold Nebulizer** – these devices put natural essential oils into your home
5. **Candles (beeswax)** – while all candles generate Ruach, beeswax tests the highest according to applied kinesiology
6. **Artwork**
7. **Symbols** – magical symbols of sun and life force elements are very beneficial
8. **Music-** high vibrational music
9. **Statues**
10. **Wind Chimes** – a cheap wind chime merely diffuses energy, although that can be beneficial too, however wind chimes specifically tuned for a purpose such as healing the heart chakra are great Ruach generators.

# CHAPTER THREE: Introduction To The Kabbalah: 3 Veils of Negative Existence & The 4 Worlds

Understanding how Ruach Healing ties into the Kabbalistic Tree of Life and how it relates to our healing work is important. The Ruach Healing Method is not strictly Kabbalistic. It draws from Hermeticism, Healing Touch, Energy Therapy, Reiki and other forms of healing that have developed out of the Western Mystery Traditions. However, there is no denying its large Kabbalistic influence.

We have some good news and some bad news. When it comes to the Kabbalah, there are a GAZILLION books on the subject! Now, that's the good news, in that there is plenty of information to keep you busy for years, but the bad news is that it could be rather confusing. If you haven't studied Hebrew, it could also be rather intimidating. My background is in the study of Golden Dawn Kabbalah. I think people like William Wynn Wescott and S.L. MacGregor Mathers did a good job of combing out the religious dogma and superstition of the Kabbalah. Their writings develop a strong usable framework for invoking the universal energies of the Kabbalah. (Please refer to the bibliography of this book for some great references of the study of Kabbalah.)

Kabbalah, also spelled QBL or Qaballah (be aware that there are many other versions of the word) comes from a Hebrew word meaning "spoken" or "oral". Kabbalah is an indication that knowledge is part of an oral tradition. It has long been associated with the mystical side of

Judaism, in addition to spiritual links with Gnosticism and other early mystical traditions. Kabbalah provides a symbolic explanation of the origin of the universe, the relationship of human beings to Divine Source, and a description of Creation where God's Light (or "D.W.B.") manifests itself in stages or degrees. These stages start with nothingness and result in the physical world in which we live.

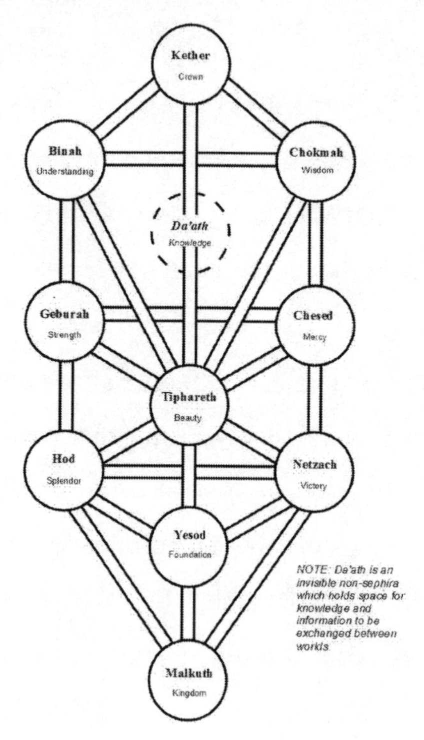


*Illustration 7: The Tree of Life*

Kabbalah also means ***"to receive."*** To receive life force from the Divine Source in a concise and consistently structured way. Kabbalah does more than just teach, as it also provides us with a path. If we follow the path that Kabbalah teaches, it leads us to unite with Divine Source and become co-creators. This path can be seen on the Tree of Life.

The diagram of the Tree of Life provides us with a mystical glyph or Mandala of the Kabbalistic path. Notice that there are Ten Emanations from the Divine on the Kabbalistic Tree of Life. These emanations are called Sephirot (plural). While it is true in Kabbalistic philosophy, there is only one sacred and Divine Source, this Divine Source radiates in these ten distinct emanations. Each Sephira (singular) is unique unto itself; vibrating at its own unique frequency. What is particularly important to you, as the healer, is grasping the concept that while you are doing healing work that depends upon you tapping into Divine Source, you are also focusing on a particular illness or part of the body as it relates to a specific emanation.

The Tree of Life is both macrocosmic, meaning "the universe as a whole," and microcosmic, meaning "the small universe or the universe within you." These are classical definitions of these terms in the study of the Kabbalah. The Sephirot are generally macrocosmic and the paths connecting them are microcosmic in nature. From our perspective within the Ruach Healing Method, the whole healing experience is microcosmic. There really is nothing outside of you. Your experience of the patient with an illness is part of your reality. So that being said, on a deeper level, it **ALWAYS** comes down to healing yourself. The Tree of Life can represent the created world in which we live, but it also emanates throughout the entire body or "sphere of sensation."

## The "3" Veils of Negative Existence

Ruach Healers recognize four Worlds of manifestation and three veils of UN-manifestation or negative existence. Taking a look back at the Diagram on the Tree of Life, you will notice the Kether Sephira. The veils are located as 3 half circles above Kether. The first veils are called Ain, which means negativity or no-thing. The second is called Ain Soph, meaning without limit. The third is Ain Soph Aur, which means Limitless Light. It is out of "Ain Soph Aur" that we have the Primordial One manifested as depicted in the Highest Sephirot on the Tree of Life called Kether.

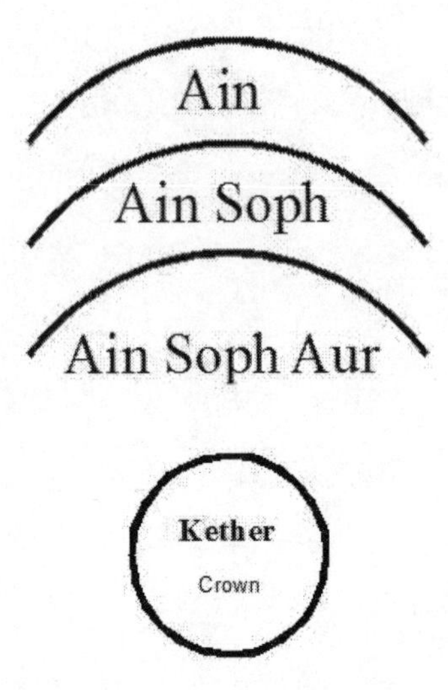


*Illustration 8: 3 Veils of Negative Existence*

Negative Existence is a tough concept to get your mind around. It is not manifested, but even more, it is not even empty space. This is the core of Divine Spark before the spark. If we think in terms of anything that we already know or could possibly know, we shall be in error. For whatever else there may be, negative existence simply cannot be, and moreover, it is UN-manifested. The Three Veils of Negative Existence suggest certain concepts or ideas to our minds. In regards to Ain, (again, meaning no-thing) this particular veil is not the same as the concept of nothingness, but rather it IS negativity. In addition, this is not to be related to the negativity of Darkness. Our minds cannot conceive of such a thing.

that is and is not. We cannot conceive the concept of existence and non-existence as being one and the same.

Yet as a Ruach Healer, it is important to empty the mind of preconceived notions of God, or Divine Source, or even the Light that provides ultimate healing and renewal. Once we as healers give up our so called understanding of the Divine, we can somehow, through no effort on our own, begin to access the expression of the Three Veils of Negative Existence. This is done through Divine expression which the mystic, magician, and healer call **"Light"**.

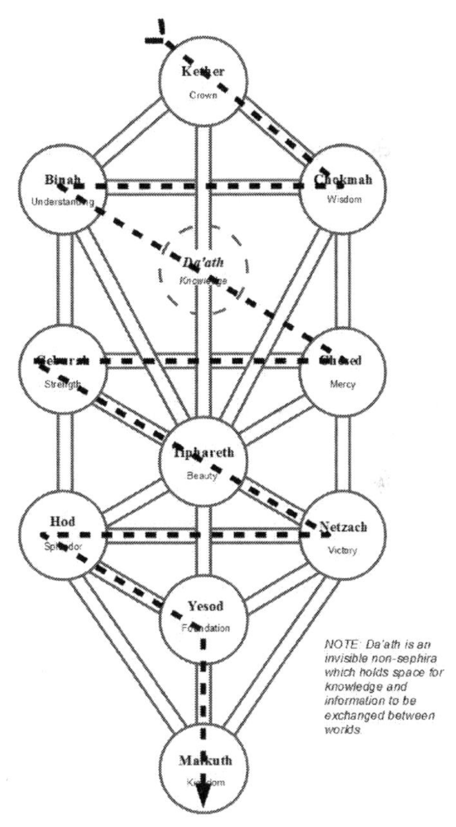


*Illustration 9: Energy Flow on the Tree of Life*

Negative existence is completely outside the realization of our ability to understand it. However, this does not mean to say that we are outside of the range of its influence. On the physical plane we have no direct access to the Divine Source of negative existence, yet all that we know as existing has its roots and origins in this negative existence. What we're trying to say here basically is that although we don't truly know of negative existence, we certainly know of its effects on our own existence and lives. The Mystics throughout history who have ventured as far back as one can safely go on this physical plane have referred to negative existence as Light or Ain Soph Aur, the "The Boundless and Limitless Light." They have spoken of the first manifestation as sound; *"In the Beginning was the Word."* (Genesis 1:1). The most exalted aspects of our Universe lies in the UN-manifest, which is the "Ultimate Source of All" or "The Great Unknowable One" which cannot be known. The UN-manifest is symbolized by the words "negative limitless Light", or in Hebrew, "Ain Soph Aur". Remember that there are three curves of radiating Light. The outer curve is Ain (No-thing), the middle or center is Ain Soph, and the innermost is Ain Soph Aur. Behind these mystical veils energy flows constantly. This is the energy that brings form from the formless. It is the place from which healing light comes into Kether and down the Tree of Life. Most of our practical healing workings deal with the manifested Universe through Tree of Life and the paths that connect them. After all, the Tree of Life is the expression of the Three Veils of Negative Existence or Divine Source. Let us re-emphasize that negative existence does have an effect on our lives as it is the Source of all that is and all that is not.

To continue understanding the veils you must have a basic picture of where the energy from the veils flows. The energy flows through the Sephirot on the Tree of Life. Starting at the top, right under "limitless light" or Ain Soph Aur is the first Sephira called **Kether**. Another name for it is "*Crown*." The second Sephira is underneath it on the right and is called **Chokmah** or *Wisdom*. To the left of Chokmah is the third Sephira, **Binah** or *Understanding*. Back over on the right is (fourth) **Chesed** or *Mercy* followed on the left by (fifth) **Geburah**, or *Power*. The sixth

Sephira is centrally located in the Tree of Life and is called **Tiphareth** or *Beauty*. Note that Tiphareth is the only Sephira that connects directly with each other Sephirot. (Except Malkuth). The seventh is **Netzach** or *Victory*. On the left, the eighth is **Hod**, or *Splendor*. The ninth Sephira, located directly under Tiphareth, is **Yesod** or *Foundation*. On the bottom, the tenth and final Sephira, is **Malkuth** or *Kingdom*. Remember these Sephirot are all distinct emanations of the vast incomprehensible energies of Divine Source which lingers behind the Three Veils of Negative Existence.

The Tree of Life shows how the Divine energies create the universe. Behind the veils is limitless energy and light in which nothing physical could possibly exist. Some method of filtering the energy and light was needed so that the physical world was not overwhelmed by the Light. The Sephirot are filters that allow us to exist in the world of Divine presence.

The basic premise in the study of the Kabbalah is that it is a pathway to light. It is the study of the purpose of life, our purpose in this life, and a study of the eternal wisdom which the Kabbalah contains. Healing is just another aspect of the light. The Ruach Healer uses the Kabbalistic wisdom through the archetypal energies in the Tree of Life. This process of learning and doing is designed to bring us closer to our higher self and ultimately to Source and Divine White Brilliance.

Divine White Brilliance is the Source of eternal light that permeates and gives life to the entire universe. As magical healers, each of us will perceive this energy in different ways. Some people can feel the light glowing in their heart. Others feel it as a wonderful weightlessness or a pouring down of energy from above. Some see the light and watch it split into many colors which are intended for various healing purposes. This is the light that illuminates the soul and illuminates our astral selves, as well as, our physical selves. It is the light that heals our bodies, as well as, our hearts and souls. Ultimately it is Life Force, for without it we could not live.

We ***all*** wish we had more Divine Light, understood it better, or saw it more clearly. You may be asking yourself the question, "How am I going to understand what to do with this light?" Don't be concerned. One of the purposes of the Ruach Healing Method is to provide you, the reader with all the information you need to determine what kind of light to use for what kind of illness, injury or disease.

## The 4 Worlds

In the Ruach Healing Method we invoke the complete power of the Divine Source through the expression of the four worlds of the Kabbalah. A simple and basic understanding will allow you as a Ruach Healer to have a deeper knowledge of where you are pulling the life healing energy from. This knowledge will allow you to tap into the incredible power of all of the four worlds to evoke powerful healing and rejuvenation.

In the Kabbalah we express the universe through the Tree of Life. The Tree represents the emanations of the Divine into levels of consciousness. These levels of consciousness are not all one same section in the world of manifestation. There are four sections called the four worlds of the Kabbalah. The four worlds are expressed in two different ways. The first way of expressing the four worlds is to simply divide the Tree of Life into four sections. The second way of expressing the four worlds is depicted with the four sections stacked one on top of each other. As a Kabbalist, I prefer the concept of stacking one Tree of Life on top of the other for a total of four Trees of Life. The highest of the four worlds, called **Atziluth,** is the *World of Pure Spirit*. Atziluth activates all the other worlds of creative force and eventually manifestation. In other words, all other worlds evolve from it. Atziluth is beyond description because it is Pure Spirit, beyond time, beyond space and in essence, beyond manifestation. Some Ruach Healers use the term Atziluth as the Divine world, or the world where the thoughts of Divine Source exist. The world of Atziluth is above all other worlds and beyond image. Therefore, when invoking the power of the Highest world we express it as a Divine Name, or title of Deity, rather than an image such as an Archangel or god. Like all the four worlds, Atziluth has its own color scale for each Sephira

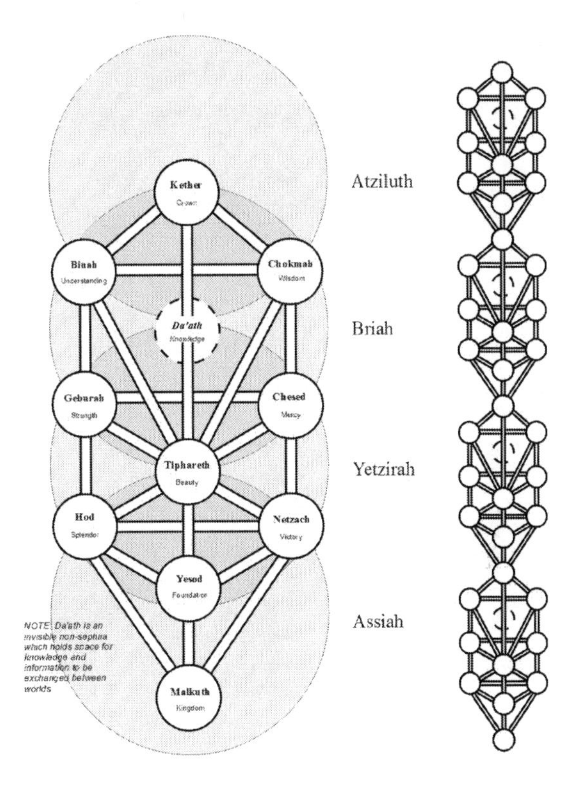


*Illustration 10: The Four Worlds*

of the Tree of Life, however because Atziluth is beyond any archetypal image, we do not use its color scale. (Only highly trained Ruach Healing Masters should use the color scale of Atziluth.) What we do use is the vibration of the Divine name of the element or Sephira invoked.

The next world of manifestation is called the world of **Briah**. Briah, which means *World of Creation*, is also beyond mortal comprehension. It is far beyond the ability of the conscious mind to understand it. It is in this world that we vibrate the Archangelic names. The Archangels are also known as the Divine names in the world of Briah. **For example, in the Sephira of Tiphareth the Divine name is: "YHVH Eloah Ve Da'ath."** The Divine name is the general name that manifests through all the worlds as emanating from the World of Atziluth. In the world of Briah or the world where we actually get to see archetypes begin to manifest, the Archangel is called Raphael. Whereas Atziluth is called the King scale of color, Briah is the Queen scale and the highest scale we can use for healing work with effectiveness. As a matter of fact, every color used in healing is of the Queen scale of the world of Briah.

The third world is the world called **Yetzirah**. Yetzirah is the *World of Formation*. It is here that the subtle and flashing patterns behind physical matter are found. This is a very important world because most healing work is done in the World of Yetzirah. The Emerald Tablet states, "As above, so below." That is why the Ruach Healer will raise his consciousness as high as he can stretch it. In other words, he or she will open their mind to the highest level of inner consciousness, and reach from the physical mundane world into the World of Yetzirah. By building and creating in the World of Yetzirah, the law of manifestation states that it must come into physical being on the physical plane. Yetzirah is the world of angels, or high level energies. In studying various diagrams on the Kabbalah, you will see Choir of Angels or Order of Angels for a particular Sephira. The Order of Angels is manifested in the World of Yetzirah. Just like with Briah, the name of the Order of Angels is also the Divine name for that Sephira for this particular world of the Kabbalah. Coming back to our example, the Divine name for Tiphareth in the World of Atziluth is **"YHVH Eloah Ve Da'ath."** The Archangel for the World of Briah is **Raphael**. The Choir of Angels is called the **Melekim**, in the world of Yetzirah.

One of the ways we activate all four worlds in the Ruach Healing Method is through vibration. Some people may not understand the concept of vibrating the Divine Name or the Archangel, or even the Choir of Angels. However it is important because it awakens the four worlds within the sphere of sensation of the healer as well as patient. The Ruach Healer will quietly vibrate these names when awakening the incredible healing power of the Sephirot. The main point now, as a magical healer, is to grasp the concept that healing power comes from the highest Source which is Atziluth and then trickles downward into form and manifestation to eventually end up in the physical plane which is our fourth and final world.

The World of **Assiah**, the physical and the mundane plane. The world of Assiah is the active world, the W*orld of Sensation*. This is the world in which physical healing must manifest in order for the patient to experience physical change within the material body. There are no Divine names associated with the world of Assiah. There are no Archangels or angels. This is the world of action, the world where you as the healer and your connection to the higher world, through meditation and vibration of the Divine names, takes on manifestation. Putting it another way, and this may sound a bit silly, but, ***you*** are the healing angel of Assiah!

**Table 1: The Four Worlds**

Atziluth – Divine Name – World of Pure Spirit
Briah – Archangel – World of Creation
Yetzirah – Angels or Choir of Angels – World of Formation
Assiah – You the Healer – World of the Physical

We have included a chart of the Divine Names related to each world. We will also explain more about how these Divine names work and are attributed to activating the four worlds in the next section. You will want to highlight this section or memorize the Divine names because we will refer to them again later in this book. Another simple suggestion is to simply write the Divine Names, the Arch Angels and the Choir of Angels on 3x5 cards.

As a side note, there is a color ascribed to each Sephirot and element of the four worlds. In the Ruach Healing Method, we primarily use the colors ascribed in this book which are the Queen Scale of Colors or colors from the World of Briah. This is the highest world our minds can slightly begin to understand, the world where archetypes and Archangels exist. In highly advanced Ruach Healing, the understanding of the four worlds and the memorization of the Divine Names is essential, so now is as good a time as any to get started. You will be astonished at the level of results you get as a practitioner of the Ruach Healing Method by quietly vibrating the name.

**Table 2: Worlds, Divine Names and Angels**

| Sephira | DIVINE NAME (Atziluth) | ARCH-ANGELIC NAME (Briah) | CHOIR OF ANGELS (Yetzirah) | QUEEN SCALE COLOR |
|---|---|---|---|---|
| Kether | Eheieh | Metatron | Chayoth ha-Qadesh | White |
| Chokmah | Yah | Ratziel | Auphanim | Grey |
| Binah | YHVH Elohim | Tzaphqiel | Aralim | Black |
| Chesed | El | Tzadqiel | Chashmalim | Blue |
| Geburah | Elohim Gibor | Kamael | Seraphim | Scarlet |
| Tiphareth | YHVH Eloah Ve Da'ath | Raphael | Melekim | Yellow |
| Netzach | YHVH Tzaboath | Haniel | Elohim | Emerald |
| Hod | Elohim Tzabaoth | Michael | Beni Elohim | Orange |
| Yesod | Shaddai el-Chai | Gabriel | Kerubim | Purple |
| Malkuth | Adonai ha-Aretz | Sandalphon | Ashim | Brown Earth-tones |

# NOTES:

# CHAPTER FOUR: Creation And Divine Names

The ancient wisdom of the Kabbalah and the Ruach Healing Method teaches that there is a Divine Energy that holds the power and possibility of everything and nothing at the same time. It is paradoxical and it cannot be comprehended, by the natural mind. That which is above and beyond our senses is also beyond our understanding. The book of Genesis expresses a metaphor with the story of creation. The Creator in the book of Genesis is known as "Elohim". In Hebrew, Elohim is a masculine noun while a feminine plural. In the Torah, the Creator is known by four letters, "YHVH," which is considered unpronounceable. Later scriptures also indicate that the Creator has multiple Divine names and in the study of Kabbalah you will see many of them. These names, as well as the names of Archangels and Choirs of Angels, are the names we will use in the healing process. These names represent the various energies of the Sephirot, the four elements and seven planetary influences which are part of the Ruach Healing System.

Why do we use a variety of Divine Names? It is because each one opens up a different portal, element, or Sephira to the specific energy of the Tree of Life or elemental force or planetary energy. The Creator has many aspects or faces and manifests itself in different ways through the use of different names, different sounds, different shapes and different colors. Knowing each of these aspects and having a basic understanding of them will help you as a Ruach healer because this knowledge will allow you to get specific with the nature of the Ruach energy being invoked.

These names are the verbal symbols of vibrations and energies that express their nature in the Sephirot of the Tree.

Recall in our teachings on the four worlds in Chapter 3, the Divine Name relates to the world of Atziluth, the world of Archetypes, and represents the world of Pure Spirit. The Archangel relates to the world of Briah, the world of Creation. The Angels or Choir of Angels relates to the world of Yetzirah. Yetzirah is, of course, the world of formation. Last, but not least, the fourth and final world is the world of Assiah, which is the physical world, where physical, emotional, and mental healing takes place. I feel the need to reiterate this, as I know from teaching it for 30+ years, it can tend to confuse even the brightest of minds.

The charts below will give you the basic relationship of the Divine Names to the Sephirot, Elements, and Planets. As you look at each Sephirot you will notice a Divine (Atziluth) name assigned to each, the Archangel (Briah) that relates to each one, and the Choir of Angels (Yetzirah) that corresponds. The aspects of Atziluth, Briah, and Yetzirah are also listed as it relates to the Elements and the Planets.

Take the time to review the charts and commit them to memory. These charts provide an essential reference to help familiarize yourself with the use of Divine names for your healing practice. Again, we suggest that you copy the information onto 3x5 cards for reference or as many are now doing, put them on your favorite portable device.

## Table 3: Sephirot and Divine Names

| Sephira | DIVINE NAME (World of Atziluth) | ARCH-ANGELIC NAME (World of Briah) | CHOIR OF ANGELS (World of Yetzirah) | COLOR |
|---|---|---|---|---|
| Kether | Eheieh | Metatron | Chayoth ha-Qadesh | White |
| Chokmah | Yah | Ratziel | Auphanim | Grey |
| Binah | YHVH Elohim | Tzaphqiel | Aralim | Black |
| Chesed | El | Tzadqiel | Chashmalim | Blue |
| Geburah | Elohim Gibor | Kamael | Seraphim | Scarlet |
| Tiphareth | YHVH Eloah Ve Da'ath | Raphael | Melekim | Yellow |
| Netzach | YHVH Tzaboath | Haniel | Elohim | Emerald |
| Hod | Elohim Tzabaoth | Michael | Beni Elohim | Orange |
| Yesod | Shaddai el-Chai | Gabriel | Kerubim | Purple |
| Malkuth | Adonai ha-Aretz | Sandalphon | Ashim | Brown Earth-tones |

## Table 4: Elements and Divine Names

| ELEMENT | DIVINE NAME | ARCH-ANGEL | ANGEL | COLOR |
|---|---|---|---|---|
| Fire | Elohim | Michael | Aral | Red |
| Water | El | Gabriel | Taliahad | Blue |
| Air | YHVH | Raphael | Chassan | Yellow |
| Earth | Adonai ha-Aretz | Auriel | Phorlak | Green |

## Table 5: Planets and Divine Name

| PLANET | DIVINE NAME | ARCH-ANGEL | ANGEL | COLOR |
|---|---|---|---|---|
| Saturn | YHVH Elohim | Tzaphqiel | Cassiel | Indigo |
| Jupiter | El | Tzadqiel | Sachiel | Violet |
| Mars | Elohim Gabor | Kamael | Zamael | Red |
| Sun | YHVH Eloah Ve Da'ath | Michael | Raphael | Orange |
| Venus | YHVH Tzabaoth | Haniel | Anael | Green |
| Mercury | Elohim Tzabaoth | Raphael | Michael | Yellow |
| Moon | Shaddai el-Chai | Gabriel | Gabriel | Light Blue |

# CHAPTER FIVE: Understanding the Dynamics of the Tree of Life

The human body on the Tree of Life is an exciting concept developed by Kabbalists who see man as a microcosm of the macrocosm. The concept of the Tree of Life and the human body can be a very deep study. The relationship between the two is expressed in a couple of different ways when it comes to the healing process. The Tree of Life can be literally laid over the body or used as states of consciousness or universal energy. Both are correct and have a place within the Ruach Healing Method. As a matter of fact, it is not uncommon for a practitioner of the Ruach Healing Method to jump from the literal concept of the Tree of Life on the human body one moment, and the very next, use the energy of a Sephira as if it were universal. Remember 75% of *all* healing work is based on intention.

In the Ruach Healing Method, we see very specific areas of the body where the Sephirot of the Tree of Life are predominant. There is a meditation that we will be sharing with you that will teach you how to awaken the Sephirot in your sphere of sensation. It is a powerful metaphysical exercise for it awakens and attunes your entire sphere of sensation or energy field to universal and Divine healing energies. This is an absolutely critical exercise for anyone participating in the Ruach Healing Method to practice on a regular basis. This exercise called the Middle Pillar, can be found later in this chapter. Each Sephira also has a consciousness that can be awakened in the body through meditation. This will be discussed in Chapter 9.

## Pillars of the Tree of Life

The Tree of Life can be split into three sections. Everything on the right hand side is said to be on the masculine pillar, everything on the left is the feminine pillar, and everything in the middle is called the Pillar of Mildness. There is a concept that the center Sephirot or the Middle Pillar must be awakened as it is the conduit of balance and healing. This can be done through simple exercise called the Middle Pillar exercise. This exercise was developed by the late Israel Regardie. Regardie wrote an entire book on the subject called *"The Middle Pillar"*. We highly suggest investing in a copy of this book.

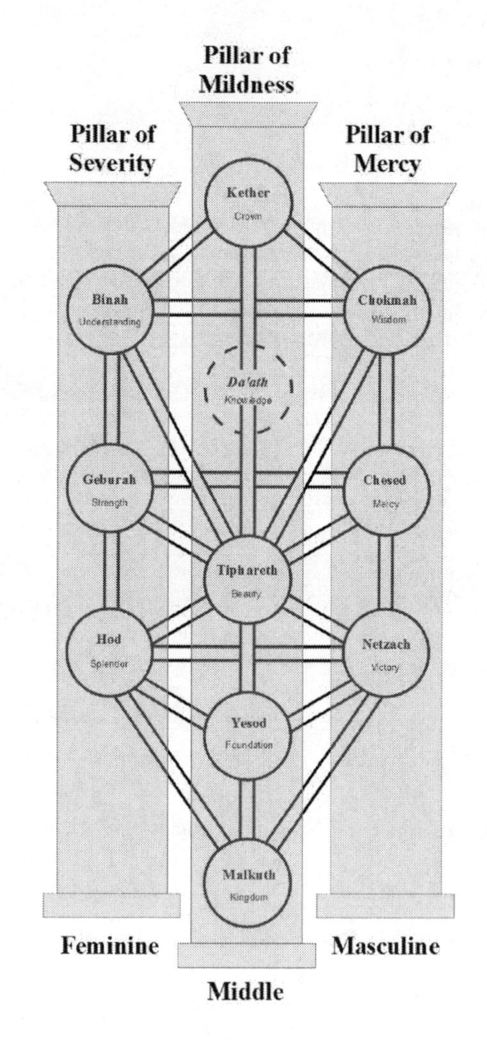


*Illustration 11: Pillars of the Tree of Life*

When we awaken the Middle Pillar in our energy field we, in essence, awaken the full and complete power of the Tree of Life. This exercise is a power source for balancing your own energy field as well as raising tremendous amounts of spiritual power.

As previously stated, this is a powerful metaphysical exercise for it awakens and attunes your entire sphere of sensation or energy field to universal and Divine healing energies found in the Tree of Life. It is most effective when done after the Lesser Banishing Ritual of the Pentagram and Kabbalistic Cross. (These exercises will be explained in Chapter 8.) Personally we believe the Ruach healer should consider doing the Middle Pillar exercise on a daily basis. The reason why doing this exercise is so helpful is that it intentionally invokes the presence of more light or D.W.B. into your energy field. This is valuable as a healer. Think about it, if you are doing this western yoga type exercise on a daily basis, your own energy field will become bright and healthy. It becomes common sense that a healer with a vibrant healthy aura is going to be far more effective in helping others. Here is our suggestion, do this exercise every morning for a month. Notice how your own maladies and weaknesses begin to heal. Notice how you have more energy and enthusiasm. We never cease to find it amazing that when people do this simple exercise they are astonished at just how good they feel after a week or two. Don't get me wrong, we are not suggesting that the Middle Pillar Exercise is alone a healing tool, but what it does do is make you the healer a better healing tool for you patients.

## Exercise: The Middle Pillar Ritual

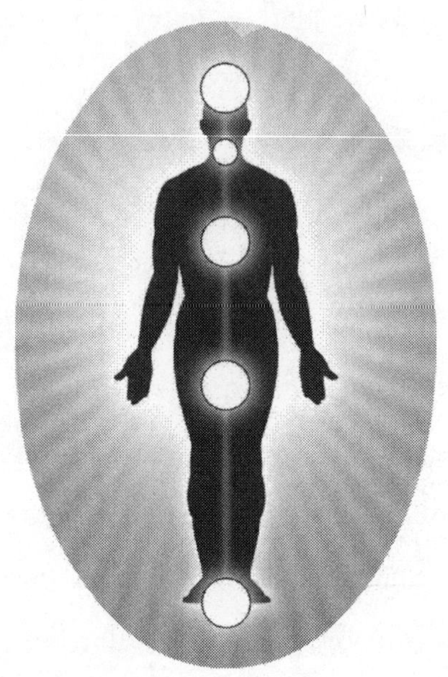

*Illustration 12: The Middle Pillar*

### Step 1:

Facing west, standing straight with feet together, begin the Four Fold Breath by deeply inhaling through the nose for the count of four, hold it for a count of four, and then release it slowly through the mouth for a count of four, and again hold it for a count of four. Proceed until you develop a rhythm. When you have achieved relaxation simultaneously, with the rhythm of breathing, say a quiet prayer to your Higher Power, Holy Guardian Angel, Higher Genius, God or whatever name you use for Divine Source. Take a moment to connect. Once you feel plugged into "Spirit," proceed to step two.

### Step 2:

Visualize a brilliant white light, the size of a dinner plate, above your head, the purest and brightest that you can see in your mind's eye. Taking your time to feel its presence, begin vibrating the Divine name **Eheieh**. Vibration should be in monotone at natural C, and elongated in the pronunciation; *Eh-heh-yeh*. Proceed by doing all the vibrations between 3, 7, or 9 times.

### Step 3:

Keeping the ball of light, bright and brilliant, visualize a line or beam of light being drawn down from the sphere above your head. Move it down through your head to the region of the throat. At this point, visualize another sphere forming, just as bright but not as large as the first. Feeling the sphere encompassing the whole region of the throat, begin vibrating the Divine name **YHVH Elohim**, pronounced *Yod-Heh-Vav-Heh El-oh-heem*.

### Step 4:

Once again, visualize another beam of light emanating from the sphere in the throat region, moving down into the region of the solar plexus. Form another ball of light a little larger than the sphere in the throat, and vibrate the Divine name **YHVH Eloah Ve Da'ath**, pronounced *Yod-Heh-Vav-Heh El-oh-ah Ve Dah-at*.

**Step 5:**

Bring another beam down from the sphere in the solar plexus to the region of the groin. Form another sphere of light, then vibrating the Divine name **Shaddai El Chai**, pronounced *Shah-die El kchai.*

**Step 6:**

Moving down once again, visualize another beam of light emanating from the sphere in the groin area and shooting toward the region of the feet. Seeing the feet completely engulfed in another sphere, begin vibrating the Divine name **Adonai ha-Aretz**, pronounced *Ah-doh-nye ha-ah-retz.*

When this last step is completed, you should have a total of five spheres, each brightly illuminated and all connected by one beam of light. Each of the spheres is attributed to a Sephira on the Pillar of Mildness on the Tree of Life. They are in order, as follows:

**The Crown** - correlates to Kether

**Invisible** (Throat) - correlates to Da'ath

**Solar Plexus** - correlates to Tiphareth

**Groin** - correlates to Yesod

**Feet** - correlates to Malkuth

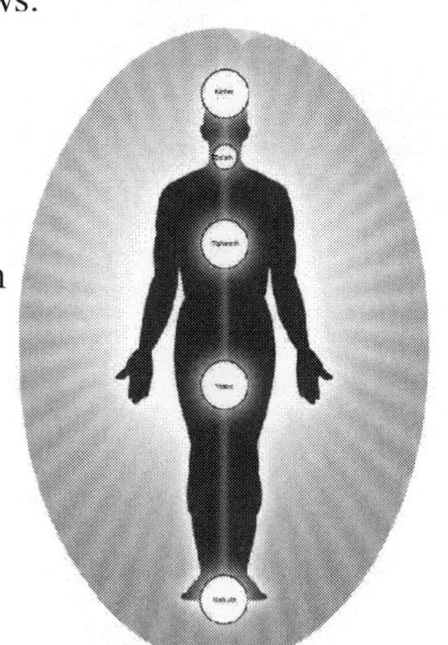

*Illustration 13: Tree of Life on Middle Pillar*

Stay in this state for as long as you desire. You may use this time to meditate or contemplate on the energies invoked. At this time you may end the ritual by taking a deep breath, and as you exhale, visualize all the spheres and lines fading, keeping in mind that the energies are still present, but invisible. Close your work with the Kabbalistic Cross. (This is exercise will be explained in Chapter 8.)

In all ritual working, it is required for the healer to be able to accomplish three things:

1. **To raise energy**
2. **To control energy**
3. **To direct energy**

Again, the ritual of the Middle Pillar obtained its name from the Tree of Life. It stands between the Pillars of Severity (the left side of the Tree) and Mercy (the right side of the Tree). In the perspective of applying the Middle Pillar to the microcosm of man, it means to say that man himself must combine the opposing forces of nature, as well as, his own self.

In performance of this exercise, the energies invoked are drawn from the Kether sphere. This is in opposition to the Eastern tradition where it is drawn from the groin, or Yesod, which is considered Lunar energy. The ritual of the Middle Pillar, simple as it may seem, is not easy. Like all the rituals, it takes time to feel the full effects and benefits. All in all, it takes hard work and practice. In truth, we draw energy from the Infinite or Fountain Gate down and also from the Foundation Gate upward. When both are done at the same time, this is what the alchemist calls the marriage of the Sun and the Moon, the marriage of opposites.

The Middle Pillar Exercise is used for a variety of things. It is used for the purpose of being able to raise magical/spiritual energy at will by a healer as already described. The same energies are used in rituals for basic, as well as, advanced healing. This may be helpful to those who are lethargic because it will give the patient a quick dose of energy. In referring to meditation, it aids in the ability to raise the mind to the higher planes as well as channeling the same energies down into the material universe and our body.

Now we are going to make a statement that will amaze many who have studied the Kabbalah for many years. This statement is not made lightly; it is made after years and years of personal study of understanding the nature of the Tree of Life on the human body. While our diagram of the Sephirot are circular in nature as if they were balls of energy, in reality, every energy *and* **every Sephirot is everywhere in the universe at the same time.** Every Sephira is a state of consciousness or universal energy.

With this in mind, we are going to share with you the traditional placement of the Tree of Life on the human body, but we don't want your brain to get locked into believing that a particular Sephira only exists in one limited place on the human body. The mandala of the Tree of Life provides us with an archetype with what the Kabbalist will often refer to as "Adam Kadmon." As each Sephira is described, visualize it as a placement on the body *and* as a universal energy.

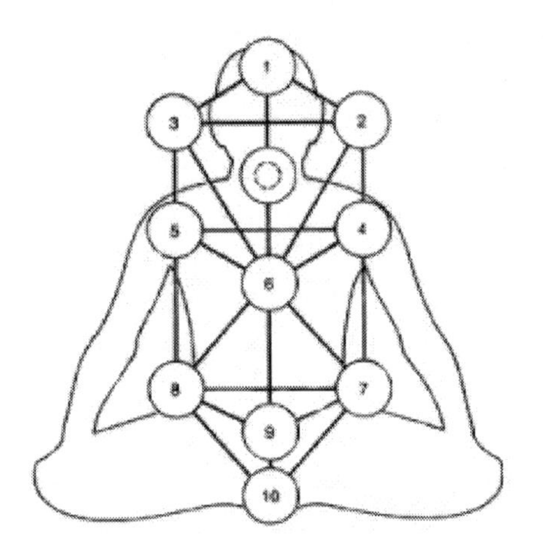


**KETHER: "Crown"**

Kether (pronounced Keter) represents the Divine Emanation that is beyond our comprehension. It is a symbol for what Kabbalists refer to as Divine White Brilliance ("D.W.B."). This is the first spark of light and exists everywhere in the universe, as well as, in the human body. It is shown primarily above the head to show that it is slightly out of our consciousness and our ability to understand.

Kether provides us healing light in its purest form. If we never used any colors or any other energy, Kether alone provides us ample healing potential and power to transform any illness into vitality. Some would refer to Kether as God, the Divine One, and the Eternal Source. The Divine name of Kether is signified by "Eheieh", which means ***"I am"***. Kether is beyond time and space and while it is always perhaps out of reach; its emanation is always within grasp. As a Ruach Healer, you have two challenges; first, to draw Kether down into yourself, second, to raise your soul and consciousness into the heights of Kether. Understand that if we did no more than stand over another human being while placing our hands over their head and invoke the Divine White Brilliance of Kether then through will, projected this cleansing light from the top of their head to the bottom of the feet, circulating it everywhere in between, you would be invoking a most potent elixir of light and life.

This is the basis of the Ruach Healing Method, the white light of D.W.B. In some traditions, gold is the highest color on the scales, but in the Kabbalistic teachings, it is the white light that holds this position of prominence. Generally, when in doubt or not sure, one can always use the healing power of white light. Kether is pure spiritual consciousness and therefore using the white light of Kether will allow you to work at the highest possible vibration. Have patience as powerful healing energies of the subtle and refined white light filter their way into the physical body; they will arrive always on time.

## CHOKMAH: "Wisdom"

Chokmah (KCHOCK-mah) represents wisdom, but it's not the kind of wisdom that deals with everyday matters. This is the wisdom of the Eternal Father of the manifested universe. Chokmah's color is gray or silver. When visualizing Chokmah's colors, we usually visualize a cloud-like gray containing a mixture of colors as transparent hued mist. Its body position is the left portion of the brain.

From a healing perspective, it is the wisdom of the energy field empowering the body. It is ultimately Divine wisdom. Chokmah is also distinguished at a planetary level as the Primum Mobile, the Sphere of the Zodiac, and the endless library of Divine wisdom. Many scholars believe that Chokmah is equally impossible to describe as is Kether. Chokmah is on the masculine pillar of the Tree of Life. The primary difference between Kether and Chokmah is that Chokmah is more tangible and tends to focus the inner attention on the preciseness of the Universe, particularly the human body and auric energy field. We tend to charge the energy field with a bright silvery color when there are phobias, anxiety and emotions that seem out of control. Think of anything that requires precision and logic and Chokmah is the energy to use.

### BINAH: "Understanding"

On the opposite pillar, called the Pillar of Severity, we have Binah (bee-NAH) which means "understanding". The color is deep indigo or shiny black. Its position on the body is the right brain. The ruling planet is Saturn and therefore anything that requires strong formation will benefit by Binah energies. It has structure, yet is creative at the same time. Saturn is also associated with the skin, bones, teeth and cartilage. Binah resides on the feminine pillar and is compassionate yet constricting.

Binah's understanding is depicted as a thick darkness which indicates that it veils the Divine glory in which all the colors of the rainbow are hidden. Do not think of Binah as the blackness of lower vibrational energies, rather as the womb that provides a wonderful safe haven for formation. We distinguish the difference between darkness and black and shiny black of Binah. Binah consciousness can be thought of as restrictive and forming. Within Binah are the mysteries, depth and silence of what is known as the Supernal Light.

The Supernals are the three top Sephirot which is the holy triad of light. Wherein Chokmah resides the Father, in Binah exists the Supernal

Mother. Often, she is referred to as Aima Elohim. Binah receives all the wisdom of Chokmah and contains it. The union of Chokmah and Binah are essential in healing, for they create a blend of masculine and feminine energies working in perfect harmony. This is critical for any healing operation.

These three Sephirot complete the triad of the Divine Source that emanates out of Ain Soph Aur. In them we have the crown, wisdom, and understanding. Together they represent the three aspects of knowledge: eternal knowledge, wisdom and knowing. It is particularly the combination and balance of the energies between Chokmah and Binah on the Tree of Life that the human body is created. This place is called Da'ath or "knowledge." Da'ath, formally is not a Sephira When we look at the human body, the neck is not part of the head nor is it part of the trunk, and so it is with Da'ath, placed within the region of the neck. It acts as a connecting link between the mind and body.

## CHESED: "Mercy"

Chesed (KCHE-sed) represents mercy. Chesed is masculine and represents the great king. Its color is royal blue. The body part attributed to it is the left shoulder or arm all the way down to the hand. Its planet is Jupiter and represents love, the quality of kindness and giving of energy from the Divine. Jupiter is associated with cellular development and integration as well as the intestines and digestive production.

Symbolically, Chesed is the first day of creation, which indicates that the rest of the Tree emanates from Chesed. This Sephira produces life giving power which manifests itself everywhere in the universe and in the individual. Chesed energy is often considered extremely expansive and benevolent.

## GEBURRAH: "Strength"

Geburah (Ge-BUR-ah) is "strength" and is seen in the color scarlet red. Geburah's position on the body is the right shoulder down to the right hand. The nature of Geburah is feminine which contains or limits the masculine energy of Chesed, giving it direction and form. The planet is Mars which represents strength or determination. It is a robust energy that includes severance or the cutting off of things no longer necessary. Mars in turn is associated with external organs, such as the ears, face and the limbs.

This Sephira may be the most misunderstood on the Tree of Life. Beginning Kabbalists often times see it as completely destructive. However, in the battle against a metastasizing cancer in the human body, there is no greater friend than the sword of Geburah. Geburah also limits the abundance of mercy emanated by Chesed. On the other hand, the severe nature of Geburah is tempered by the mercy of Chesed. So, like Yin and Yang or opposite twin powers, these two Sephirot provide a mighty balance on the Tree of Life. Many people believe Geburah is a harsh energy, but as mentioned earlier, sometimes this force is necessary to remove some of the disease out of a patient's energy field.

## TIPHARETH : "Beauty"

Tiphareth (TI-fear-et) is in the center of the Tree of Life. Its meaning is beauty. Its color is yellow-gold. Tiphareth balances Chesed and Geburah, providing a state of mildness between mercy and strength. When the giving energies of Chesed are met with the energies of strength from Geburah, the result becomes one of beauty. This beauty is true purpose of Tiphareth. On the human body it is the heart center. As the heart beats outward, it becomes more akin with Chesed, for Chesed is expansion and giving. As the heart beats inward, it becomes more Geburah in nature, constrictive. Tiphareth is the heart at rest. Thus, for most heart and circulatory conditions, we use a combination of Geburah, Chesed and Tiphareth. Tiphareth is the heart at rest. Its planet is the sun. The sun is associated with the heart, the circulation of blood, and the regeneration and maintenance of life energy.

It is from Tiphareth you can truly experience healing gratitude. From this magnificent vantage point you have access to all creation both in the world and within yourself. Tiphareth located in the center of the heart, if nothing else as a metaphor that you can experience all the Tree of Life, all its glory, and all its beauty. Notice that Tiphareth is connected with every Sephirot directly except Malkuth. In one sense, everything flows through Tiphareth. Looking at Tiphareth from an esoteric perspective, we could claim that to know Tiphareth is to know Kether, for Tiphareth is a direct reflection of Kether.

In the Ruach Healing Method, we talk about the healer attaining Tiphareth consciousness. In esoteric schools such as the Golden Dawn, Tiphareth represent the grade of Adeptus Minor. Several years of study and preparation go into obtaining that grade. However, from a healer's perspective, as we begin to live in a state of gratitude allowing this gratitude to flow into our life and our healing work, we are operating in a state of Tiphareth consciousness. Through gratitude you align yourself to that part of your soul that is linked to every other part of your being. Gratitude takes us out of the chair of judgment and into a centered and balanced place where healing can manifest. This is important as a healer, for it is in Tiphareth consciousness we are receiving the direct reflection of Kether, or Divine Source. This Divine Source connection is essential for a Ruach Healer.

## NETZACH: "Victory"

Netzach's (Net-ZAKCH) meaning is victory. It symbolizes perseverance, energy, passion, and overcoming adversity. Its color is emerald green. It is attributed to the left leg on the human body. The planet is Venus, which is associated with internal organs and the lymphatic system. This is one reason why the emerald green color is so often employed in the Ruach Healing Method when the body needs to overcome infections. It's a very cleansing, fiery and purifying energy, akin to that of spiritual antiseptic, if you will.

Netzach is connected to your passions and emotions giving you balance to the more logical side of your personality. Medical science now knows that the human brain cannot function without the emotional nature, even when logical decisions are being made. Through Netzach you have connection to emotions and passion that give you drive toward the Divine causing you to strive toward ascending in vibration. There can be no victory without passion. We see in history moments of high intellectual peaks in mankind of great art and music in celebration of the victory of human passion directed to higher pursuits. Netzach allows us to connect with the fiery aspects of our emotions, the empathetic, and the intuitive aspect of the self.

## HOD: "Splendor"

Hod (Hode) is the Sephira of splendor and the intellect. Its color is orange and it is feminine. Hod is associated with the right hip and leg on the human body. Its corresponding planet is Mercury, which is associated with the nervous system and all that it involves. Hod enforces sacrifice and works in harmony with Netzach to keep all options open. The energy of Hod is very mercurial in nature so is therefore another very cleansing energy. It reflects the purity of the mind without the influence of emotional or mental disease.

Hod is the realm of reason and therefore is attributed to the planet Mercury. In legend, Mercury was a messenger of the gods that delivered the Divine Holy Word into the world of man. Through reason we begin to ascend beyond our animal instincts. The ancient philosophers Plato and Socrates were striving to do just that; to use reason in order to elevate themselves above their animal nature.

It is interesting to note that in alchemy one of the seven primary stages of alchemical (spiritual) development is called "the Marriage of the King and the Queen". Put simply, this is the marriage of intellect and mathematical nature with the emotional, passionate, and creative nature. It's fascinating to observe that on the Tree of Life, Hod is on the feminine pillar, and Netzach is on the masculine pillar. This indicates a type of symmetry and balance that the Tree of Life provides as a spiritual mandala.

## YESOD: "Foundation"

Yesod (Yeah-SOWED) means is "foundation". This is the foundation that relates to the groin area associated with the genitals and womb area on the human body on the Tree. Its color is purple. Its planet is Moon, which governs bodily secretions and fluids. Yesod represents both sex and death and it contains all prior experiences of the mind. Many of our subconscious memories and thoughts are caught up in the Yesodic center. It is no secret that most people spend a great portion of their life thinking of death and sex. It represents the astral plane which seeks to enlighten, as well as, deceive us. This is an extremely powerful center of the body that can be used for healing and transmutation. It is the seat of the Ruach Elohim, the Divine energy akin to the Kundalini of the East.

In Eastern philosophy, Yesod is the rising serpent of power called the "kundalini," or life force. In the Kabbalah, this powerful energy is referred to as the Ruach Elohim. It is from Yesod that emanations of your astral body are projected from you. Also, this area represents the lower or animal nature that serves to empower and protect the human body. If we did not have the instinct to survive, for example, and run when afraid, we would parish quickly. All emanations of the Tree gather and are codified in Yesod. This codification makes this Sephira act as the backdrop to Malkuth; the symbol of the physical body.

## MALKUTH: "Kingdom"

Finally, Malkuth (Mal-KOOT), is known as the kingdom and represents the totality of your body. Its color is divided into four, which are citrine, olive, russet, and black. Also earth-tones are used. The body association on the Tree of Life is the feet. This is our foundation on the planet, which is of course, Earth. Malkuth is the sum of all proceeding energies that have traveled down the Tree of Life. It is the expression of an aspect of God known as the "Shekinah", which means the feminine principle of Deity. The Shekinah could be said to be the Source of healing on the physical plane. In a sense we see the physical body as Malkuth. It is the feminine aspect of the Divine Source, also defined as the Divine Presence or God.

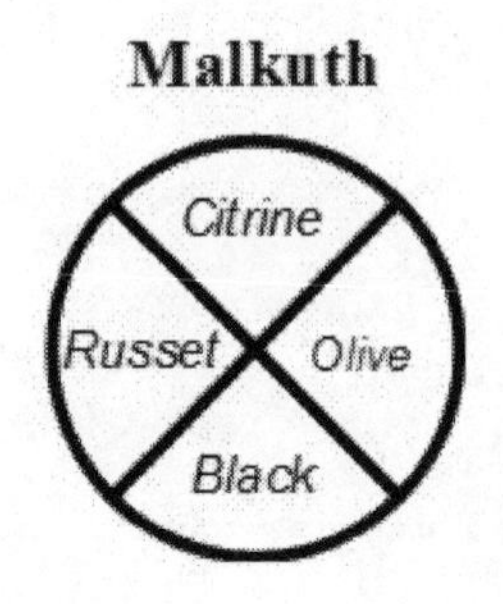


*Illustration 14: Colors of Malkuth*

Malkuth indicates the vessel from which we receive the light from all other parts of the soul and aspects of the Divine Source. This light is then put into the world of actions. Malkuth is the domain of the manifested universe, the immediate environment and the plane of physical reality. As a consequence, all inner journeys of spiritual consciousness begin symbolically in Malkuth. It is absolutely essential that the healer provide a firm base from which to build his or her personal Tree of Life. This means that in order to optimize your healing potential, it is important to optimize the power and magnetism of your physical body. There's no need to become Jack LaLanne (American fitness, exercise, and nutritional expert;

1914-2011). Simple things like clean water, fresh air, and exercise will all serve the healer in fortifying his or her own Malkuth.

### Putting the Sephirot Together for an Understanding of Self

Now that we have defined the Sephirot, let's study the Tree of Life more closely. The Tree of Life is what we call a map of the macro-cosmic or objective universe, but it is also a reflection of your own soul. Therefore, it is also a map of your subjective self or what you truly are on the inside. This shows each of the Sephira represents the Divine aspects of your soul in a perfected state.

**The lower qualities are not part of who you truly are.** They are incorrect choices we sometimes make due to our egoistic concerns. Part of the spiritual evolution we go through is that we raise ourselves up and strip away the lower qualities to live in a perfected state. This is Spirit revealing itself by un-cloaking itself of all the things that are not part of it. Similarly, as you are rising on the Tree of Life you are tuning yourself in to the purest aspects of which you are, stripping away what you are not. This process continues as you shed beliefs, fears and emotions that you have acquired by choice. In many instances you have latched onto lower energies that you mistakenly think are part of you. You may think, **"I am my fear. I am my hatred. I am my anger"**. But it is not true. **You are not these attitudes.** As you raise yourself on the Tree of Life, you acquire the energies that exist there and they replace the lower energies. Remember that the Tree of Life is a pure reflection of you, a reflection of the Divine Spirit within you. You are a reflection of the Divine act of Creation in its entirety and in its glory!

# NOTES:

# CHAPTER SIX: The Vitality Gates on the Body

The Vitality Gates on the body are similar to the chakras in the Eastern system, but not exactly the same. In Ruach Healing Method, the Vitality Gates are based on the metaphysical concept of the city of Jerusalem. This becomes a philosophical model of the physical world and the human body. This model is used to check the energy flow of the body. Traditionally, Jerusalem had seven gates.

In ancient times, map makers had a horrific challenge in creating an accurate map of the world. It was believed that Jerusalem was the center of the world. As a matter of fact, Jerusalem and the planet earth were considered to be at the center of the galaxy. Naturally, modern science has disproved this. Jerusalem certainly is the Holy Place, therefore metaphysically, the center of the world. Many deeply spiritual meta physicians consider Jerusalem the heart chakra or the gate of the *entire world*! It is the birthplace and holy city to three of the world's major religions: Christianity, Judaism, and Islam.

I never could get a complete grip on this concept until I visited Jerusalem. While in Jerusalem, I was standing in the Holy Sepulcher, just at the entrance to the Greek Orthodox section of the Sepulcher, and I noticed a stand with a black stone resting upon it. On this black stone was an equal armed cross etched into it. Naturally, the sepulcher and the equal armed cross caught my attention, so I had to ask somebody what it meant. The old Orthodox monk pointed out to me that this was, metaphorically speaking, the center of the entire world. This one little spot was exactly half way between the place of Jesus' crucifixion and his point of resurrection. I became entranced with this whole concept of dying and rising, which in truth expresses the whole concept of initiation and metaphysical healing. As healing practitioners our job is to help our patients die to illness and rise to a new level of health and vitality.

***"Let me enter the path of darkness per adventure there shall I find the light."* – Golden Dawn Initiation**

Jerusalem is a microcosm of the macrocosm. Put simply, this is the idea that Jerusalem represents on a small level what exists throughout the entire world. Since the human body and energy field is a reflection of Divine presence or higher Source, it too is a microcosm. The human body is a type of old Jerusalem which must be healed and rectified internally to bring peace unto the land. In the book of Revelations, St John claims to see a New Jerusalem descending from heaven. We believe the cleansing and activation of these holy gates, the Vitality Gates on the Body, help the healer to prepare the patient who is about to be healed, to move through this path from darkness to light. You must first remove all lower vibrational energies that cause physical sickness and decay. Next, by invoking the presence of spiritual healing light, into these "holy centers" located on the energy field of the body you will be restoring the spiritual body, the Vitality Gates and of course the human body.

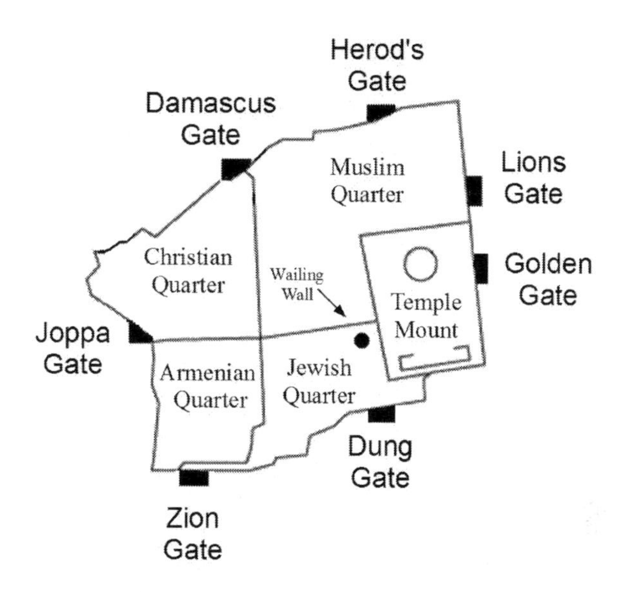


*Illustration 15: Gates of Jerusalem*

In the Eastern tradition, the Vitality Gates are called chakras. In fact, if you attend a Ruach Healing Workshop, you will see and hear students using the terms “chakras” and “gates” in an interchangeable fashion. The truth of the matter is, while they may be expressed in an interchangeable manner, there is a difference in how we conclude the Vitality Gates work to help the human body function. In order to understand this subtle, yet important difference let me return back to our model, the city of Jerusalem.

While in Jerusalem I visited each gate. Some of the gates were very narrow. It became easy to see how energy, or people in this case, could become clogged going in and out of a narrow gate. I also felt a specific energy at each gate. Different gates exist within different portions of the city. Some are within the Christian quarter, some within the Jewish Quarter, and others within the Muslim quarter. In essence, the gates allowed for garbage and UN-useful energy to leave the city, or "quarter", and allowed for life giving energy such as food and water to be brought into the city. This is exactly what the Vitality Gates on the human body do. We believe and many spiritual healers agree that the gates of Jerusalem are a powerful metaphor for the human body.

The "Vitality Gates" are similar to chakras, in that they are energy centers of the energy field. However, the movement of the gates is seen as slightly different in the Ruach Healing Method. In the chakra system the energy seems to flow almost in the same fashion as a vortex. In the Ruach Healing Method the practitioner observes that the energy flows much like a paddle wheel, bringing specific energy into the sphere of sensation and bringing the negative energy to the surface to be released.

As energy gets clogged within the "Sphere of Sensation" and particularly within a gate, the "paddle wheel" or energy stops moving within that gate. It becomes stagnant and stuck resulting in a whole host of problems and illnesses! (Please refer to Chapter 20, "Most Common Illnesses And How To Heal Them")

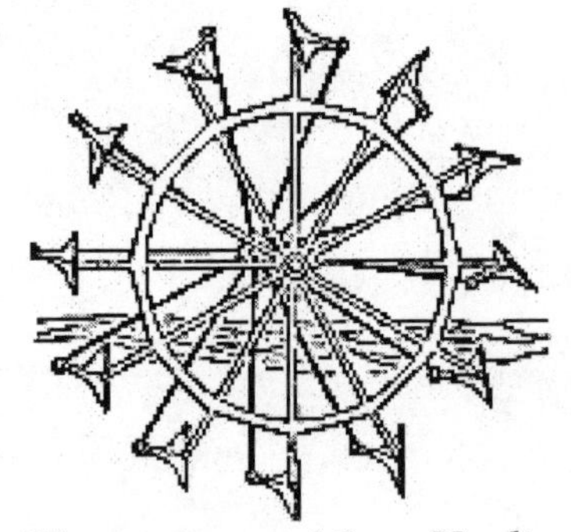

*Illustration 16: Vitality Gate as a Paddle Wheel*

Interestingly enough, through countless spiritual and astral investigations by an untold number of magicians, mystics, shamans and healers, we have found that these gates vibrate at approximately the same rate as depicted in the eastern chakra system. Therefore, the colors are about the same. The difference is that the Ruach Healing Practitioner not only works within the color spectrum of the gate but also works within the colored light of the specific Sephirot to which the gate is assigned. (Note that is Kabbalistic tradition, the gates begin with the number 1 above the head rather than at the base of the spine.)

### Gate #1 – Foundation Gate

**Location: groin and base of spine**
**Color: light red tint**

The Foundation Gate provides foundation, spinal health, prosperity, security and presence. It relates to male/female sexual energy. Both the testicles and vagina are considered feminine. It is only through heat that their natures change when resolution of the Foundation Gate is brought about with the Fountain Gate. When this occurs, the Vesica Piscis is created in the Sphere of Sensation thus, an alchemical marriage takes place within the human being. The separation of masculine and feminine, strong and weak, hot and cold is no longer felt. All dichotomies are overcome, all oppositions are resolved and the Light of the Holy Spirit reigns. In regards to the Foundation Gate, the imbalance or clogging of this gate can be the cause of financial problems, material gain or loss.

**Gate #2 – Navel Gate**

**Location: lower abdomen, lower back, sexual organs (ovaries and/or womb)**
**Color: light orange tint**

The Navel Gate relates to self-gratification, through deep emotional influx, sexuality, sensuality, feelings, desires, sensation, movement, and purification through the bowels.

**Gate #3 – Solar Plexus Gate**

**Location: solar plexus**
**Color: light yellow tint**

The Solar Plexus Gate relates to personal power, creativity, the ego identity, and will/autonomy. It affects our metabolism, immune system, energy levels and cooperation/integration with the rest of the self and with others.

**Gate #4 – Heart Center Gate**

**Location: heart and lungs**
**Color: light green tint**

This gate affects our ability to unlock universal, unconditional love. It is related to the deeper will of the soul. The gate pertains to social identity and empowers the Rose Cross within the healer. On a physical level, it relates to the heart, lungs and governs the circulatory system of the body. It is also considered the "HUB" of the "7 Vitality Gates of the Human Body".

### Gate #5 – Throat Gate

**Location: throat**
**Color: light blue tint**

This is the gateway that pertains to sound and creative identity, and is oriented to self-expression in connection with Da'ath, the invisible Sephira in between Binah and Chokmah. This provides energy transit from the lower body to the higher mind, represented in sound and speech. The health of this gateway is vital for conditions that affect the thyroid, depression, or schizophrenia. The Throat Gate is particularly important when working with people who have suppressed emotions---such as anger. Here are a couple of examples. One would be young girls who have been told to be quiet, smile, and look pretty. Another example is children who were, "better seen then heard," whom oftentimes fill this gate with emotions that have never been verbalized. It is not unusual to be clearing this gate, or the throat in general, and have your patient begin screaming, crying, and verbalizing deep emotional pain. Go slowly when working with this gate. It is the connecting link between mind and body.

### Gate #6 – Third Eye Gate

**Location: Third Eye, spot between your eyes on your forehead**
**Color: light violet tint**

This gate relates to the Yesodic influence within the Supernal triad of the Higher Self. Self-reflection, and intuition are what this gate primarily activates. This gate is responsible for both physical sight and more importantly astral or spiritual sight. When this gate is clear and healthy, it allows us to see the bigger picture, rather than our own narrow needs. The

Third Eye Gate relates to eyesight, the pituitary gland, physical growth and other related areas of the human body.

### Gate #7 – The Fountain Gate

**Location: resting on the top of the head**
**Color: brilliant white/golden tint**

This gate relates to thought, universal identity, and self-knowing. It is the awareness and union with your Personal Holy Guardian Angel as the connecting link to the Supernals. This is the doorway for Divine White Brilliance. This gate is located slightly above the head; in the place of the crown.

**NOTE:** ***If you've been an working as an Eastern Practitioner and have become proficient with using the standard colors of the chakras in your healing work, you may find variations in using the color attributions of the Gates. You will likely find that using lighter, almost white, tinted light is more effective than dark colors. Light colors are especially good for healing people who have very refined, high-vibrational light bodies. Some dark colors are carefully implemented for the purpose of destroying disease. Trust your instincts as to which hues to apply and which specific conditions are appropriate for which color application.

## Exercise: Activating your Vitality Gates on your Body

This exercise is designed to activate your own personal gates. Healers require a great deal of energy and life force to be effective, and this exercise will help raise more power. In addition, you will discover that in doing this exercise you'll begin to rise to higher spiritual consciousness.

### Step 1:

Begin with the Four Fold Breath. After a minute or so, focus on the base of your spine... visualize a very pale vivid red light about the size of a softball at the base of your spine...keep up the visualization for at least two minutes.

### Step 2:

Visualize the very pale, yet vivid orange light about two inches below your navel. After a minute, pause and visualize both the Navel Gate and Foundation Gate simultaneously.

### Step 3:

Continue following this pattern one Gate at a time until you reach the Fountain Gate.

**Step 4:**

Continue breathing in the 4 fold count, and visualize all 7 Gates lit up at once. Pause to feel your spiritual connection, continue as long as you wish. When finished, open your eyes. It is interesting to note that in the Middle Pillar Exercise we work from the top down and when activating the Gates we work from the bottom up.

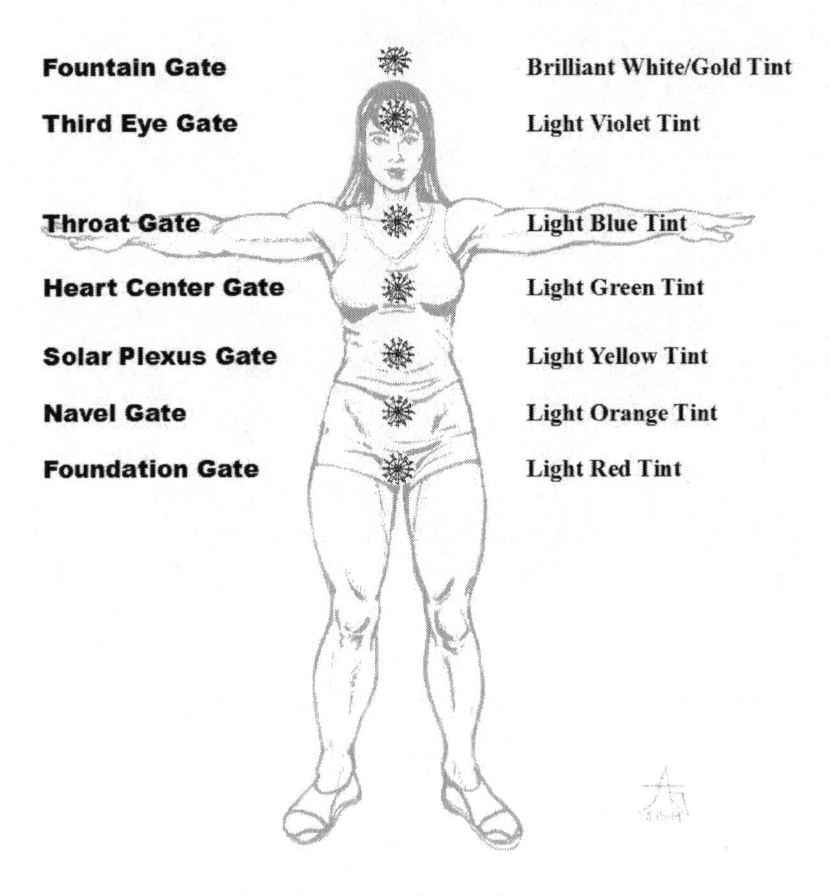


*Illustration 17: Vitality Gates on the Body*

# CHAPTER SEVEN: The Nature of the Astral Body

Interaction between the subtle body and the physical body is such that a disease from the astral body can affect the physical body and vice versa. The function of the astral body is to absorb, distribute and energize the whole physical body with the Divine Ruach. It also helps organs of the body to function properly. Understand that without Divine Ruach, the body would die. Through the Sephirot and the Vitality Gates, the astral body controls, as well as, takes responsibility for the function of the whole physical body.

No doubt you have seen someone who after a hard day's work looked as if they were drooping. There is really nothing physical about them that is drooping, it is there Vitality Rays that emanate from the energy field that are drooping. The interaction between the subtle body or the energy field and the physical body is extremely intimate. It is in this unique connection, between the energy field and the physical body that we see perhaps the greatest expression of the Emerald Tablet of Hermes. **"As above, so below, and as below, so above."** The whole of spiritual healing in general, works on this premise, that if we can affect the subtle body, we can also affect the physical body. Interaction between the subtle body and the physical body is so intimate that disease from the astral body can affect the physical body and vice-verse. We must always be cognizant of the adage that states; "we are spiritual being having a human experience." The astral body serves on a spiritual level some very specific duties that aid the physical body and provide it with the vitality it needs to live. In essence, the astral body absorbs, distributes and energizes spiritual energy into the whole physical body. Putting it simply, Divine Ruach finds its doorway into the physical body in part through the astral body and through the Vitality Gates.

The astral body also helps the organs of the body to function properly. For without Divine Ruach or spiritual sustenance the physical body would die. The astral body is created in part, by a regular action of breath and the electromagnetic energy of the heartbeat. This alone however is not enough to create an astral body. Our astral bodies according to many are created before our physical bodies are forming in the womb. The astral body, Kabbalistically on the Tree of Life, is an extension, of the Supernals; Kether, Chokmah, and Binah; into the planes of lower manifestation. The bottom line is that the astral body, through the Sephirot on the Tree of Life and the Vitality Gates on the human body, is responsible for the function of the whole physical body.

The energy field or astral body is divided up much like an onion. There are numerous layers to the energy field or energy fields. Some hold that there are ten layers, 12, even as many as 32 layers, to the astral body. For the purposes of Ruach Healing at this level, we are primarily working with an inner layer, an outer layer and what are commonly known as the ganglia. The ganglia are called "Vitality Rays." These are feathery rays of light extending from the outer energy field, the part of the energy field that reaches well beyond the inner part of the energy field, or energy fields. One of the primary purposes of these rays of light or Vitality Rays is to react to astral contaminants.

There is an extended energy field, that in some people reaches outward twenty or thirty feet. Most people's energy field is only about 8 feet outside of the body. In general, the inner energy field reflects the outer energy field. In other words, if there is a depletion of energy at the inner energy field level, the same will be true of the outer energy field. Working at a range of about six to eight inches from the physical body when scanning, cleaning and charging the astral body is very effective. However, with extremely sick individuals, virtually all of your work will take place at the two to three inch level away from the body. The reason is quite simple, sick people do not produce a healthy vibrant or strong energy field. Their energy field is closer to the body because it is sick.

As a Ruach healer, you will begin to notice the difference, between a vibrant energy field and a weak energy field. Here are some signs of a vibrant healthy energy field. The inner energy field closest to the body, feels warm and energetic. Even if a patient's skin is cold from being in the outdoors, if they are healthy, you should still feel that sense of vitality and warmth. Another sign of a vibrant, healthy energy field is that the secondary energy field extends out farther than eight inches. In a healthy vibrant individual the energy field will extend for two feet or more. The ganglia/Vitality Rays that extend outward beyond the secondary energy field are generally pointed upwards, almost like the branches of trees reaching towards the sun.

The mind, or more specifically our thoughts, is very influential over the energy field because we are connected though the Divine Source first and foremost through our thoughts. The energy field acts as a gauge for our thoughts measuring each thought and responding according. Our thoughts affect first our energy field or our astral body and then our physical body. Negative emotions can have serious effects on the gates especially, depleting them and possibly leading to psychosomatic or even physical illness. For example, expression of anger, frustration, depression, phobias and bipolar behaviors are signs of the Ruach in the area around the solar plexus being depleting. Negative emotions are often responsible for causing congestion in the Tiphareth portion of the body and the Heart Center Vitality Gate.

Some common problems or indications for treatments manifest as weaknesses or clogged Vitality Gates on the human body. In the energy field of the aura or astral body are emanations of feathery rays of Light. The rays extending from the human aura will often droop if the body is weak and become very perky if the vitality of the patient is strong. We have all met people who have a powerful astral body. Maybe we can't see it but we can certainly feel it. A clogged Vitality Gate indicates that too much energy is trying to enter or exit, thus leaving the energy field depleted in some area of the body. The energy field can become suffocated with too much energy, and thus not allowed to breathe in the healing Light, and allow negative toxins to escape.

*Illustration 18: Healthy Vitality Rays*

Fundamental treatments using the Ruach Healing Method are used when there is a depletion, congestion or clogged energy current in the astral body. Ruach Healing is also used on the astral body when a gate is malfunctioning in a manner which the gate is not allowing clean energy and Light to enter and negative energy to escape. When the energy field emanations called the Vitality Rays are drooping or tangled, there is a leak in Ruach energy through a hole in the energy field. The general protocol in treating depletion is to energize the problematic area. If there is congestion or if a gate is found to be malfunctioning, it is best affected by cleaning and disentangling followed by energizing and strengthening. Finally when Ruach life force energy is leaking out through a hole in the energy field, that area needs to be sealed.

Applying this to practical application can be seen when treating a cut. With a physical cut within the body, it is critical that you are aware, that there is equally a cut within the energy field. When these kinds of situations occur especially in emergency situations, step one is to physically stop the bleeding; step two is to charge the tear or the hole in the energy field with as much Ruach Light that you are able to invoke. If there is congestion or blockage in the energy current, the energy or blockage must be removed before charging or energizing commences. It is important to note, that if someone cuts themselves physically and you are the one that is treating the cut, (provided medical attention is not needed!) skip all the previous steps and immediately go to charging!

Another practical application is found when working with somebody that is chronically or severely ill. While they may be suffering from congestion of blocked energy of their Gates or in their energy fields, the healer must be aware that this energy, even though it is corrupted, may be the only thing keeping the chronically ill patient alive. If you are working with someone in the hospital who is very sick and you observe a very weak and listless energy field, you might want to consider charging them until the body starts to regain some strength. Then, lightly perform cleansing of the energy field and scanning of the gates. Make sure to be extra cautious not to remove too much energy at one time.

The astral body can be healed using variations in Divine names, colors relating to the Sephirot, and planetary energy. These variations may be helpful for specific types of illnesses; working with white Light is always safe and effective. Remember, the Emerald tablet of Hermes teaches: **"As Above, So below"**, but it also teaches, **"As Below, So Above."**

**Literally all problems of the astral body that Ruach Healing changes manifest in the following ways:**

- A weak energy field
- An unbalanced energy field
- The symmetry of the Vitality Rays is unbalanced and uneven
- An energy field that droops and is not collecting positive vitality
- Vitality Gates are either clogged or not functioning well, or weak and listless.

I have had the good fortune to meet some people that have overwhelming dynamic energy fields filled with positive magnetism. One of those people is a legendary Siegfried, from Siegfried and Roy. I was sitting in Las Vegas in a midnight meeting for entertainers. When he came walking in the door. Moments before he entered the room I felt this powerful solar energy field. His energy field emanated incredible health and vitality but there was something else that emanated as well; it emanated incredible magnetism. Truly vibrant and alive people that have this magnetic quality, such as Siegfried, are able to motivate and attract people in ways the average person cannot. They work hard to maintain the magnetic energy field by eating a healthy diet, exercise, drinking clean water, and time in the sun,...so on and so forth. Most importantly, I believe, magnetic people practice the **Law of Attraction**. They think positive thoughts about themselves, their health and their lives.

I would like to mention a few other people, that share this super magnetic and healthy energy field, namely, John F. Kennedy, (I saw him at a young age) and Mother Teresa (of whom was said to have incredible magnetism even when she was getting older!). I am sure you have heard that the Dali Lama possesses the same quality as well.

## Exercise: Expand your Astral Body or Energy Field

Previously, we provided you the Middle Pillar exercise. This is a powerful exercise that will help you develop more Light or Ruach in your Energy Field. A strong and powerful astral body or energy field is essential for vitality. As a healer you will want to be able to expand your aura and contract it at will. The very exercising of the energy field is an effective way of strengthening it. You can think of it as pushups for your astral body.

**Step 1:**

Perform the Middle Pillar exercise

**Step 2:**

Begin to expand your energy field to fill up the entire house or building. Strongly feel it pushing on the walls of the house.

**Step 3:**

Contract your astral body back to normal size

**Step 4:**

Repeat Step 2 & 3 several times.

**Step 5:**

Practice separating your astral body away from your physical body. Don't worry you cannot separate all of it.

**Step 6:**

Practice putting your seed of consciousness into your astral body and explore your environment.

**Step 7:**

Come back to your physical body and allow your astral body to mesh with your physical body.

Doing the above exercise will greatly expand your aura, and strengthen your astral body. The portion where you separate your astral body from yourself will greatly help your intuition. It will help give you special abilities, especially in the area of long distant healing. As I was healing a patient, I experienced a feeling of someone joining me. As I looked over to see who it was, I noticed it was me. My astral body had separated to help me and working in harmony with the healing objective. Amazing!

## NOTES:

# CHAPTER EIGHT: The Importance of Self-Protection

The Ruach Healing Method is different from other systems of healing. Ruach is more energy oriented, based on actual energies within the energy field of the patient, rather than on a mystical attunement as in some traditions. This doesn't mean that the Ruach Healing Method does not have specialized moments of advancement called “Awakenings”. In the Appendix, we cover the levels of Awakening that can be obtained by a Ruach Healer. The Ruach Healing Method is an alchemical system of healing based on the philosophy of the Emerald Tablet of Hermes. The Ruach Healing system works from the top down and the bottom up. The Tree of Life flows from the top down, while the Vitality Gates rise from the bottom up.

Ruach Healing is focused on healing the actual problem, rather than just the symptoms. We are working from the higher levels of existence down to the lower manifested forms. The patient being healed also usually experiences a spiritual healing counterpart as well, and becomes more awakened.

With all the energies and Divine power used in Ruach Healing it is extremely important to protect yourself from unwanted forces. To protect yourself before you perform a healing operation, the healer must go into a meditative state and connect to the Divine White Brilliance (D.W.B.). The Lesser Banishing Ritual of the Pentagram is important in creating a personal circle of protection for your work. The Pentagram circle of protection is followed by lighting up the Tree of Life in your personal sphere with the Middle Pillar exercise, using the appropriate Divine names. In the process of protection and Divine connection the healer lights up the Vitality Gates of their body. After connecting yourself to these protective sources, some healers take additional steps to purify and consecrate their healing space before proceeding onward.

For our own personal work, we prefer the using the Lesser Banishing Ritual of the Pentagram (L.B.R.P) for our protection ritual. We specifically, find connection to the Archangels important before beginning a healing operation. This Archangel connection is easily found in the L.B.R.P. There are some people however, that are not comfortable with pentagrams. That is fine.

We have taught thousands of people around the world the Ruach Healing Method. In our teachings we discovered many students have their own way of protecting themselves and their sphere of sensation before embarking on a healing session. As an eclectic student of the spiritual mysteries, we certainly have no problem with this. Many of our students like to smudge themselves with white sage. Our pagan students often times do a short invocation to the Goddess. Our Christian students will pause and say the Lord's Prayer. Whatever protection ritual you use, we think the most important point is the intention of the healer.

If you are a person that is not comfortable with the pentagram, it could be because you are only familiar with the Hollywood version of the pentagram. In truth, the pentagram is the Signet Star of the Microcosm, or sphere of sensation of the individual. The pentagram is also the symbol of Light of the Microcosm. It represents a balanced and healthy position of human kind stretched out before the cosmos. When all of the elements in our Sphere of Sensation are working in balance and harmony, we are at optimum health; physically, energetically and spiritually.

The symbol of the pentagram is our desire to govern the elemental forces of nature through, in, and under the rulership of the Divine Source. It becomes a wonderful symbol for balance, integration, and protection. Think about it for a moment, if every element in your body is in perfect harmony under the guidance of the Divine spirit, nothing can be a threat to you. In reality, it is only when we allow ourselves to become unbalanced that we open to the influences of unwanted Sources.

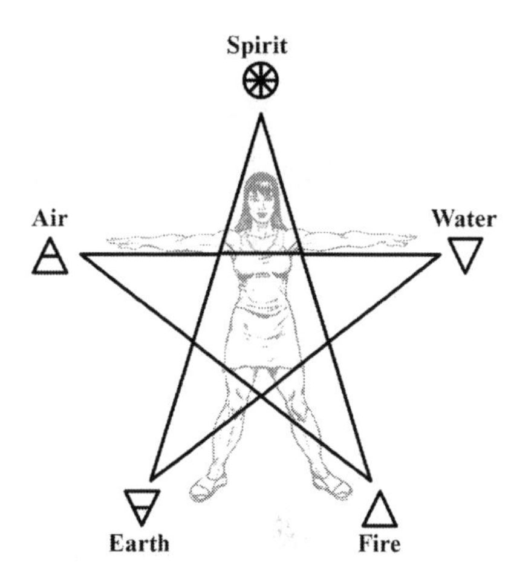


*Illustration 19: Signet Star*

Again, the following protection exercise of the Lesser Banishing Ritual of the Pentagram is not mandatory, as some of you follow a different set of beliefs. Whether you use it or not is up to you. We do recommend the preparation exercises to the L.B.R.P. even if you use your own protection ritual.

### Exercise: Protection Preparation 1 - Calming

You should begin the Lesser Banishing Ritual of the Pentagram protection ritual and all rituals by first calming your interior self and relaxing your whole body. You always want to be sure you are calm so that you are protecting and not trapping anxieties and fear in your sphere of sensation. Calming yourself is easily achieved by performing the Four Fold Breath. The detailed instruction on the Four Fold Breath can be found in Chapter 2.

### Exercise: Protection Preparation 2 - Expanding

Upon completion of the Four Fold Breath exercise, begin visualizing yourself growing taller and bigger. In Chapter 7, you did an exercise to expand your astral body or energy field. This exercise is very similar. This expansion exercise connects you the Ruach or Light from Divine Source. The Light is then used in protecting the Ruach Healer.

Close your eyes. Let your entire body grow upward toward the sky and into the infinite space above. Allow your mind to drift into that vast region of the infinite which presides above all things and time. Literally see the Earth shrinking beneath your feet. See the planets, the solar system and then the galaxy becoming smaller. Your body should be so enormous that even the Milky Way has no significance to your size. Above your head, as you continue to grow, you should begin to visualize a bright sphere of light coming closer and closer to you. This light is only a small portion of that infinite light which is beyond our comprehension. Allow the sphere of light, which appears to be no larger than a dinner plate, to hover above the crown of your head. Feel its majestic power, its vastness and the infinite love that it has for all that is created.

### Exercise: Protection Preparation 3 - Kabbalistic Cross Prayer

*"Ateh Malkuth*
*Ve-Geburah, Ve-Gedulah,*
*Le-olam*
*Amen"*

The Kabbalistic Cross is how we begin and end all of our "Ritual Exercises." It is prayer that brings down the Light of Divine Source vertically and extends the Light horizontally.

#### Step 1:

Stretch both of your arms straight out to your sides into the form of a cross. Take your right hand and gently plunge your index finger into that light which is above your head (see expanding visualization above) and will it to be drawn down as you touch your forehead. Have it rest upon your forehead as you vibrate, **"Ateh"**, pronounced *Ah-TAH.* This should be pronounced elongated. This means: ***FOR THINES IS...***

**Step 2:**

Bring the point of your finger firmly down your body while willing the light on your forehead to follow along as you point toward the ground at your feet. Visualize the light now covering your feet and vibrate, **"Malkuth"**, pronounced *Mahl-KOOT.* This means: ***THE KINGDOM...***

**Step 3:**

Now bring your finger up to your right shoulder, touching it gently. As you do this, visualize the sphere of white light running up through the center of your body, forming a beam of light into your heart area shooting out to your right side to the end of your right hand. Focus on this beam and vibrate, **"Ve-Geburah",** pronounced *Vih-Gi-Boo-RAH.* This means: ***THE POWER...***

**Step 4:**

Move your finger and the sphere of light to your left shoulder, touch it gently. Visualize all through this process another beam of light connecting from your heart area ending at the tip of your finger on your left hand. Vibrate, **"Ve-Gedulah"** pronounced *Vih-Gi-Doo-LAH.* This means: ***AND THE GLORY...***

**Step 5:**

Clasp your hands together at your chest in a praying stance while visualizing within you a cross made of light that covers your entire body. Vibrate, **"Le-olam"**, pronounced *Lay-Oh-LAHM.* This means: ***FOREVER & EVER...***

**Step 6:**

End by vibrating **"Amen"**, pronounced *AH-men.* This means: ***AMEN.***

With all of these words put together it forms the prayer: ***"For Thine is the kingdom and the power and the glory forever. Amen."*** Does this sound familiar? It should! For it is derived from one of the oldest prayers in the Bible. You will find this same phrase found near the end of the Lord's Prayer.

The word "Amen" in Hebrew translates into "so be it." Amen is a notarikon. A notarikon is made by taking the first letter of each word of a sentence and forming a new word. Amen is taken from the phrase: El Melech Neheman, which means "God is our faithful King." This is the mystical meaning behind the word "Amen".

**Exercise: Performing the Lesser Banishing Ritual of the Pentagram**

The Lesser Banishing Ritual of the Pentagram, (L.B.R.P.), is a simple protection exercise that can be memorized quickly. Some say it only takes an hour to memorize. We certainly hope you will apply the L.B.R.P. to your healing practice. If you are about to provide healing for someone, be sure that even if you are not using the Lesser Banishing Ritual of the Pentagram that whatever method you use invokes the power and the presence of the Divine Source to guide you and protect you. Our personal preference is the L.B.R.P. with an Invocation of the Archangels. We believe this should be included in your pre-healing protection work. We will leave that choice up to you.

**First, start by performing the Kabbalistic Cross which is above.*

**Step 1:**

Stand in the East and face East. Draw a pentagram in a brilliant flaming blue. Draw it in front of you, at the distance of one full arm's length. Using your right hand begin at your left hip. See the line being drawn and following the line up to the apex of the pentagram at the level of your head, down to your right hip, then across your body to the furthest left of your body at the level of your shoulders, across your body

*Illustration 20: Pentagram of the L.B.R.P.*

again to the furthest right of your body at the level of your shoulders, and completing the pentagram by ending it where you first began at your left hip.

**Step 2 :**

Inhale through the nose. As you do, drawn into you the sphere of light above your head and let it mend with your breath. Feel the energy coursing and rushing through your lungs and body. Step forward with the left foot. At the same time, lift up both arms above your head, then bring your hands down to ear-height, palms facing in, and thrust both of your hands forward with all fingers extended outward with index fingers almost coming together as a point, palms facing the ground, pointing at the exact middle of the glowing blue pentagram in front of you. This is the Sign of the Enterer. As you do this, vibrate YHVH: **"Yod Heh Vav Heh".**

*Illustration 21: Sign of the Enterer*

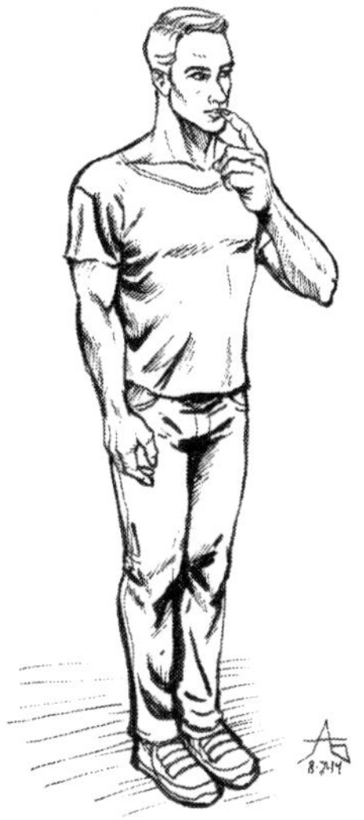

*Illustration 22: Sign of Silence*

Remember, when vibrating be sure to elongate each word in a continuous flow, using one full breath. As you vibrate this vocally, mentally hear the name echo throughout the eastern ends of the Universe. The same will go for the South, West and North. Revert your left foot back. Now place the point of your left index finger to your lips, in the form of silence. This is the form of Harpocrates, the Sign of Silence.

**Step 3:**

Once again, point at the center of the pentagram that you have just drawn, using the index finger of your right hand. Trace a brilliant white line from the center of the pentagram and follow it to the South. This will form an arc of ninety degrees so that you end up in the south, facing South.

**Step 4 :**

Now in the South, repeat Step 1 and Step 2, but vibrate:

**"Adonai"**, pronounced *Ah-Doh-Nye*

**Step 5 :**

Draw the brilliant white line connecting the pentagram in the south to the west. Repeat Step 1 and Step 2, but vibrate:

**"EHEIEH"**, pronounced *Eh-Heh-Yeh*

**Step 6 :**

Draw the brilliant white line connecting the pentagram in the West to the North. Now in the North, repeat Step 1 and Step 2, but vibrate:

**"Agla"**, pronounced *Ah-Glah*

Complete the circle by connecting a white line from the north to the east where you began. Then, moving in the same clockwise direction, return to where you started the ritual. You should once again be facing east. If you do not have room for a circle, simply pivot where you stand.

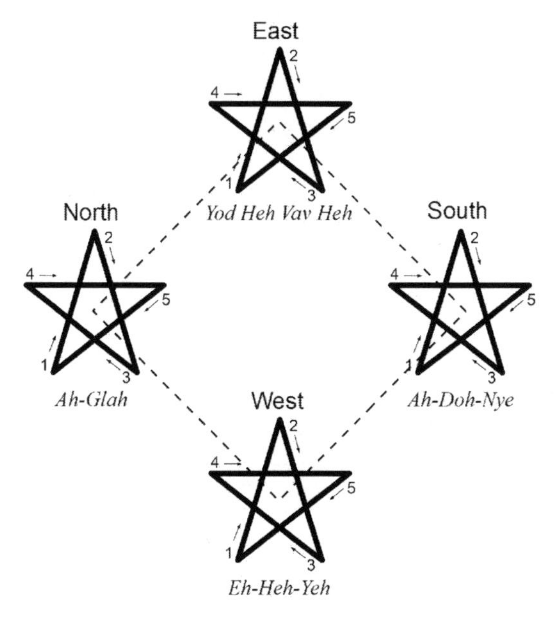


*Illustration 23: Lesser Banishing Ritual of the Pentagram*

**Step 7 :**

Now visualize the brilliant white circle expanding up and down to form a sphere above, below and all around you. What you have done is created a sphere in brilliant white all around you with electric blue pentagrams at the quarters which have been charged and sealed with God names.

## Exercise: The Evocation of the Archangels

### Step 1:

Stretch your arms straight out to the sides, so that your body forms a cross. Take a second or two to once again feel the energies that you felt when performing the Kabbalistic Cross. Re-create a cross of light within your being (the cross also represents the four archetypal elements: Air, Earth, Fire and Water).

### Step 2:

**Say: "Before me, (vibrate) Rah-fay-el."**

Visualize the Archangel Raphael on a hill in front of you. He is dressed in a yellow robe which has purple highlights. He carries a Caduceus Wand (the symbol used by doctors, a wand entwined by serpents, which represents the life force). Feel a breeze coming from behind him.

### Step 3:

**Say: "Behind me, (vibrate) Gah-bree-el."**

Visualize Archangel Gabriel behind you, dressed in blue with some orange highlights. The figure holds a cup and is surrounded by waterfalls or the ocean. Try to feel the moisture in the air.

**Step 4:**

**Say: "On my right, (vibrate) Mee-chai-el."**

Visualize the Archangel Michael dressed in a scarlet red robe with green highlights. He is holding a flaming sword. Feel the qualities of fire emanating from him.

**Step 5:**

**Say: "And on my left, (vibrate) Oh-ree-el."**

Visualize the Archangel Auriel dressed in earth tones on a fertile landscape. He holds a bundle of wheat.

**Step 6:**

After you have invoked the Archangels move your feet slightly apart, still with both arms stretched out to the sides. Now visualize yourself within a large pentagram and say:

**"For before me flames the pentagram."**

**"And behind me shines the six-rayed star."**

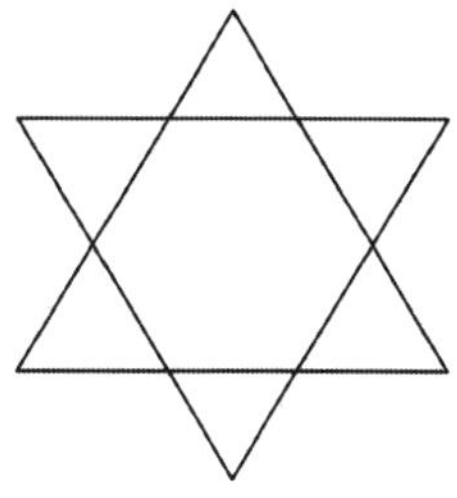

*Illustration 24: Six-rayed Star*

**Step 7:**

Repeat the Kabbalistic Cross

Other people have different versions of the Evocation to the Archangels. In one version you would say, "Around me flames the pentagram, behind me shines the six-rayed star". There are little differences between what is said, but you might like to try them and see which works best for you.

**Archangel Names and Their Meanings:**

In the East: Raphael, God has healed.
In the West: Gabriel, God is my strength.
In the South: Michael, Who is as God.
In the North: Auriel, Light of God.

Note: There are many people who perform this ritual that have problems visualizing. If you are one who has problems seeing visual pictures, just know in your mind that it is there. For example, as with the pentagrams, although you may not be able to see the lines or the color being in brilliant blue, just affirm to yourself that it is there. Some will encounter that they have problems feeling the energies. Don't worry, this is common. One reason that this may be occurring is that you may not be accustomed to the ritual so the energies it invokes may be too foreign to you. It just takes time and persistence to work through this. On a more positive note, those who think of themselves as being "numb" will be glad to know that over a long period of performing the L.B.R.P. daily, your sphere of sensation is slowly but surely becoming accustomed to the energies. So when you have internally reached a state of openness, you then judge for yourself that the presence of the Archangels are truly powerful and present.

# NOTES:

# PART II: HEALING

# NOTES:

# CHAPTER NINE: Practical Applications Before Getting Started

Before we get into practical applications of Ruach Healing, assure your best effort in gaining a firm grasp upon the theory. It's important to have a base established before we begin to actually expand on the work. Essential to this integration is the importance of understanding the concepts of the Sephirot. As they become thoroughly ingrained into your mind they will become a powerful aid when working with another person using the Ruach Healing Method.

We have talked about the Tree of Life and the Sephirot, and while they represent ten separate emanations of energy or spiritual vibration, they also represent different states of consciousness. As a matter of fact, for the most part, we use the Sephirot on the Tree of Life as consciousness. Thinking about these different states of consciousness is a way of learning how to take mastery over yourself and to help others using the Tree of Life. The following is an exercise you can use to start practically applying and experiencing energies on the Tree.

## Experiencing the Different Variations of Energies on the Tree Of Life

Take a few minutes to feel and think of moments of generosity and giving. Perhaps you may want to elicit a memory where you felt particularly generous. Maybe there was a time in your life when you felt so open that you wanted to give everyone almost anything. Let's give this feeling a definition. For the sake of discussion, we will call it "compassion." How do you express compassion? It's through your emotions.

In order to truly express this, we need to awaken our *memory* to times we felt loving, generous and compassionate. Let *all* your emotions flow freely; hold nothing back. If you are really engaged in this exercise, you should be feeling incredible love, happiness and joy. You may even feel a tinge of sadness because as you open your compassion to others, you're going to experience a whole host of emotions. Keep these feelings strong in your consciousness. This is a powerful place to experience spirituality because you are connected to Source.

This is what we would call the state of Chesed, because from this state an almost unlimited stream of mercy flows through us. Remember in our discussion of Chesed, our primary definition term was "Mercy." When we look at this Sephira on the Tree of Life, we see one state of consciousness that can be extremely useful in the healing process. We can choose to be merciful just like King Solomon, who cared deeply for his kingdom. In other words we are acting as co-creators.

The state of consciousness of Chesed can be extremely powerful, yet every state has its own set of attributes. As you begin to meditate on each Sephira on the Tree of Life and its nature, you will learn how to assume its specific energy. This will eventually become second nature to you.

Now, let's try the "Geburah" state of consciousness. Here, you can feel powerful and confident. You might feel even a bit of anger.  Geburah is a powerful and a necessary state of consciousness in the healing process. You can't really be an effective healer without Geburah. You certainly won't gain much healing ground by using the consciousness of

Chesed when it comes to stubborn diseases such as cancer. Every state of consciousness found in the ten Sephirot has its own purpose in healing others.

To tap into Geburah consciousness, go back to a time in your life when you were absolutely certain about something. Return to a time when you knew exactly what you were going to do, and how you were going to do it. In your meditation, this was a time when you were absolutely sure, with a strong and powerful sense of certainty and authority. Now, allow those feelings of power, might, will and certainty to permeate your mind and your body. You are super powerful and confident. Now is a time to act with confidence, determination, and will! This is a vital state of consciousness for any healer to develop. There will certainly come a time when you may feel overwhelmed by the healing task at hand. Taking on Geburah consciousness will aid you in your task.

By understanding these states on the Tree of Life, you become able to move from one state to another by choice rather than happenstance. At any time, you possess the ability to switch from one place of consciousness on the Tree of Life to another within seconds. You can switch how you think and feel to determine the meaning to any given situation in life. You also determine how you will choose to react to it. When you are engaged in all out warfare against disease, it's absolutely critical that you have mastery over your emotions and states of consciousness. Take the time to meditate on one Sephira every day, until you feel you can master the vibrational state of that Sephirot. Naturally with practice and experience you will get better.

There is another reason why we need to have a deep understanding and connection to these states of consciousness. The reason is when we are doing healing work and invoking the power of a Sephira, we want to instill in the patient's energy field with not only the healing properties of the Sephira but the consciousness of the Sephira too! This is an important point because we want the energy field, including the very cells in the body, to take on the mindset of the Sephira we are using. This will cause the patient to have a cellular level of consciousness not directed by disease or fear, but rather directed by health, and vitality.

The following provides only a broad stroke of the ideas and concepts of the states that can be achieved with the various Sephirot on the Tree of Life.

### Kether, Chokmah, Binah (Supernals)

The top three Sephirot on the Tree of Life are called the Supernals. Kether, Chokmah, and Binah make up the Supernals. Kether, Chokmah, and Binah are considered ONE, in that the three of them operate harmoniously as the higher self. When opening up to the Divine or Higher Self, a state of deep universal connectedness becomes mentally and emotionally apparent within you. This is an extremely difficult state to describe. In connection to the Supernals, it is a type of gnosis (knowing) that goes beyond words. One of the things that is apparent in this state is the feeling of the presence of God in everything and everyone. The healer while performing the Ruach Healing Method should always be open to the influx of Divine guidance and connection to the Supernals.

## Chesed

Universal and unconditional love, a feeling of mercy towards yourself and all life is found in the consciousness of Chesed. As a healer, we must first be merciful with ourselves, understanding that we are a conduit of Divine love. When we have this connection we can be open to sharing our mercy with everyone and everything.

## Geburah

The state of Geburah is confidence, conviction and power. As healers, taking on this Geburah state is essential because it provides us the engine to move forward when all the signs and symbols of the world say to give up.

## Tiphareth

Tiphareth consciousness is perhaps one of the most esoteric states on the Tree of Life. In Tiphareth, there is a realization of uniqueness and brilliance to your life. It is also about understanding that you are a reflection of the Divine White Brilliance in Kether. As a reflection you are willing to sacrifice your own ego in order to become a pure conduit for healing light. One of the important natures of Tiphareth is that of integration. Tiphareth connects the entire Tree of Life together.

## Netzach

Within Netzach, burning passion flows through your sphere of sensation, and your desire is only towards the higher consciousness of helping and healing others. Developing Netzach consciousness is about taking the brakes off your enthusiasm and your passion for healing.

## Hod

Extreme focus, and attention to detail, is found in Hod. Detail is important and logic plays an essential role in the healing process. There's a kind of Zen that takes place in Hod, where all that is unessential is blocked out so one's focus is sharpened.

## Yesod

Each of us has intuitive powers. Some of us experience déjà vu, others get hunches or feelings, and some people see visions. Yesod relates to the astral plane, allowing yourself the freedom to open to the consciousness of Yesod is a huge advantage in the healing process. Learning to develop your intuition *and* listening to it will aid you as a healer.

## Malkuth

There are different types of Malkuth consciousness. Things we do daily in the mundane world are part of this Sephira. There is another aspect to this consciousness where we become solely in tuned with our physical bodies, such as when we exercise, eat, dance, etc. Malkuth is where physical action takes place.

Before concluding this chapter, you've probably discovered that it's not uncommon to have a blend of Sephirot states at one time. That's perfectly normal. Part of being a successful healer is to be able to choose which state you want to be in at any given moment.

**NOTES:**

# CHAPTER TEN: Fact-Finding & Applied Kinesiology

We often wonder why healers, of all kinds, seem to want to do things the hard way. When you go to visit the doctor, the doctor will likely ask you a number of questions about your condition; what happened, where is the pain, so on and so forth. Then your doctor will likely either perform some tests on you or send you out to get some tests performed. Honestly, this is common sense. As magical healers, we must ask the patient, in need of healing, a series of questions, helping us to better understand the nature of their distress.

**Questions to Ask During Fact-Finding**

1. **Have you been diagnosed with any physically/mentally/emotionally damaging illnesses?**
2. **What is the nature of your diagnosis?**
3. **Are you in pain?**
4. **How long have you had this condition?**
5. **Have you employed other forms of healing?**
6. **Are you on medication for your condition/ailment?**

As a Healer it is not your duty to diagnose a health condition. Your job is to provide spiritual healing. Your focus is to concentrate on returning balance to the energy field. We want to know what the physician has diagnosed the patient/client with, because this knowledge can and will help when you begin healing with a specific Sephira, color or Gate. Knowing what the physician has diagnosed gives us a specific target in the energy field of the patient receiving the healing.

This does not mean we will not do our own full scan of the energy field. We still scan the entire aura as there may be contributing factors in the energy field that are causing the physical problem. We also want to know up front if the patient is in pain. Pain is something we want to address right away.

The Ruach Healing Method can be used to reduce pain. Pain is often an over abundance of Ruach in the energy field. It is important that the Ruach Healer knows if the patient is taking pain medication. Pain medication will often droop the aura. The Vitality Rays tend to close down. Combing the Vitality Rays upward may cause an intensity of pain so we avoid doing this. We also focus our scanning and muscle testing on the energetic source of the pain.

Ask the recipient various questions to narrow down details about his or her ailment. It is important to ask the recipient questions about any pain or discomfort he/she may be feeling, as well as, his/her emotional state, energy, and mood. Fact-finding is also done during "scanning" when the aura or gates show signs of being blocked, clogged, weak, or over-energized. It is also important to ask recipients about their previous medical history. Problems such as congestive heart failure or diabetes may be present, knowing about these will be important clues for providing treatment.

## Applied Kinesiology

Another technique that can be used in conjunction with fact-finding is called, "Applied Kinesiology" or, muscle testing. Kinesiology is used to check for weaknesses in the gates or various organs and even testing for allergies.

Dr. David Hawkins has done extensive research in the area of kinesiology. We highly recommend any healing practitioner to read his research found in his book entitled, *"Power vs. Force"*. We will share with you a simple yet extremely effective method of Applied Kinesiology as it relates to the "Vitality Gates" (although Applied Kinesiology can be applied to any part of the energy field, but is most effective in testing the gates.) Remember, it is important that these gates be functioning, both expelling negative energy and providing the life force energy of Ruach for optimum health and vitality. If any one of the gates is clogged, the results can range from a sluggish energy system, mood swings, anxiety, or even disease. The combination of fact-finding questions along with scanning and kinesiology, gives healers extremely powerful tools in analyzing the nature of the disease.

**Exercise: Basic Kinesiology Muscle Testing Method**

**Step 1:**

Have the patient stand up, if possible.

**Step 2:**

Give the patient a clean glass of water to drink. The water helps to clear the patient out, prior to doing the muscle testing.

**Step 3:**

Using 3 fingers, give the thymus gland (located under your Adam's apple at the base of the neck) a slight thump.

**Step 4:**

Have the patient hold out either his/her right or left arm.

**Step 5:**

Place your middle finger upon the gate to be tested; tell the patient to concentrate on the particular spot that you are testing. Next, place two fingers on the back of the patient's wrist of their outstretched arm.

**Step 6:**

Tell the patient, that when you say the word, "Resist", s/he is to literally resist the practitioner pushing downward on their outstretched arm. Make certain that the patient understands that they are not to push upward, but to merely resist the pressure the practitioner is applying. If the arm goes weak, it is an indication that there is either a lack of energy, or too much energy through the specific gate being tested. Also, we like to test the strength of our patients arm first, before testing any specific chakras, gates, areas of the body, *etc*.

Today Applied Kinesiology is becoming more and more accepted as a vital tool within the treatment of the body. Thousands of doctors, chiropractors and acupuncturist are now employing one form of applied kinesiology or another. We urge anyone serious about the healing arts to develop skills in the area of applied kinesiology.

Sometimes, when we are doing healing work on a patient, the energies can seem muddled. What happens is that after a long period of working in someone's energy field, the sensitivity of the healer begins to get confused between his or her own energy field and the energy field of the patient. This is where applied kinesiology really is very effective. The advantage of doing some muscle testing when uncertain about the information you are obtaining when performing fact-finding or scanning will great help you as a healer to make important decisions in regard to the healing process.

Here is one of the most amazing concepts that you can employ when engaging in the Ruach Healing Method with a patient. Say you have a patient who is sickly or has cancer and is generally weak all over. Naturally you can't test them because you likely will not get any kind of a reading. In some cases it might be too painful to test the patient. So here is what you can do. Drink a glass of water, tap your own thymus and test yourself for the patient. Now at first glance this sounds absurd, but it really works and is absolutely effective. Here is how it works. We tend to think that we are separate from each other as human beings, but the fact is that the energy matrix that is behind the physical illusion we call reality is an expression of ONE. In other words we are all connected via the energy matrix. (Recall that in Chapter 2, the meaning of A.R.A.R.I.T.A. and the Lord being One was discussed.)

This oneness that is the true expression of the universe is not limited to distance either. You can use this test in long distant healing on a patient who lives on the other side of the world. In this case, it is helpful to be looking at a picture (current is best) of the patient, as we begin performing muscle testing on ourselves to get a better idea of what kind of healing techniques to invoke.

### Exercise: How to Muscle Test Yourself for Your Patient

#### Step 1:

Open up your hand flat so you are looking at the back of your hand. Bend just your thumb and middle finger together so that you are forming a circle or ring.

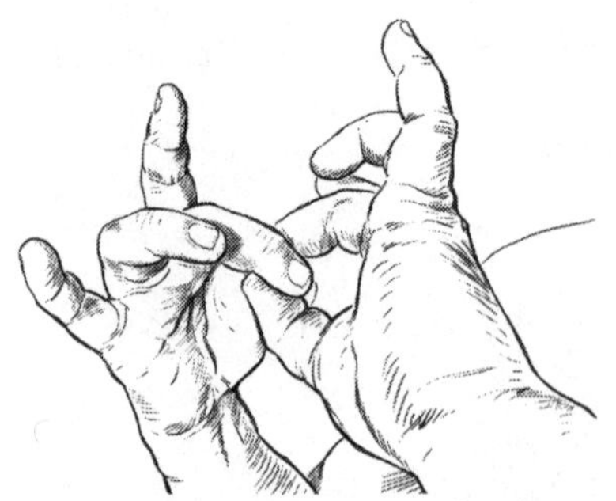

*Illustration 25: Interlocking Fingers Muscle Test*

#### Step 2:

Turn your hand so you are looking through the circle you just created. You will be making the same circle with the other hand but interlocking it with the first circle. So, bring the middle finger of the second hand to the back of the circle on the first hand. Bring the thumb of the second hand to the front of the circle on the first hand. Connect the middle finger and the thumb on the second hand. You should have just created two interlocking circles with your hands.

**Step 3:**

Both rings from each hand are interlocked. Now pull your hands apart in opposite directions, and try to separate your hands. Do this quickly. If you are strong, or if the patient is strong, your fingers will be difficult to separate, on the other hand if you go weak and slide apart, that means there is an area for concern.

**WARNING:** *In some states, within the United States and perhaps some countries around the world, physically touching a patient without a massage license may be a violation. Be sure to understand the laws of your area. When this is the case, simply have the patient touch, using their middle finger, the gate area that you are testing while you do the muscle testing exercise described above.*

**NOTES:**

# CHAPTER ELEVEN: Scanning the Aura and Gates

There is perhaps no part of the Ruach Healing Method that is more important than developing the ability to scan. Scanning tells the practitioner exactly where to work and how to approach the condition. We will be referring to scanning, on and off, throughout the remainder of this book. The development of this skill is absolutely critical.

Scanning is the process of gentling running your hands, palms, and fingertips over the different layers of the aura or energy field of the patient's body feeling for bumps of congested energy and dips of depleted energy. This allows the Ruach Healer to detect imbalances in the energy field of the patient and detect possible illnesses that have physically manifested, or are about to manifest physically. There are different techniques and methods for scanning that will be discussed further in this chapter. Though scanning sounds like an easy process, it requires deep focus and sensitivity to energy. Scanning starts with you, the Ruach Healer. Thus, this chapter on scanning begins with helping the Ruach Healer connect to the energy of Divine Source and the patient's energy in order to provide accurate scanning in the healing process.

## Connecting to the Patient's Energy Field for the Purpose of Scanning

You may recall in the beginning of this book that I spoke of one of my first patients, Jim. For over a month I had been doing healing work on him, including full ceremonial healing invocations. My healing was having a limited affect. However, one day as I pointed out, I became sensitive to the energy he was emanating. That sensitivity gave me the keys to providing him the restoration of balance and health he deserved.

The techniques and practices we are going to share with you here will save you a great deal of time and struggle in developing this sensitivity. In addition to healing, you will likely develop an auric sensitivity (seeing auras), allowing you to understand and read people better in everyday life. This is a powerful skill to develop in almost any field that involves working with other people, especially healing.

Our energy fields are generated by the beating of our heart and the influx of Divine Brilliance into our sphere of sensation. The heart beat provides the charge and the influx of Divine energy. This energy does not enter the patient's energy field in a smooth manner, but rather much like the heartbeat, it pulses or vibrates. Everything in the Universe vibrates. Therefore, the energy field is never stagnant. It is always in motion, always expanding and contracting. This gives the healer an advantage. If the human energy field were stagnant, as some healing practitioners believe, it would be far more difficult to sense or attune.

One of the secrets of attuning to the patient's energy field that is used in the Ruach Healing Method is to raise the patient's heart rate slowly while observing and tapping into their aura. This can be accomplished through a number of simple methods. One of these methods is having the patient do a few deep knee bends while breathing deeply. Another method is have the patient do a few jumping jacks. It can also be effective to have the patient stand inhaling deeply as they lift their arms up above their head, and as they exhale they lower their arms slowly. With each of these exercises, you will be able to strengthen the vibration or pulse of the patient's energy field so that you can easily connect with it for the purposes of healing. Of course, do ask the patient if they feel well enough to do any of these activities before attempting them. If the patient cannot or will not try these activities, you can just observe the patient's breathing to help you connect with their energy field.

Often the Ruach Healer will discover something in fact-finding that they believe may have relevance to healing the patient's physical condition. If it seems relevant for the Ruach Healer to accomplish their healing intent, the patient may be asked to recall a story. By the Ruach Healer simply putting, in a comforting way, a hand on one of the patient's shoulders while asking them to share a little bit of their own personal story, the Ruach Healer begins to notice where the patient's energy field is erratic and, most importantly, where it is congested. The erratic parts of the energy field are then confirmed through scanning. While intuitively, it is possible to scan a patient's energy field by just looking at them without using your hands or any touching at all in order to obtain information about their energetic state, the Ruach Healing Method is based on letting your hands become instruments of your intuition. The hands become a receptacle for Divine Source and higher sensitivity.

One of the factors that is clearly different between the Ruach Healing Method and Usui Shiki Ryoho Reiki, widely propagated today, is Ruach Healers are equally concerned with overabundance of energy and lack of energy. Healing is not just about sending people energy, or filling them up with a spiritual force as if you were filling a water balloon. Filling them until they pop could bring results which are serious and damaging, therefore scanning is mandatory. Generally speaking, in a complete healing session, we are spending as much time scanning as we are withdrawing and/or projecting energy into the patient's sphere of sensation. With every little bit of energy that we are either projecting into the patient, or removing from the patient, we must pause to re-scan.

We have discussed extensively about connecting to the energy of the patient. The following are exercises that will physically prepare you for the scanning process. You will be activating your hands, creating a ball of light, activating your fingers and palms, as well as, increasing your sensitivity to different types of energy. Instructions on scanning will follow these exercises.

### Exercise: Activation of Energy in the Hands

Place your hands, palm to palm, in a prayer like fashion. Begin rubbing your palms together slowly in a circular motion. While doing this, simultaneously activate the Divine White Brilliance at the Fountain Gate, located directly above your head. Be aware that while you can rub your hands together quickly and harshly, it certainly will warm them up, but it also has the ability to numb the hands. Rubbing them slowly and for a longer period of time is more effective. There is no need to be in a hurry.

Begin breathing in through your nose and out through your mouth. Hold each portion of the breath for about 4 seconds. This is, as you remember, is called the Four Fold Breath. As you are slowly rubbing your hands with the Divine White Brilliance glowing above your head and breathing rhythmically, begin to separate the palms of your hands about an inch. Continuing the Four Fold Breath, exhale into the space between the palms of your hands. Visually, you should see and feel yourself pulling in the Divine White Light from above your head, circulating throughout your body, and then exhaling into the space between the palms of your hands.

Now something exciting should be taking place! You should begin to feel the energy/light in between the palms of your hands. FYI: You are also feeling your own energy field. Keep breathing, and circulating the light, between the palms of your hands. Now, while maintaining the breath exercise, slowly move your hands apart. Bring your hands 3 inches apart, keep going until they are 6, 12 and up to 24 inches apart.

*Illustration 26: Ruach Ball of Light*

***You have essentially created a ball of energy, a spiritual ball of light!*** This exercise when done on a regular basis, will condition your mind, your hands, and your entire sphere of sensation to be hyper sensitive to another person's energy field. This is more than just an exercise, this is how we prepare for every Ruach Healing Session.

Conclude this exercise by raising your hands above your head, and slowly pulling the ball of light down onto yourself. Bring the energy down with your hands by making a sweeping motion from your head all the way down your body to your toes. In long distance healing, you will discover how this simple exercise will be used to create a ball of energy that can be sent to anyone around the world. The ball of energy can positively bring anyone, anywhere in the world your healing intention and the incredible healing light that you have created with your hands.

## Exercise: Finger Activation

In the Ruach Healing Method, we perform general scanning of the body and of the gates, with the palms of the hand. However, sometimes it is essential that we use our fingers to scan smaller and more delicate areas of the body. In addition, we find that the fingers are far more sensitive.

Let us share an example with you. I had a patient who had a detached retina, he was clobbered in the eye by a high heeled shoe. We won't get into the details here of the "WHY" this story took place, but I am sure you can use your own imagination! Anyhow, due to the nature of the injury, the doctor's gave him a couple of months to recover and the possibility of needing surgery. His main concern was that he was flying to China to compete in an international sport's competition. Literally, all of the scanning work that I had done on his eye involved the use of my fingertips. The palm of the hand is just too cumbersome to scan the eyes, the ears, the nose, and even some areas that are reachable by the palm of the hand. The fingers are just more sensitive than the palms. Let your best judgment and intuition guide you. While some people may scan more often with their whole hand, others, because of being ultra-sensitive, depend more often on their fingertips.

Turn your right hand palm up. Use your thumb and first finger of your left hand to gently press the base of your little finger, and then slide your thumb and first finger up to the tip of the little finger. Give the tip of the little finger you are activating a nice little squeeze. Continue with each finger on the right hand, including the thumb. This will activate your fingers. Repeat with the left palm up, pressing and squeezing with the right hand.

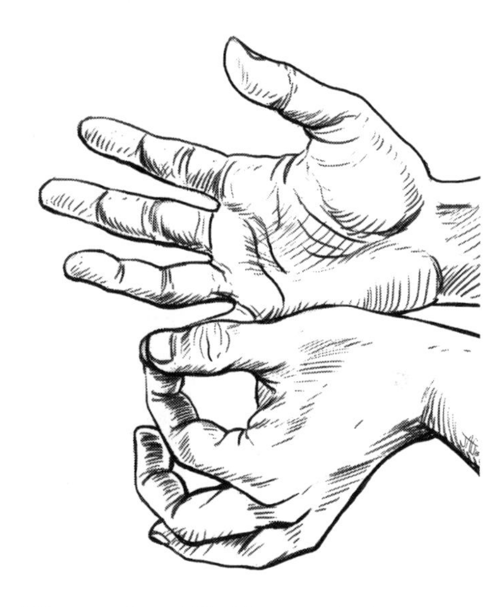

*Illustration 27: Finger Activation*

In addition to finger activation, palm activation is important. Activate your palm by applying pressure with your left thumb on your right palm, and the other four fingers applying pressure to the top of the right hand. Repeat this on the left hand with the right hand applying the pressure.

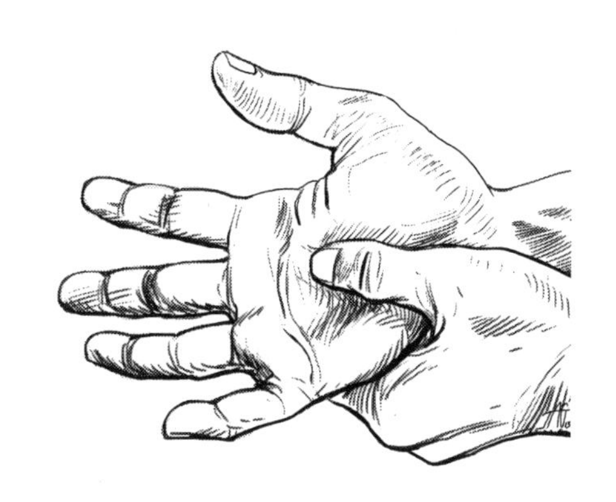

*Illustration 28: Palm Activation*

Activating your fingers and palms can cause great sensations and energy shifts in your body, especially if you are highly sensitive. If the sensation of gentle pressure, along the length of each finger, is overwhelming, start with just squeezing the finger tips. We use our hands in countless ways everyday but rarely do we take time to massage them. As you practice activating your fingers and palms, the energies and sensation will balance out into a healing intuition.

**Exercise: Increasing Your Sensitivity To Different Types Of Energy**

This exercise is primarily a training exercise. Acquire 5 or 6 different types of stones. Perhaps a rose quartz crystal, an amethyst, a river stone, hematite, or any number of precious stones, that may be available to you in your area. Practice your hand/finger exercises as described above. Then, proceed to scan one stone at a time. Pause in between each stone, and reactivate your hands if necessary. Make a mental note of the energy that you feel emanating from each stone. Is it Light? Is it Heavy? Does it make you feel more open or closed? Is the energy free flowing or sluggish? Upon finishing all of the stones and noticing the difference in each type of stone, place them in some salt water, preferably sea salt. Let them sit in the sea salt water for a minimum of one hour, then place them in the sunlight to dry. Now take the time to reactivate your hands and rescan the stones. Observe whether you feel a difference of energy, within the stones. They should by all accounts feel lighter and cleaner. Within a short period of time, and with a little bit of practice, you likely will develop the ability to become so sensitive to the energy of the stones that you can identify them with your eyes closed. While this certainly is not a goal, it is a byproduct of increased sensitivity.

I once knew a Reiki Master who was quite adept at feeling and creating energy. She was in attendance at a Ruach Healing Method workshop I was teaching. During our break for lunch I noticed that she had her hands about twelve inches apart. She was noticeably feeling the energy that she had placed in between her hands. I said to her, "It is good that you are practicing your scanning sensitivity." She replied, "I have been doing this for years." I teach all of my students to, as often as possible, spend time creating and feeling the Ruach Ball of Light of energy (or chi-ball as some traditions call it) in between their hands. This lady's connection to energy is well developed; it is so well developed she is known as an exceptional healer. As a matter of fact, she initiated me as a Grand Master of Usui Teate Reiki.

There are a lot of factors that go into making a great Ruach Healer. Certainly one of the most important factors is sensitivity and scanning ability. So, if you skimmed through the previous chapter, we seriously suggest you go back and practice and take part in the exercises provided. The scanning of the aura is absolutely mandatory, if you wish to become proficient in the Ruach Healing Method.

## General Scanning Of The Human Aura

Before proceeding with details on scanning, it is important to help the patient become comfortable and relaxed. As a Ruach Healer you can scan patients standing up, sitting down, and lying on a massage table. Having the patient standing up can be a preferred method. The simple reason for this is that you can feel and scan both sides of their body (front and back) at the same time. When the patient is lying on a table you must have them roll over to scan the back of the body.

***Now, let's dispel a myth before we proceed.*** We have had many healers try to convince us that the projection of energy and healing light comes from the right hand, and that the reception or scanning ability comes from the left hand. This just simply is not true. If you can only scan with one hand and project energy with the other, this will critically limit your abilities, particularly in the area of scanning. The healer's goal is to create wholeness, not duality.

Not long ago, I was brought a patient, who had stage four bone cancer, which had metastasized throughout her body. She was a 26 year old woman, who had the worst kind of pain imaginable. Even scanning her energy field too closely sent her into excruciating pain. She was on a high dosage of morphine, controlled by a little box that was plugged into her body. She was given less than a week to live, when I began working with her. There was only one or two positions on the bed that she could lie in that would allow her any kind of comfort at all. I had to scan her lying down next to her, with one hand. If I had been trained that only my left hand was usable for scanning, I would not have been able to scan her.

Lying on my left side facing her, only allowed for my right hand to be available. You have no idea what kind of situations you may find yourself in, people in wheel chairs, hospital beds, with equipment all over the place. So make certain that you take the time to activate both hands, so you have the ability to scan with both hands.

Begin by having the patient get comfortable. Earlier it was mentioned that it is preferred to scan people standing up, as this is due to the fact that you can scan both the front and the back at the same time. This gives the Ruach Healer the ability to look for imbalances. However, scanning a patient standing up is not always practical, most of the time you will scan someone sitting or lying down on a massage table. This is usually most comfortable for the patient. It also helps the patient relax so you can scan without a layer of anxiety surrounding your patient.

As the patient gets comfortable, begin activating your hands. Remember to wash your hands first, with soap and water. Use some Ruach Healing Mist on your hands as well. (Later in the book you will find directions on how to make your own Ruach Healing Mist)

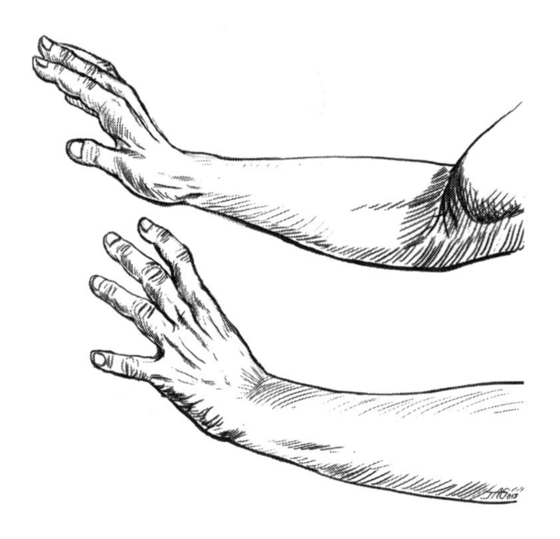

*Illustration 29: Hands Scanning*

As we previously mentioned, the energy field is like an onion with multiple layers to it. Again these layers vary from system to system. In some

Western Systems there are approximately 30 layers to the energy field but in other Kabbalistic belief systems, there are about 10 layers. The truth of the matter is most people are only going to be able to feel about 3 layers. As a Ruach Healer you are scanning the inner aura, and the outer aura. The inner aura is about 3 inches away from the body. The outer aura is about 12-24 inches away from the body. Again, scanning is the process of gently running your hands, palms, and/or fingertips over the different layers of the aura or energy field of the patient's body feeling for bumps of congested energy and dips of depleted of energy.

Now, scanning with the palms of your hands, focus on any areas where you notice a bump or dip in energy. Anytime there is a bump or dip in energy, this is an indication that there is a healing problem that needs to be addressed. Begin scanning the top of the head, continue slowly down the body from the neck, to the torso, down the legs, and to the feet. Keep your hands fluid and in motion about 2-3 inches away from the body. Scan the inner aura, and then proceed to scan the outer energy field. For scanning the outer aura, start at the head again but allowing your hands to float 6-12 inches away from the head following the energy field down the body.

After looking for bumps and dips, the next thing to look for in general scanning is symmetry. This generally requires using both hands at the same time. When checking out the symmetry of the head on the body, both hands will be about 12 - 18 inches away from the head. One hand is on the right side and one hand is on the left side. For example, if there is an imbalance of energy you will feel too much energy projecting out of one side of the head or the other. This is an issue that we would want to address when we move into the cleaning and charging phase of our work.

Whether we are scanning the inner aura, the outer aura, or looking for symmetry, we start with the head. We scan the back of the head and the neck with the palms of our hands. We will pause for a moment, to scan the face, using only our fingers. Often times, in patients with congestion or severe allergies, you will notice a stiffness, or kind of a thickening of the energy field around the nose. Be careful not to directly scan the eyes. The eyes have a very sensitive mucus membrane and direct eye scanning could cause problems with the retina. Therefore be sure to keep your fingers moving when scanning around the eyes.

Next, scan down into the neck and shoulder area. The neck area is extremely important. Particularly with patients that have anxiety disorders, weight problems, diabetes, and a number of other ailments. Many people who were raised in an environment where they were told to keep their mouths shut or their opinions to themselves, metaphorically end up choking on their own emotions. This is particularly true for women, who in society have been told it is better to "look pretty and keep your mouth shut". This can also be true for men as well.

This type of negative emotional energy is trapped in the neck, and will usually display itself as a total absence of energy, almost as if there is a void of energy at the neck. However, in some cases just the opposite is true. The energy field will feel like the patient is wearing a cement turtleneck. Also, the neck area is where the thyroid is located. Imbalances in the thyroid can result in severe weight problems, not to mention other conditions such as painful migraines.

I once had a close friend who suffered severe migraines. She had been to over a dozen doctors and healers, with no apparent result as to why she was getting these migraines. In scanning her body, I noticed the cement turtleneck around her neck. I asked her when the last time she had her thyroid checked. She said she had it checked about a year prior and it was fine. I told her to go back to her doctor and demand another test. She did so and the result was that she had an imbalanced thyroid that acted as the perpetrator to severe migraine headaches. When they adjusted her thyroid medication, her migraines disappeared. I think this story is a showcase example of how the Ruach Healing Method can work hand in hand with western medicine.

Continue your scanning downward. If you have done your fact-finding correctly you will already know if there are broken bones or other kinds of ailments that will present themselves in your scanning. A broken arm, for example, will generally present itself as a thickening in the energy field where the arm is broken. The energy field and the physical body tend to mirror each other. Primarily, we are looking for general flares in the energy field and/or voids. As a Ruach Healer, we are also looking for cold/hot spots in the energy field as well. A hotspot in the energy field will indicate that too much energy is flowing into that portion of the body's energy field. Whereas a cold spot indicate not enough energy is flowing into that part of the body. Make sure to take your time in scanning the spine, heart, lungs, stomach, intestines, liver, kidneys, and reproductive organs. Scan the kidneys from the lower back portion of the body. You should have a general idea of where these organs are on the body. In preparing to scan a specific part of the body, just simply announce the intention in your mind. Such as, "I am now scanning the liver seeking to know its' condition." Continue your scanning all the way down to the base of the spine, the legs, the ankles and the feet. There is no need to spend a lot of time scanning the arms or the legs; unless of course, in your fact-finding you have come to know of an already previously existing condition.

Some Ruach Healers like to have a notepad handy. They will pause for a moment to write down an abnormality in the energy field, location, and description of the abnormality. Another idea is to have an image of the human body on a cork board in which you place different colored tacks/push pins into represent the finding of the scanning process. Others tend to just simply keep the info in their mind. Whatever method is used, Ruach Healers are firm believers in scanning, charging, scanning, charging. In other words, you are constantly scanning to check your results and your progress.

## Scanning the Vitality Gates

In Chapter 10, we discovered the importance of fact-finding. This chapter provides you with skills to activate and condition the energetic sensitivity in your fingers and hands for scanning. Together, fact-finding and scanning provide two tools essential to diagnosing the patient's aura. This knowledge prepares you for taking scanning to a deeper level. After a general scanning of the patient's body, a deeper scan of the Vitality Gates is necessary. Scanning the Vitality Gates of the patient is extremely important in the Ruach Healing Method. (Feel free to review Chapter 6 for a the description of each gate.)

The Vitality Gates act like a paddle wheel pulling in vital energy, from the etheric and spiritual planes, which feeds into the energy field, and ultimately into the body. It is essential that these gates be operational and free flowing. When scanning the gates one should never feel a resistance, a thickness, or any heaviness of any sort.

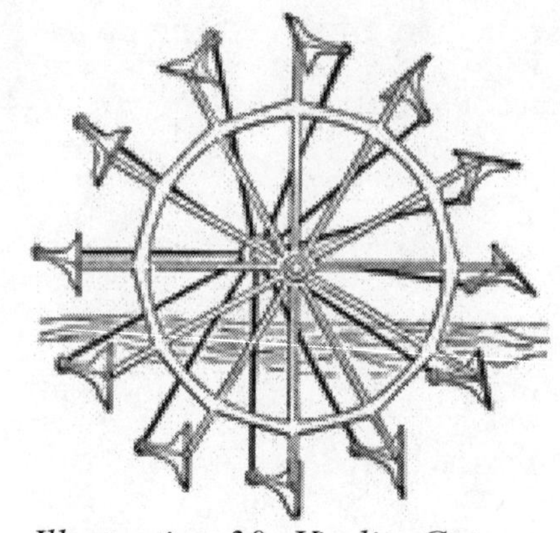

*Illustration 30: Vitality Gate as a Paddle Wheel*

The gates generally, on most people, provide a small bump in the inner aura, a section where there is an increase of energy flow. However, if the bump is too thick, too large, perhaps even stagnant, the result is a gate that is clogged. Energy can neither enter nor exit smoothly.

Here is an example to illustrate my point. Imagine people with their cars trying to enter a gate, while people with their cars and trucks are trying to exit the same gate. This becomes a clogged or congested gate. On the other hand, the gates can also become depleted of spiritual energy. When scanning a gate that is depleted, it feels almost as if there is a sinkhole in the energy field. Your hand tends to want to drop down or be pulled into the gate when depletion is present. In this case, the gate is lacking vitality. The result is a body that is listless, tired, lacking in energy and likely sick or becoming sick. A healthy gate should feel vibrant, filled with free-flowing energy that protrudes from the inner aura. This gate is not thick or clogged in any manner.

**Table 6: The Vitality Gate's Location and Colors**

| Name of Gate | Location of Gate | Color of Gate |
|---|---|---|
| Foundation Gate | Base of the spine/groin | Light Red Tint |
| Navel Gate | Lower abdomen/two inches below navel | Light Orange Tint |
| Solar Plexus Gate | Solar Plexus/base of rib cage | Light Yellow Tint |
| Heart Gate | Chest/Heart | Light Green Tint |
| Throat Gate | Neck/Throat | Light Blue Tint |
| Third Eye Gate | Pituitary gland/forehead | Light Violet Tint |
| Fountain Gate | Crown of Head | Brilliant White/ Gold Tint |

## Gate 1: The Foundation Gate

This gate relates to the base of the spine. Scanning this gate is most effective with the palms of the hands. People that are very weak and sick, sometimes even dying, have an extremely depleted Foundation Gate. People that are celibate or have not had a healthy orgasm for a period of time will often have a congested gate. This oftentimes shows up as listlessness and a lack of passion for life. If a patient states that they are constantly feeling “BLAH-ZE” (for lack of a better word) it is generally necessary to spend more time scanning the Foundation Gate. An overabundance of energy in this gate will reveal itself as being hot and erratic in the palms of the hands. The danger of too much energy in this gate is that the individual becomes solely focused on present moment thrills and unbalanced in the management of their lives. A patient that has an over active Foundation Gate may also have difficulty connecting to spiritual concepts and ideas. This is the gate of the animal self. Or, as it is often called in the Kabbalah, the Nephesch.

### Gate 2: The Navel Gate

This gate is a very emotionally charged gate is located just below the navel. Remember, while the Navel Gate and the Solar Plexus Gate are very different and have very different independent tasks within the sphere of sensation, it is equally effective to scan them together. Scan to see if both gates are about the same size and level of intensity.

It is important to scan the Navel Gate slowly. Take care and caution while working with this gate because emotions can easily be stirred up.

With tender loving care the Navel Gate can be completely emotionally free. Without love and care the Navel Gate can easily become as clogged as a Louisiana Bayou swamp. Be sure to give the Navel gate attentive loving care.

## Gate 3: The Solar Plexus Gate

The Solar Plexus Gate is located at the solar plexus, at the bottom of the rib cage, several inches *above* the navel. The Navel Gate is located about 2 inches *below* the navel. While these gates have very different and independent tasks within the sphere of sensation and body, it is equally effective to scan them together. To scan these gates together, use the palms of both hands and look for both gates protruding at about the same level. Check to see if both gates are about the same size with the same level of energy and intensity. If both feel free flowing, we move on to the Foundation Gate. If there is a difference between the two, then we begin to scan each gate individually, using the palms of our hands.

While you are scanning, take note as to the circumference of the gates. As you become a seasoned Ruach Healer, the circumference will give you clues as to whether the gate is clogged or whether there is an over-abundance of energy. When the Solar Plexus Gate becomes clogged or stuck there is a thick or hard feeling to the energy. This can be an indication that there are immune disorders within the body.

If the patient is having difficulty with their digestive system there will be depletion or an over-abundance of energy within the Solar Plexus Gate. Working directly on the Solar Plexus and Navel Gate together optimizes the health of the liver, stomach, intestines and kidneys. Again, most of the time we are using the palms of both hands to scan for equality in the Solar Plexus and Navel Gate.

### Gate 4: The Heart Center Gate

Scanning the Heart Center Gate is generally done using the entire palm of the hand. This is a fairly large gate that affects the condition of the heart and the circulatory system and the lungs. When this gate becomes congested, it feels almost like a hard lump above the chest on the patient. Due to the fact that this gate affects the central part of the body, it is important to scan both from the front side and the backside. We are also scanning for temperature when we are scanning the Heart Gate. There are cases where a little energy field or depletion of energy is felt on the front side, but on the backside the energy field feels hard and cold. This combination of feeling can be a sign of bronchitis or sometimes pneumonia. With a heart condition we are looking for a weak, erratic, or congested gate. A Heart Center Gate that feels hot one moment and cold the next is an indication of a heart condition. Other systems of healing avoid charging and/or direct scanning of the heart, if the patient has a heart condition. However, the Ruach Healing Method is so gentle that Ruach Healer have experienced no difficulty or danger in scanning the Heart Center Gate directly.

### Gate 5: The Throat Gate

The Throat Gate is also a very sensitive gate, especially to women who have been told that their opinions do not matter. It is the connecting gateway between the body and the mind. It is important to understand that within a healthy human being, there is *no* noticeable separation between the mind and the body. The body IS the mind. Recent scientific discoveries and many Eastern systems of healing conclude that the mind is more than the brain, it includes the whole body. Scientific evidence demonstrates that the heart muscle cells actually think in the way heart muscle cells think. Brain cells think in certain ways that are specifically designed for thinking. Each cell within the body thinks within the parameters of its cell type. Your body is your mind, and your mind is your body.

The Throat Gate when flowing freely and effortlessly creates a wonderful link between the body/mind. A depletion of energy is often found as you scan this gate. Depletion in the Throat Gate often indicates a condition in which energy is not flowing well thorough any part of the body. This is often the case with people who have thyroid conditions. In addition, special attention should be given to the Throat Gate, in people who have schizophrenia and/or bi-polar conditions. Schizophrenia and bi-polar disorders are a clear indication that the body/mind is not in harmony functioning at one unit.

We generally use three fingers when scanning the Throat Gate. I found a secret many years ago, when scanning this gate. Using the palm of my hands, I would place one in front of the Throat Gate about eight inches away from the Adams apple, and one palm about eight inches away in the back of the Throat Gate. (This works best if the patient is standing or sitting.) I discovered that if I could push the energy field in the front of the neck then feel the energy come out the back of the neck, similar to the rocking of a ship, back and forth; that the gate was fluid, healthy and free flowing. If the energy was stuck, it was an indication that there was difficulty with this gate and that it was in need of attention.

### Gate 6: The Third Eye Gate

The Third Eye Gate, for the most part, should only be scanned with the finger tips. It is located in between your eyebrows, at the pituitary gland. The clogging of this gate, particularly in children and teenagers can result in stunted or diminished growth. A congested Third Eye Gate in an adult can also result in severe mental problems, including delusional behavior.

I had the opportunity to work on several AIDS patients prior to widely-accepted medical treatment for HIV. Back in the 90's, it was an automatic death sentence. In working on these patients, I noticed that they, for the most part, had over-active pituitary glands. Like the Fountain Gate above, this gate has a direct connection to the brain. Many of these HIV patients were suffering from paranoia and anxiety that stemmed from drug use, rather than the HIV itself. I had one patient whom I kindly told to stop having promiscuous sex and to stop using drugs as it was disrupting his body's natural energy flow and vitality. He refused. The result was death, shortly thereafter. He was living in a delusional state of reality. While he certainly had a lot of other problems, including skin cancer, I took note of the fact that his Third Eye Gate was completely erratic and unbalanced.

Over the years, I have worked on several intuitive people and psychics. I noticed they had a third eye that was exceptionally large and contained an overflow of energy. The difference between an intuitive and a drug user is that the third eye's overflow of energy in the intuitive is steady, while the energy of the drug user is erratic and unsteady. The drug user thinks he is psychic but it is a result of the drug affecting his/her brain by over exaggerating the third eye with a quick high. This leads to an overabundance of feelings, thoughts, pictures, and ideas that are not based on any form of reality. As the high diminishes, these feelings and thoughts are trapped in the Third Eye Gate in an ungrounded state. Whereas, the intuitive has an over abundant third eye as well, but his or her feelings, pictures and ideas are brought into the third eye by a quick drug high. The intuitive's feelings and thoughts are constantly flowing. If you notice, within your scanning, somebody with an exceptionally large third eye and an abundance of energy, it is a fair fact-finding question to ask them about their intuitive abilities and/or drug use.

## Gate 7: The Fountain Gate

Generally, we scan the entire head first with the palms of our hands. Then, after scanning the entire head area, we switch over to our fingers, and begin scanning the actual Fountain Gate itself. The Fountain Gate is located in about the same location of what was once the soft spot on the top of your head. It's directly in the center of the head. People that lack spiritual connection and a deep sense of purpose in their life oftentimes have a depleted Fountain Gate. We use our fingers to scan the area of the Fountain Gate, lightly. If the energy feels clogged or congested this can lead to a whole host of illnesses; mental, emotional and physical. There is no illness or disease that exists within the body that does not have some effect on the Fountain Gate. We know of healers who primarily work only on the Fountain Gate or the crown chakra. They believe that they can affect the entire physical condition of the body by increasing the clean free flowing energy of the Fountain Gate.

Several years ago, I had the privilege of providing healing on an Armenian woman, who had stage four lymphatic cancer. For whatever reason, she chose not to receive any chemotherapy or radiation. This was a unique healing experience because I had no direct communication with my patient. Every time I worked on her, I was working through an interpreter to inquire on her condition. In the process of completely healing her, over a three month period, I worked on the lymph nodes that were most congested and required immediate attention. However, there was never a treatment that did not include a complete and thorough scanning of the Fountain Gate. Generally her Fountain Gate required a certain amount of energetic charging. Many healers would have sadly ignored the Fountain Gate. It was this healing that showed me beyond a shadow of a doubt the importance of the Fountain Gate. Even though I could not verbally communicate with my patient without an interpreter, the healing I brought to her Fountain Gate eradicated all the cancer from her body. As a Ruach Healer you are urged to include Fountain Gate scanning and energetic work with each patient.

# CHAPTER TWELVE: Creating Your Depository: Alchemical Healing

Early on in my healing career, I became perplexed as to why some people had what appeared to be miraculous recoveries from life threatening illness but would relapse. They seemed to be doing better and going about their lives in a normal fashion. After what appeared to be a few days to a couple of months, these people who had previously made a remarkable recovery were now sick again. Many times the illness would return worse off than before. I was also perplexed when I also noticed that after giving a Ruach Healing treatment there was an elongated period of time whereby all the rituals in the world and all the showers with soap and water had no effect at cleaning away the gunk that was attached to my hands and on occasion my entire body. Some healers reported to me that they felt emotionally and physically drained after a healing session. Other healers wondered if they were hypochondriacs because they seemed to be taking on the symptoms that they were removing from the patient. The return of illness in the patient and the drain on the healer's vitality poses a serious problem.

I began working on this problem by increasing spiritual banishings and clearings prior to a healing session. Not as much for the patient, but for myself the practitioner. This became time consuming and cumbersome. Certainly there had to be an easier way to dispose of the negative energy that was removed from energy field of the patient so that it would not take root in the Ruach Healer.

Seeking a solution to this problem, I had a healer from a different primary path come to my house and speak to a handful of high level healing adepts. (I am primarily a Ruach Healer but I have also been trained and enjoy working with Pranic Healing and am a Grand Master in Reiki.) The visitor was a representative of Master Choa Kok Sui, the architect of Pranic Healing. One of the ways practitioners of Pranic Healing dispose of negative energy is through a large bowl of water with several cups of sea salt; either dissolved or partially dissolved into a solution. The Pranic Healing practitioner pulls negative energy off the patient, then disposes of that negative energy and places it into the bowl of salt water. This method is helpful because it's easy and anyone can do it but it is effective only to a limited degree.

While it is true that water and salt are natural purifiers, oftentimes the amount of negative energy extracted from a chronically ill patient quickly overflows the bowl. Any healer using this method must constantly check the clarity of the water. Once it becomes extremely cloudy, it needs to be disposed of and the bowl should be cleaned and refilled.

One final thought on this method is that the disposal usually takes place by flushing it down to a toilet. This doesn't seem too dangerous, since the water goes through a city treatment process then purified water is released to the ocean. However, if the water is flushed into a septic tank system I would be less likely to use this method. In a septic system the negative and diseased energy would remain trapped underground in your own backyard.

***"All Nature is regenerated through Fire."***

Due to my influence in Golden Dawn studies, it became apparent to me that a portal of fire was going to be the most effective way to permanently dispose of and alchemically transform harmful negative energy. The whole concept that purification comes through fire finds its root belief amongst the medieval scholars and Rosicrucian alchemists.

The alchemists understood the whole process of elevating a substance to its highest potential. You might recall this as a metaphor of lead being transformed into gold, or the human being transformed into Divine Spirit. This process involves the separation of the alchemical principles of the original element and the purification of each alchemical principle through fire. A simple example of this is the process of distillation, where an impure element is purified through heat. In the process of distilling, certain aspects of the element that are no longer positive or appropriate are burned away. One only has to venture to a liquor store for a few moments to see alcohol that has been distilled once, twice and even three times. The alcohol that has been distilled only once has a higher level of water and impurity. Another short example, is the blacksmith who puts his steel rod into the fire, only to pound out the impurities and all of which is necessary, thus creating a beautiful horseshoe or dagger.

Most of us have seen the letters **"INRI"** hanging over a crucifix of Jesus hanging on the cross. Traditionally, it means ***"Jesus of Nazareth, King of the Jews"***. However, there is a deeper and more esoteric meaning to this phrase. Ancient medieval alchemists, Rosicrucian alchemists and Kabbalistic healers express **"INRI"** as the following.

**"INRI" = "Igne Natura Renovatur Integra"**

*Which means:* ***"All of Nature is regenerated through fire."***

The answer to eliminating the negative energy and disease as you heal now becomes clear. All impurities must be placed into fire. This fire is not a physical fire of a candle but an astral fire. An astral fire can be invoked and contained with a simple exercise. In this exercise you build a container encoded with the symbol of fire to transform all the negative astral energy that you clear from your patient.

### Method of Creating Your Astral Fire Container

The astral container creation is an essential part of the Ruach Healing Method. If we did not create a container, the negative energy would likely snap back to the patient. (Sadly, this is what happens in many other healing systems.) The Invoking Fire Pentagram is the sacred symbol we use to create the astral container in the Ruach Healing Method. If you recall in an earlier chapter, we discussed how the pentagram is the symbol of the perfected man and a symbol of the microcosm. Therefore, the pentagram becomes an incredibly powerful symbol used for purifying and transformation. This is especially true when using the *fire* pentagram. Each elemental type of pentagram is drawn differently. In this book we only need to know two kinds of pentagrams, the earth pentagram used in the Lesser Banishing Ritual of the Pentagram and the fire pentagram used for the creation of the astral fire container. The actual pentagram looks the same except for the color and the way it is drawn in the air.

## Exercise: Creating Astral Fire Container

*Illustration 31: Drawing the Astral Fire Container*

**There are a few things to remember when using the Astral Fire Container. First, keep it always in the same location. South is the preferred location for the fire container. Elementally, as we spoke of earlier, the South is symbolic of fire. Second, create your Astral Fire Container a little bit lower than your waist. The Astral Fire Container should be at the level of the lower vibrational energies which are being placed in it.**

### Step 1:

Draw a circle, in the air, with your right thumb, beginning in the eight o'clock position, and drawing clockwise (The 8 o'clock position is the first house in astrology.) Use your thumb, the symbol of spirit, for the drawing the circle because the circle is symbolic of spirit. What the circle does metaphysical is keep the astral container in one place. Without the circle the pentagram would tend to fade away over time. Remember *never* draw the circle counter-clockwise. Make the circle using Divine White Brilliance.

**Step 2:**

Draw the invoking fire pentagram as shown in the diagram above using your fire finger, ring finger, for the drawing of the pentagram. You can also draw the pentagram with a fire wand, stick of incense, sage bundle, frankincense and myrrh, or even a garnet crystal. Draw the pentagram, starting from the top uppermost point, (relates to Spirit), drawing downward and to the right.  Visualize drawing the pentagram in a bright scarlet red within the Divine White Brilliant circle. While drawing the pentagram, vibrate the Divine Name: **"Elohim"**, pronounced, *El-oh-heem.*

**Step 3:**

In the center of the fire pentagram, draw the Kerubic symbol of fire. The Kerubic symbol is also the symbol for Leo. Draw it in bright green with your fire finger, while vibrating the Arch Angelic Name: **"Michael"**, pronounced, *Mee-chai-el.*

**Step 4:**

Point to the center of the Kerubic Leo symbol and vibrate the name of the great Angel of Fire: **"Aral"**, pronounced, *Ahh-ral.*

## How to Use Your Astral Fire Container

Your container is actually a portal of fire more than it is a container. As the practitioner extracts the negative energy from the patient, the negative energy is projected or thrown into the container with a slapping/brushing motion of the hands. As the negative energy hits the container, it will be immediately contained, transformed and regenerated. There is no longer any worry of the negative energy remaining stagnant within your patient, your energy field, or healing workspace. It is absolutely necessary for the practitioner to take these tools and make good use of them. The Ruach Healer never wants to find that he/she acting as a human waste receptacle for a patient's emotionally charged, unwanted energy. Using the astral fire container is a very simple enough process to learn and practice. This is just another tool in your toolbox of small precautions that are beneficial use, for all Ruach Healers and other healing practitioners. Next, it is important to learn how to properly dispose of the Astral Fire Container filled with negative energy.

### Exercise: How to Dispose of Your Astral Fire Container

*Illustration 32: Disposing of the Astral Fire Container*

**Step 1:**

Draw the banishing pentagram of fire pentagram with your fire finger. Notice that to banish you start as the fire point and go toward the point of Spirit. As you draw this, vibrate the Divine Name: **"Elohim"**, pronounced *Yod-Heh-Vav-Heh El-oh-heem.*

**Step 2:**

Draw the Kerubic sign of Fire, the Leo symbol, as you did above, and vibrate the Arch Angelic Name, **"Michael"**, pronounced, *Mee-chai-el.*

**Step 3:**

With your fire finger draw an equal armed cross over the container. Start with a vertical line from top to bottom, and then add the horizontal line from left to right. As you draw the cross vibrate the Angel of Fire, **"Aral"**, pronounced, *Ahh-ral*.

**Step 4:**

Preform the Sign of Silence as taught in Chapter 8, Kabbalistic Cross or simply bring the palms of your hands together as if to pray. Either gesture will seal the container closed.

**Step 5:**

Make sure to remember to close the banishing of your astral fire container with a final prayer of release.

***"Oh Lord of the Universe, Divine Source of All, Lord of fire, we bless thee, and we thank thee for the purifying fire, and the aid of your angels, Michael and Aral, and the countless Angels that serve them, and aid in this operation of purification. Thank you, Amen."***

All too often, I have witnessed unseasoned Ruach Healers finish the healing work and leave their container open. While there is likely no immediate damage in leaving it open, there can be serious long team consequences. It is a good habit to close your astral fire container as soon as you are finished working. We also like to end with a final prayer. The prayer we have provided you above is a traditional prayer that you are free to modify to your own believes and needs.

## NOTE: Warning About Your Astral Container

I have a friend in Southern California who is a marvelous healer. He works on people from all over the region who need healing from chronic diseases. I'm proud that I was able to be his mentor for over twenty years. I became concerned when he came to me lacking vitality and energy. I scanned him finding he had an outrageous amount of sluggish lower vibrational energies within his energy field. I was stumped. After a thorough scanning and extensive fact-finding, I determined he was probably picking up negative energy from people he was doing healing work on. I could not get a clue as to what was hurting him. Later we went to a patient's home to do some healing work. I immediately noticed that he was not creating his astral fire container to dispose energy into. Later that evening when we returned to his home I suggested that because he was not invoking an astral alchemical container the negative sludge he was removing from the people he was healing was snapping back on him. To put it simply, being a healer was hurting him. I did a complete cleanse on him and charged his gates. By the next morning, his energy field was restored to health and vibrancy. The moral of this short true story is that you run the risk of doing yourself harm if you do not take the time to create your astral fire container disposing of energies extracted during the healing process. Reminder: ALWAYS create and close your astral container before and after healing.

# CHAPTER THIRTEEN: Cleansing The Aura

**NOTE: For our purposes in this book the "aura" and "human energy field" are synonymous.**

The entire concept of the Ruach Healing Method revolves around having a clean energy field with well-functioning healthy gates. When the energy field is clean, energy is able to move in and out of the energy field in a natural fashion. As energy moves in and out of the energy field, the energy field holistically begins to pull in vibrant life force. It also pulls in Ruach that gives the body energy, vitality and allows the body to operate at an optimum level. The energy field knows what it needs. It knows the kind of energy it needs to attract and pull in to heal disease and deficiency thus keeping the body healthy.

We have all experienced that feeling of sitting out in the sun, after a long winter or perhaps an extended time working indoors, and just closing our eyes and enjoying the sunlight. There is more going on here than just the warmth of the sun. What is taking place is that the energy field and the Vitality Rays are opening up and receiving the vital life giving energy of the sun. In the Golden Dawn Tradition, it states, **"The sun is the visible dispenser of light to the world."** In other words, the sun is the material representation of an inward reality and that reality is that nothing can live without light.

Cleaning the energy field is an essential part of the healing process because it removes negative, unwanted, lower vibrational forces and energies that are stuck in the energy field. These lower vibrational forces/energies either can lead to sickness/disease or oftentimes, are the result of sickness/disease. Remember the adage, **"as above so below"**. By gently cleaning the energy field in the proper manner, the Ruach Healer is in effect cleaning the body. Healing and vitality are then brought to the body simultaneously.

In many healing traditions, the focus is charging or sending energy. As a Grand Master in Reiki and a healing practitioner in many healing modalities, I understand this belief, however I believe it is a little unbalanced. Remember in the Kabbalistic Tree of Life, there are two primary pillars. These are the Pillar of Severity and the Pillar of Mercy. It takes a certain amount of severity to balance out the benevolence of mercy. So to draw a parallel, charging the energy field with energy could be said to be merciful whereas cleaning the energy field could be akin to being severe. *(Mercy: Masculine – Severity: Feminine)*

Our goal as a healer is to work in concert with the Middle Pillar, the Pillar of Mildness. From a healing perspective, this means cleaning and charging the energy field. Without trying to over emphasize this point, it needs to be made clear how important cleaning the negative lower vibrational energy away from the energy field is. This is fundamental to the whole Ruach Healing Method.

Not long ago, one of my students asked me if I would examine someone he had performed healing on. This patient had a slow growth cancer and a weakened immune system. I began the process through a little fact-finding and moved right on to the scanning process. The whole energy field seemed weak and listless. Upon further examination, I noticed that the energy field was heavily clogged, particularly his Vitality Gates.

They were like lumps of hard energy attached to his energy field. Even in a weak energy field, there is a certain amount of movement that takes place within the energy field. You can always feel the patient's energy flowing and vibrating, even if it is only slightly moving. If the patient is alive the energy field is never stagnant.

My student had been treating his friend for 3-4 months, with no noticeable improvement. As a matter of fact, he had been getting weaker. I immediately decided that his entire energy field needed a general cleaning. Particularly, his gates needed a thorough cleaning to get them functioning again. Before I began the work, I asked my student in private what kind of healing work he had been doing specifically. He pointed out that mostly he had been charging the energy field and the gates with Divine White Brilliance, as well as, doing extended amounts of Reiki on him. Typically, this healing approach would be a good decision, however there was just one thing missing. He hadn't *cleaned* the energy field every time before performing charging or Reiki work on him! When a patient has a chronic disease, such as cancer, their energy field is in constant need of cleaning. The chronic disease is a reflection of the condition of the body. So, we began cleaning the patient's energy field with Divine White Brilliance. We immediately noticed and could feel an influx of energy flowing through the energy field. This happened particularly when we cleaned the Fountain Gate, the Crown Chakra around the head. The gate began flowing again in a healthy fashion. In this case, we spent upwards of an hour just on cleansing his energy field. I only had one chance to work on him, but all reports from my student indicated that the cancer receded. His health and vitality also returned. This is the importance of cleaning.

## Getting Started

After you have done a thorough job of scanning the energy field, you are ready to begin cleaning. Don't put your scanning skills away yet. Most Ruach Healers are scanning and cleaning almost simultaneously. It's easy! You clean the energy field and then you go back and scan your work. At this point, scanning is almost like proof reading. If the patient needs more cleaning, you continue cleaning; if scanning shows that patient doesn't need more cleaning, you move onto another part of the body.

Metaphorically speaking, lower vibrational energy is downward and higher vibrational energy is upward. Therefore, when cleaning the energy field, all of our cleaning action is accomplished through a *downward* motion. For this reason, that the Astral Fire Container is created little bit lower than our waist.

Begin cleaning by creating your Astral Fire Container, then, slightly above the Fountain Gate (Crown Chakra) hold your hands about six inches apart, creating a ball of light. Create the cleaning Ruach Ball of Light by breathing in deep through your nose and while breathing it in, vibrate the divine name of Keter, in the world of Atziluth Eheieh, and the Archangel Metatron, in the world of Briah. Lastly, you will vibrate the name of the Choir of Angels, Chayoth ha-Qadesh. The Choir of Angels is pronounced *Ki-ot-hoc-odesh.* Now, as you breathe in the light from the top of your head downwards and back out your hands, the ball of Divine White Brilliance will begin to form above the head of the patient you are healing.

I like to think of the D.W.B. as a reservoir that I can tap into for the cleaning process. Remember, as a Ruach Healer it is always the Divine that you are calling upon during the healing process that is doing the healing.

The cleaning process always begins with literally calling Kether so vibrating the sacred names from Kether is appropriate and empowering for the patient. As the cleaning process continues down the rest of the body the names of the Divine, Archangels, and Choir of Angels can be vibrated in the appropriate spots on the body. Please note, there are times you will choose not to vibrate the divine names. If you are in the process of cleaning and using a variety of colors from the Sephira or gate, you may not vibrate all the names of Sephira. Your intention and sensitivity, during cleaning, will be felt by the patient whether you are vibrating the name or not.

Now, with your right hand, or left hand if the situation calls for it, begin creating a type of hand shovel with your fingers and thumb. Simply bend your fingers slightly, so your hand is cupped, as if something were about to be placed in your hand. Turn this hand so that the cupped palm is facing the floor. This is your shovel hand. Cup your opposite hand, typically the left, in a similar fashion. Turn this hand so that the cupped palm faces the ceiling. This is your bucket hand.

*Illustration 33: Cleaning the Aura*

You are going to slowly use the Divine White Brilliance to cut through the energy field and "dig" out the contaminants and negative energy in the aura with your shovel hand. As you dig, transfer the dirt into your bucket hand. You are moving energy from one hand to the other. Continue cleaning the top of the head and the sides of the head. Using your fingers as mini shovels; dig out energy around the nasal passages, and the Third Eye. Pause for a moment, as your bucket hand should be full. Now brush the energy off your hand into the Astral Fire Container. Do this as if stating that you are "done" or "finished" with something; slap your hands both ways, as if brushing dirt off of them.

Continue cleaning the back of the head and the Throat Gate thoroughly, again using your hand like a mini shovel or rake. Go slowly and gently. It is perfectly appropriate to pause for a moment and scan the area you are cleaning. Make certain that it isn't clogged in any way. If areas of aura or the Vitality Gates are still clogged or congested continue cleaning. We might mention here, that we like to spend a lot of time cleaning the back of the head and the crown in the Fountain Gate. In Kabbalah, the back of the head is represented by the letter "QOPH" which is significant of the subconscious mind. Since many of the diseases and illnesses a patient may be suffering from tends to attract to, and attach to the patient's fears, anxieties, and doubts, cleaning the back of the head and neck is of extreme importance.

Now, with your left hand you should be sensing a number of feelings that indicate that you have been successfully pulling off negative energy. Usually a heaviness in the hand is felt. Note that the negative energy has weight, this is the heaviness in your hand. It can feel like a stickiness, or a kind of, for lack of a better term, "YUCKY" energy. This energy may make you want to go wash your hands and/or take a shower. In the beginning of my Ruach Healing days, I realized that I needed something to keep my hands fresh and clean during the process. Certainly some fresh running water would be appropriate. This however, is not always available. I tried bathing my hands with rubbing alcohol, but that just made the patient sick, due to the horrid smell. Finally, I created my solution in what I call Ruach Healing Mist. It is refreshing and cleansing. It smells like fresh lemons, limes and lavender (recipe included later in this chapter). We mist our hands with a little Ruach Healing Mist, after we empty the energy into the astral waster receptacle. This allows our hands to stay fresh as we clean the lower energies out of the patient.

If, for whatever reason, Ruach Healing Mist or running water is not available, simply hold your hands above your head, and begin invoking the Divine White Brilliance downward thru your sphere of sensation and outward through your hands. Make sure to allow the Divine White

Brilliance to build, and accumulate. This will clear your hands of the negative energy you are removing from the patient.

You can recreate another ball of Divine White Brilliance at any time during the cleaning process. We like to stop after we finish the head and neck and pause for a moment. After we brush all of the dirty energy into the Astral Fire Container and clean our hands with the Ruach Mist, we begin creating a ball of light at the base of the neck. This second ball of Divine White Brilliance is used in our general cleaning process for the middle portion of the body. As you clean, work on the front of the body first. Cleanse from the Fountain Gate down to the Foundation Gate. After the front is clean, clean the back of the body in the same fashion; from the head to the feet.

From the neck area, generally we will sweep over the arms, lightly. Unless there is a problem with the arms, or a circulation issue, not too much time is spent cleaning the arms. Cleaning the neck and arms flows into cleaning the chest, heart, and lungs. Next, cleaning is done in the region of the stomach, the bladder, the liver, and the spleen. In the areas of the body that are reflected in the energy field we are looking for a lumpiness, congestion, and/or depletion. It is not uncommon for the Solar Plexus gate to be heavily clogged, in people with deep emotional illnesses. This gate generally has chronic illness and needs a through cleansing. It is not uncommon to clean it, scan and re-clean, several times. In addition, look for energy that is projecting in an uneven manner, by projecting out one side of the stomach area and not the other. When you notice this lack of symmetry, clean the whole area thoroughly in preparation for charging. Continue your cleaning all the way through the bladder, and the groin area. Continue down to the Foundation Gate, located at the base of the spine. There is perhaps no gate on the body having such a wild energy swing as the Foundation Gate in the groin area. We do not spend a lot of time on the groin directly, as people tend to feel uncomfortable, while working on that area. Even if you are not touching the body, the easiest way to work on the groin area, is through the base of the spine. We generally do a thorough cleaning on this gate, but don't be surprised if with some people you cannot seem to clean all the energy. You will continue to dig out the energy, only to have it replaced, moments later.

**NOTE: If the patient is extremely sick, we will hardly ever clean out the Foundation Gate or this region of the body. Too much cleaning of this area can weaken the patient's vitality.**

Finally clean down the legs. Remember, the legs take all the weight of the body. In the last 25 years, there has been an onset in type two diabetes, often times resulting in swollen legs, with poor circulation. We spend a lot of time cleaning the legs thus ensuring that there is no clogged energy around the large thigh muscles and the ankles.

When you have finished cleaning the front side of the body it is time to clean the backside of the body. The patient's backside is usually different than the front. Don't be surprised if an area on the back requires more or less cleaning then the same area on the front of the body.

As you clean the back, clean down the shoulders and particularly the spine. The back area, in between the shoulder blades, is a very good area for cleaning the lungs. Make certain that you clean all the way down. Clean thoroughly the kidneys and the lower back. This is an important area to clean. It is absolutely vital that the liver and kidneys are functioning at an optimum level in order to maintain a healthy body and energy field. Be sure to brush the hands into the Astral Fire Container several times, making certain that you are eliminating all of the lower vibration and negative energy into the container. Use the Ruach Healing Mist as necessary. Continue cleaning down the backside of the body in the same manner as cleaning the front.

Now, move around to the front side of the body, and again scanning the chest and, particularly, the Heart Center Gate. This gate is the conduit for all of the organs in the chest area. Specifically, the heart and lungs. Focus on cleaning the chest thoroughly, removing all unwanted congestion and contaminants. The process of cleaning the patient's backside may have loosened energy that can be cleaned from the front of the body.

Oftentimes, with organ conditions there will be noticeable cold spots within the energy field; this happens with cancer as well. Contrary to popular belief, the cold spot does not indicate a lack of energy. More often than not, it's an indication of congestion; or too much energy that is clogged, or not moving with fluidity.

Anytime during the healing process, especially during cleansing and charging, that you are uncertain as to whether to continue cleaning or not, pause. Place your right hand on that part of the energy field in order to muscle test the area. Focus your attention on the part of the energy field that needs to be tested, and/or have the patient you are healing touch that part of their body. When the patient touches the area, it activates it. The act of touching, by the patient, causes a chain reaction bringing the patient's focus to the area thus awakening the energy field of the area being tested. When you perform the muscle test, the nervous system and the muscles of the patient know which area you are testing. This gives you the information you will need, to either keep cleaning or not. If you feel the existence of negative energy or congestion, continue clearing and cleaning. It is not uncommon in the first session, with a new patient to muscle test 2-3 times as we are cleaning the energy field.

After you are done cleaning the entire energy field, you are ready to rescan, and see if there are areas that you may have missed, or additional areas that may have needed additional cleaning. Remember to keep brushing that energy into your Astral Fire Container and using the Ruach Healing Mist. If everything seems in order, and the energy field feels smoothly free flowing with little or no congestion, you are now ready to move onto the charging operations of the Ruach Healing Method.

## Recipe for Ruach Healing Mist

You will need the following ingredients. Note: all natural or organic works best.

**Orange Oil**

**Lemon or Lime Oil**

**Lavender Oil**

**Frankincense or Sage Oil**

**1/5th of unflavored Vodka (Triple Distilled)**

**Clean, Dark Colored, preferably glass spray bottle**

First, pour half your vodka into an empty 2 liter bottle, or your preferred bottle. This bottle will be used for mixing purposes only. Next, blend in 1 cup of Orange Oil. Add 1/4th of a cup of Lemon or Lime Oil. Add about 1/3rd of a cup of Lavender oil. Add a few drops of Frankincense. Mix and pour into a dark bottle with a mist top.

**That's it!** You are ready to begin using your Ruach Healing Mist to clean and enliven your hands and the patient's energy field.

***NOTE:*** *At Ruach Healing workshops, the oils are blended in advance and then mixed with vodka at the workshop. Vodka is used because it is antiseptic in nature, and also natural. If any mist should end up in the mouth, no harm would come of it.*

# CHAPTER FOURTEEN: CHARGING THE AURA

Before jumping right into some techniques on charging the energy field of our patient, a word or two is essential on the need to prepare your own vessel, before you transfer D.W.B. into your patient. Our experience has been that placing great emphasis on preparing the vessel of the healer is absolutely critical for maximum success. Sadly, we often notice that many healers have skipped this very important step. It seems that many healers place little importance on keeping their own vessel vibrating at a high rate. The bottom line is that you, as a healer, are a conduit for healing energy or Ruach. While it enters your own sphere of sensation pure, if you are not optimizing your own energy field by cleaning it and raising its vibration, then the energy will likely be tainted. This does not mean that the energy is not usable and effective, but as the following example will illustrate there might be a few side effects. More importantly, you will not be maximizing the full potential of the Ruach energy that you are transferring to the patient.

Years ago, when I was working on 2-3 patients a day, I was also a 2 pack a day smoker. I regularly brought a bucket out into my healing room with me, so that my patients could vomit. The patients were vomiting after I was charging them for a short period of time with my dirty and negative energy field. Later, I quit smoking and I spent the time necessary before every patient to light up my entire aura, with the Middle Pillar Exercise. We encourage you to do the same. We are not fanatics, but don't convince yourself that you can eat greasy hamburgers, drink beer and smoke cigarettes and still be an effective healer. We are not saying that you need to cut everything out of your life. A Ruach Healer can still enjoy a beer or glass of wine from time to time but regular consumption of lower vibrational substances will weaken your own energy field. Regular alcohol and cigarette consumption will absolutely affect the energy field of your patients in a negative way. It is simple, everything you do affects your energy field, so do things that help empower it, rather than weaken it.

As an effective Ruach Healer you absolutely must prepare yourself energetically before projecting energy onto your patients. Now, many of the Ruach Healers that we have worked with and trained, do not light up there entire energy field with the Middle Pillar Exercise. They choose some other method such as deep meditation or some form of yoga or even tantric breath work. Feel free to discover what method of raising the energy field works for you. The Ruach Healing method is for all, so this book is not the place to tell you how to connect with Higher Source and how prepare your vessel. In fact, no one should ever tell you how to connect with Spirit. Only suggestions for connection can be shared, which are all based on personal experience and traditions.

Some Ruach Healers almost always perform a complete ritualistic herbal bath before healing as a means of preparation. More traditional Ruach Healers prefer to light up their entire energy field by activating every Sephirot on the Tree of Life. Naturally deep and sincere prayer or invocation is an effective method for many as well. The secret is to prepare. Sometimes we believe that the intention of preparation is more important than the actual method. The secret is that whatever method you use to connect with Divine Source and invoke power into your body, make certain that the method you have chosen does exactly that. It must help you connect. It must invoke Ruach or DWB into your energy field to eventually be transferred to the patient.

## Methods of Charging the Aura

### Method 1: Breath Control

Breath control is very important in the process of charging the aura or energy field, of your patient. As you should well know by this point in the book, Ruach Healers like to do the slow, deep breathing of the Four Fold Breath. Breath exercises can be done while the healer is charging the patient's body and energy field. The breath work helps to to do a few things:

**1. Breath is used to invoke the Ruach or DWB.** As you breath in with your nose, you are concentrating on the the Light above your head. Focus on seeing it brightly. Some healers like to see it as a ball of white light above their head as in the Middle Pillar Exercise; others see an infinite cloud of healing light. Now, breathe in with your nose slowly, feeling your entire body being filled up with this incredible healing light. After about a 7 to 8 count, slowly breathe out with your mouth, allowing yourself to feel the Ruach Healing energy flow out the palms of your hands. You will likely notice your hands become very warm, almost hot. That is the healing light, the Ruach flowing out your hands into the sphere of sensation of the patient.

**2. The rhythm of breath work is similar to the natural pulsation of the universe.** Everything in the universe vibrates. The energy of your breath vibrates from a very *active* force when you are breathing outward, to a *passive* energy when you are breathing inward. The inward breath revitalizes or fills up your own sphere of sensation in preparation for the exhalation when the energy will flow out of your hands with more strength and power. This directly ties in with the Kabbalistic construct that "Spirit" is both an active energy and passive energy. To better understand this, realize that when you are breathing in, the Ruach is simply trickling out of your hands and into your patient's energy field. When you are full of Ruach or DWB and begin to focus your breath out, the energy flows with great intensity. You are in a sense acting as a bellow, filling up and sending out light and energy. Naturally as you because a seasoned Ruach Healer, you become less aware of this. Even after you are a seasoned healer, if you manage to stay consciously connected to your breath, while charging, you will have exact focus what you are doing at *every moment* in the charging process.

**3. There is something about slow, deep breathing that allows your patient to open their aura to you.** People are naturally guarded because our auras are designed to close down and tighten up when we are around someone we don't like or when we feel threatened. The same thing happens to the aura when a patient is in a state of fight or flight, or when the aura of the patient is ill or sick. The Vitality Rays droop and the aura gets tighter and more confined. This is a natural reaction to illness but it *always* acts as a wall to the Ruach healer. As a healer, you don't want this closing down, or closing in your patient's aura; you want your patient to open up as much as possible.

Breathing allows you to be more effective when you are in the process of charging a patient. An open aura allows the healing energy that you are invoking to penetrate more easily into the deeper layers of the energy field, thus becoming drastically more effective. There is something interesting that happens when you begin to breathe slowly, in through your nose and out through your mouth. Your patient begins to follow your breath pattern without even knowing it. They tap into your breath pattern and little by little they follow it. As they follow your breath, they become more open to you and the healing work you are doing, especially in the charging process.

## Method 2: Hand Placement

For about 90 percent of all our work we focus the energy coming out of the palms of our hand. There are a few ways to place your hands when you are charging your patient.

**1. Hands Side by Side.** This is basic and generally the most effective. Hold the palms of your hand side by side with fingers and palms turned slightly inward. The inward tilt should result in your side by side hands looking like a very wide letter "V". It is like the sides of the "V" are open twice as wide as normal. This allows the energy from each palm to mix with the other. The result is that you have one powerful and effective healing ray emanating from your hands onto your patient. In this position you can naturally slide your hands up and down the patient to the area that is in need of the charging.

**2. Hands Parallel With Each Other.** Parallel hands is an effective method when charging areas of the body such as the limbs, the neck, and even the heart and lungs. This method, of charging is simple, putting one hand on one side of the body and place the other hand on the other side of the body. Use both hands and charge the body part from both sides. For example, say you have a patient that has a bad knee and you determine that charging the knee, will be effective as a healing protocol. Put one hand on the outside of the knee and one hand on the inside of the knee and charge the front and the back at the same time.

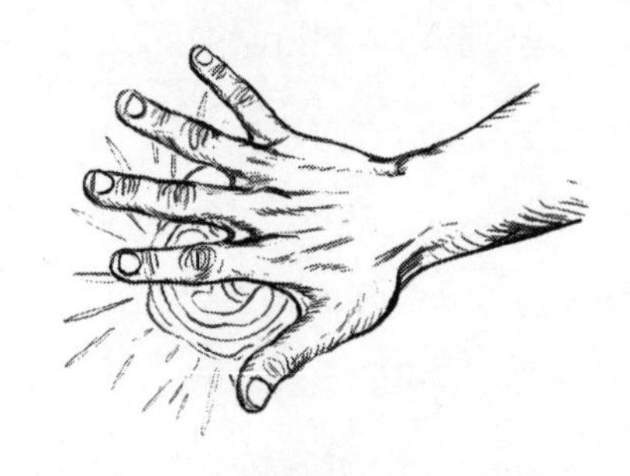

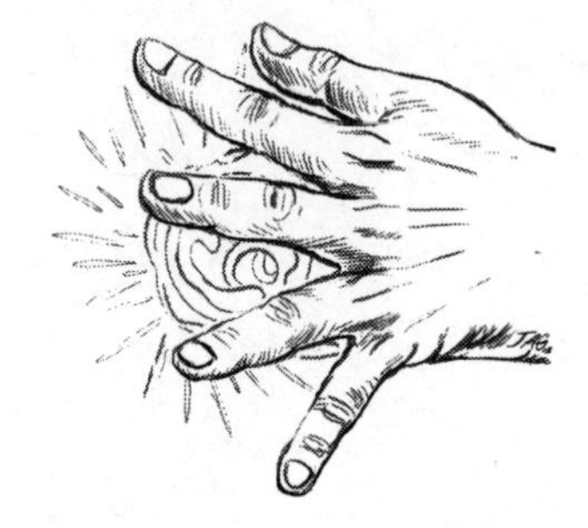

*Illustration 34: Charging Through Hands*

**3. Charging With the Fingertips.** There are a number of areas on the body that are sensitive to charging, in particular the eyes and anywhere on the face. Never use the palms of the hands for charging the face. The more effective method is to use your fingertips. You can use one finger or two or all of the fingers; such is in the **Beak of Thoth**. The Beak of Thoth gets its name because the hand position looks like the beak of an Ibis, the

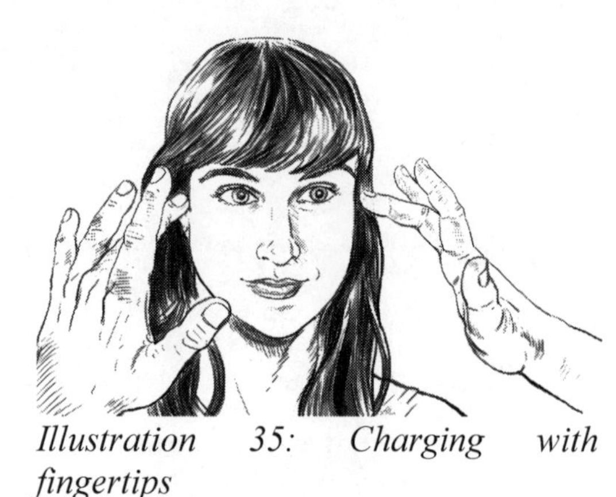

*Illustration 35: Charging with fingertips*

sacred bird of Thoth to the ancient Egyptians. The Beak of Thoth focuses all of the elemental energies under the direction of Spirit into a laser like ray. There is nothing else like it. It is extremely powerful for situations where a small but focused ray of healing energy in required. You might consider using the Beak of Thoth on the gates when they are depleted. The Beak can also be used on the spine for general healing and back spinal injuries. Ruach Healers particularly like to use the Beak of Thoth on anything that has to do with the nervous system, especially the spine. Energy from the Foundation Gate often runs up the back of the spine to the top of the head using the Beak of Thoth. The Fountain Gate is then charged with a Ball of D.W.B. From this point, draw the white light tinged with the red of the Foundation Gate down the entire body, like a loose fitting blanket. Naturally, mixing the white and red makes the color flowing down an extremely light pink color. If you only master this one technique you will have a powerful tool for almost any kind of healing.

Also as you become more sensitive to energies, you will naturally want to use your fingertips in several parts of the body simply because it is more precise. You can use one finger, as in charging the face, or the Beak of Thoth for a precise ray of powerful Ruach. You are limited only by your imagination and inner spiritual guidance.

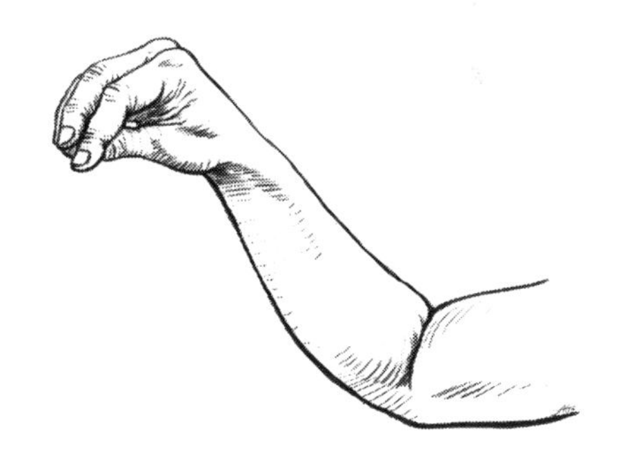

*Illustration 36: Beak of Thoth*

## Method 3: Charging the Healing Cloud

This is a method of charging that can be used on extremely sensitive people. It is also the preferred method for group charging as well. When you have a group of healers, you don't want everyone charging the patient with Ruach at the same time, as it could be overwhelming. The secret is to charge a white healing cloud above the patient's head. Everyone sends the energy to the cloud rather than directly to the patient's energy field. This allows the cloud, to become filled up with Ruach and D.W.B. Then all that is necessary for the Ruach Healer to do is gently comb the cloud energy down into the patient's energy field. It is really quite effective.

As mentioned above, this method can be used for people that have very sensitive energy fields. For some reason about 1 in 10,000 people simply cannot take direct charging, so when you run into one of them, use the healing cloud. Children, that some light workers consider "rainbow" or "crystal" children, are also extremely sensitive and do well with the cloud method.

## Prove the Power of Charging with Ruach to Yourself

Practice makes perfect when it comes to charging. There are a number of ways you can practice charging. Take two apples, making sure they are from the same batch. Twice a day, charge one of the apples gently with the palms of your hands, or your fingertips. With the other apple, simply do nothing. Continue to do this for about two weeks or so. Cut both apples open and proving to you the power of Ruach Healing energy.

You will be amazed that the apple you have been charging is still healthy and vibrant, while the other apple will likely be mushy, and brown on the inside. Naturally you will want to advance beyond fruit and vegetables, so why not practice light charging on the family cat or dog. Trust me they love the energy and usually beg for more.

Practice charging lightly your sinuses, with your finger. Then gently charge your third eye and your neck. If you have hearing problems you might want to charge your ears gently with your fingertips. Remember to only charge for about 5 minutes or so. It won't take long to get the hang of charging.

One final note, Ruach is life force, the same as Prana or Reiki. It is the very substance the universe is created from. Therefore, consider developing a deeper connection with the universe by charging everything. You can charge your meals, clothing, even furniture. Imagine how pleasant it will be to enjoy a visit with the in-laws having them spend an evening sitting on Ruach charged furniture and eating Ruach charged food. Charging your entire environment with Ruach will positively affect you and those you interact with.

# NOTES:

# CHAPTER FIFTEEN: Untangling the Vitality Rays Of The Aura

Have you ever walked into a room when you thought nobody was in the house, but felt you weren't alone? You somehow instinctively knew that there was someone else in the house. These are the “Vitality Rays”. They extend from your aura. Most of the Vitality Rays are about 18-24 inches long, but there are some that extend upwards of 18-22 feet. These extremely long Vitality Rays are especially found in highly intuitive people.

These health rays serve the body in a variety of different ways. One, they act as a filter for the outer and inner aura. They detect negative energy and then send a pulse back to the aura which connects with the various gates. Each gate has its own psychic type of awareness, or its own intuitive strength. The primary gates that deal with intuition are the Third Eye Gate and the Foundation Gate. When the Vitality Rays sense something that could be dangerous or contrary to the health of the body, the Vitality Rays sends a vibration back to the appropriate gate. Usually it will be one of the two we have just mentioned. This information is then transferred into the nervous system, or the thinking pattern of the physical body. For example, have you ever heard somebody say, “I have a gut feeling about ____________?” Gut level feelings are usually, or generally beyond the scope of thinking and happening long before the brain becomes involved.

As a Ruach Healer, aiding the Vitality Rays in becoming untangled and open, exponentially increases the patient's energy and vitality. It is equally advantageous for tuning the patient's intuition. Intuition is absolutely necessary for the self-healing process. Having healthy and vibrant Vitality Rays are an absolute benefit to not only functioning better in the physical plane, but also functioning and connecting on the spiritual plane as well. There are spiritual forces all around us, ALL the time. As we assist the creation of a spiritual connection, while bringing healing to the physical body, balance is brought to the patient.

As stated earlier, most of the Vitality Rays are roughly 2 feet in length. These rays are the primary focus of the Ruach Healer. They connect all the way from the inner aura, to whatever their length may be. Highly intuitive individuals can oftentimes see these Vitality Rays. I have spoken to these intuitives all over the world. There is a general consensus, when the Vitality Rays are tangled and not flowing freely, health and vitality are not optimized. The task of a Ruach Healer, is to act as a spiritual comb for these Vitality Rays. Of course, the primary tool for combing the Vitality Rays, are your two hands.

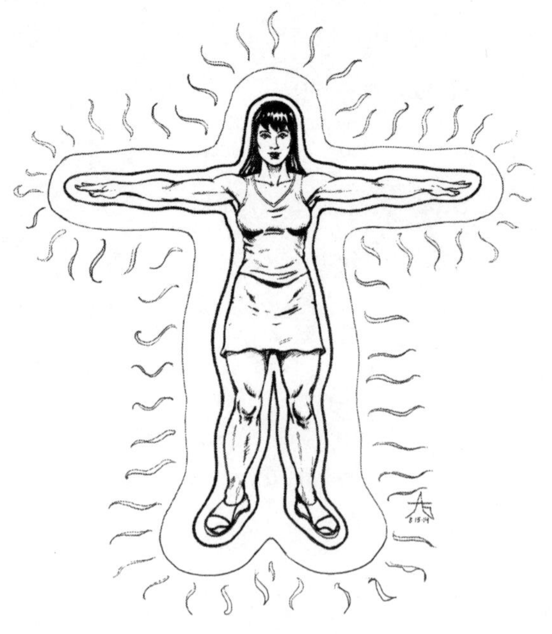

*Illustration 37: Healthy Vitality Rays*

### Directions for Combing the Vitality Rays

Begin by washing your hands. This is a time when we really like to use the Ruach Healing Mist, because the lemon and lime combination provides an extraordinary power of cleanliness and invigoration. Lightly and quickly scan the aura at the level of the Vitality Rays. Notice where the Vitality Rays may be tangled and/or drooping. The difference between this type of scanning and the scanning we do early on in the healing process, is that we are scanning a foot to two feet away from the patient's body. The scanning is done very lightly and very softly and quite rapidly. Keep in mind, we are not scanning for congestion or deficiencies. Rather, we are scanning like a high priced hairdresser who is running his or her fingers through his client's hair, feeling the texture and the tangles. Generally, if we have been working on someone for any length of time, our hands are pretty well activated, but activate your hands again if need be.

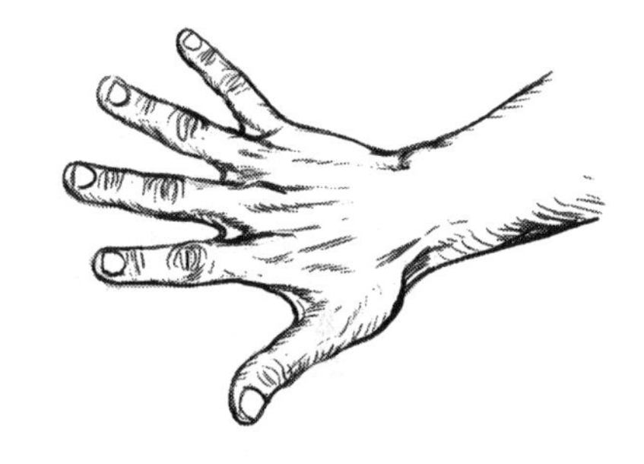

*Illustration 38: Combing or Untangling the Vitality Rays*

After washing your hands, open our fingers apart on both hands, and begin combing the Vitality Rays by lightly pulling straight out, while untangling the rays as you go. The pulling outward motion allows the aura of the patient to expand. The sensation is like that of running your fingers through hair.

If in your scanning, you found the Vitality Rays to be dirty, or have a lot of negative energy particles attached to them, the light untangling can be done first with downward strokes. The downward stroke gently combs the Vitality Rays toward the feet. Combing the Vitality Rays pointed toward the feet allows negative energy to slide downward to be grounded. The Ruach Healer should always keep in mind that downward brushing of the Vitality Rays removes any unwanted negative energy.

In the case of upward brushing toward the head, it does not remove negative energy, but the untangling gives the patient a greater sense of energy and vitality as their aura makes a spiritual connection. That is why in the beginning, we generally brush straight out, which has a more neutral effect, then towards the end of our combing we will brush the aura in an upward motion.

**Table 7: Combing the Vitality Rays**

| Combing Direction | Affect on the Vitality Rays |
|---|---|
| Strait outward from the body | Neutral – expanding the aura |
| Downward toward the feet | Cleaning – removing negativity |
| Upward toward the head | Energizing – spiritual connection |

## Relaxing the Healing Recipient

One of the things you can do to help relax the patient, who may be nervous or feeling anxiety, is to gently brush the Vitality Rays downward. Brushing the Vitality Rays downward, will put a patient in a very calm and relaxed state, as well as, making them oftentimes feel sleepy and tired. We have advised a countless number of parents to brush the aura of their crying baby downwards in the evening. This ensures sleep for the baby as well as the parents. We have seen children fall asleep in less than two minutes from simply brushing the Vitality Rays downward.

***It is generally not a good idea to comb the aura downward on anyone who is running a fever. It tends to encapsulate the body, and perpetuates the fever. Never comb a patient's aura downward if they are driving, or using heavy machinery at the time. Brushing the aura downward is like giving your patient an astral Valium.***

## Tips on Combing the Vitality Rays

Start combing at the head and work your way downward. Even when you are combing upwards, start at the head. When you want to provide extra vitality to your patient, brush the Vitality Rays upward from the head all the way down to the feet, then continue to brush upwards from the feet all the way back up to the head. When brushing with your hands, don't stiffen them up, keep your fingers relaxed and limber. Allow them to feel the Vitality Rays with a high level of sensitivity. One of the strongest experiences the Ruach Healer can give a patient is to gently intermingle light charging of the Divine White Brilliance ("D.W.B.") with brushing or combing of the aura and Vitality Rays. You can gently rotate between charging and combing, back and forth, for as long as needed. Please note, there are times when just a light combing of the Vitality Rays can revitalize someone and give them an uplifted feeling. It is not always necessary to go through an entire healing process, if your primary goal is just to recharge by combing the Vitality Rays.

# CHAPTER SIXTEEN: Sealing the Aura – The Power of the Rose Cross

Healing work is never finished until the aura is completely sealed. Sealing the aura works to keep in positive energy that the healer has invigorated into the aura. Sealing also acts as a protective shield, keeping out negative energy, specifically energy that could cause the disease to return or worsen. It amazes me that a number of people have shared with me over the years they were successful with the healing work that they had performed only to have the disease return in about four months. As a matter of fact, one evening I was watching the Larry King Show on CNN has he interviewed the famous healer Benny Hinn. Benny Hinn suggested that if a disease returns it returns after about four months. I have talked to other healers as well, who wrote off the return of disease as karma or something else. When I first began as a healer, it seemed I was constantly being called back to heal people that I thought were completely healed. So, the whole concept of cleaning and charging an aura is not a complete work, until the aura is firmly sealed. I was even more amazed that in sealing the aura of patients who have undergone deep emotional trauma, after a complete spiritual and emotional cleaning, seem to drastically improve after a sealing of the aura. Let me explain what I mean.

Much of the time, the illness that the Ruach healer is treating has an emotional core. As the energy field of the patient is cleaned and charged, you are not only cleaning the outward sickness, you are also cleaning the inward emotional core. So, after the healing work is complete, by sealing the aura, you not only invoke healing into the physical body, but you have also awakened new potential and power into the emotional body as well. Thus, by spiritually sealing the aura, neither the physical illness nor the emotional can return. This is astonishing because the patient not only gets free of the illness, but has new emotional empowerment. This is what true spiritual and Ruach Healing is all about! I can't over emphasize the importance of finishing the work by sealing the patient's aura.

To get an idea of what sealing is, I will explain a very basic sealing technique and then go into detail about using symbols with the sealing process. When you are finished doing your entire work with a patient, you will, of course, brush the aura, as explained earlier in the book. The very last thing we do is back up a few feet and draw an entire Rose Cross covering the entire energy field. This seals the entire aura, putting it in a high vibratory state. This insures that your healing intentions will be safe until the next time you begin your work on the patient.

In the Ruach Healing Method, a very specific symbol is used for sealing the aura, called the Rose Cross. The basic symbol appears astrally as a golden yellowish cross with a red circle in the center of it. I have done extensive research on the Rose Cross over the years and I can tell you, it is almost impossible to find when the Rose Cross appeared in the collective conscious. Perhaps on some esoteric level it has always been present. Variations of this symbol extend beyond antiquity. While we can not tell the time the Rose Cross appeared, we can talk about what this symbol means on a variety of levels.

It is important that the Ruach Healer, who chooses to use symbolism in their healing, understands the symbol as much as possible. There is a great debate among metaphysical scholars as to how a symbol works. Some would argue that it is the knowledge of the symbol that gives it power. Others report that the knowledge is inconsequential, because in truth, the symbol wakes up an energies in the subconscious which is the connecting link to the universe. In Ruach Healing, both constructs of symbolism are experienced. It is both the knowledge of the symbol, as well as its inherent power, that give it life.

The Rose Cross is a particularly interesting symbol because it is a symbol hidden within the symbol. What I mean by this is, "Does the rose sit upon the cross giving life to the cross, or does the cross give life to the rose?" If you were to answer either way you would be right. It is truly a mysterious symbol.

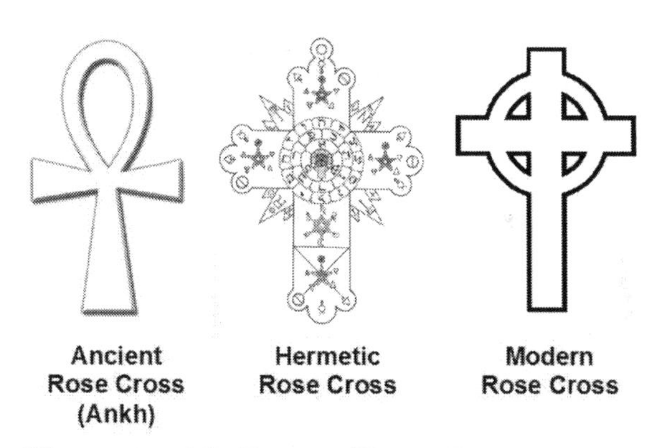


*Illustration 39: Types of Rose Crosses*

The symbol of the Rose Cross begins to show up in human conscious in a big way in ancient Egypt. Most Egyptian gods, can be seen holding the ankh or Crux Ansata. The ankh, like the modern version of the Rose Cross, is a symbol of light and life. Next, the Rose Cross is seen in the more modern form, appearing in Rosicrucian orders around the 16th and 17th century. These orders were groups of dedicated mystics and magi that traveled the world in search of hidden wisdom and knowledge. They also looked for secrets of alchemy and healing. The mystics more sacred symbol is the symbol used in the Ruach Healing Method called the Modern Rose Cross.

## Symbolism of the Modern Rose Cross

Most think of the cross as having two arms, a vertical and horizontal. Amongst other symbolism, the arms of the cross can be divided into four instead or just two. Therefore, it makes sense that the symbolism of the cross represents the four elements of nature as well as the four directions. The circle in the center of the cross represents the changeless Eternal Spirit, or Divine Source, binding the two arms and the four elements of the cross together. The circle also represents infinity or the alpha and omega, the beginning and the end. *"I am Alpha and Omega, the beginning and the end, the first and the last."* (Revelations 22:13 KJV). To put it succinctly, the circle represents the changeless nature of the god head.

Another way of looking at the cross, is having two arms or four arms, depending on how you look at it. If it has two arms vertical and horizontal it is the vertical arm, which is usually a bit longer, this represents humankind's connection to the divine. The horizontal arm represents humankind's marriage to the physical plane. From time to time, you will interact with a patient in whom you can vividly see this imbalance. Some people are so engrossed in the physical world they have no interest in spirituality at all. They have a strong horizontal arm, but no vertical arm. On the other hand, I am sure you have all met people that cannot figure out how to feed themselves, but they have an amazing connection to a spiritual component. The cross is a scale measuring equilibrium between the physical world and the spiritual plane. When the horizontal and vertical arms are in perfect balance, then and only then, the rose of creation is formed in the center.

The place of equilibrium in the cross is the place of ultimate power. It is here that the symbol of the rose is found. In the Hermetical Rose Cross, the rose is symbolized by three tiers of petals. The first tier consists of three petals representing the three alchemical principles; salt, mercy, and sulfur. The second tier consists of seven petals which refer to the seven planets of the ancients. The third tier has twelve petals, which relate to the twelve astrological signs of the heavens. Thus, we have 22 petals in total. These 22 petals equal the 22 letters of the Hebrew alphabet or the 22 paths of the Kabbalistic Tree of Life.

*Illustration 40: Hermetic Rose Cross*

The Rose Cross also has many other meanings, as we look more closely at the rose. In addition to the changeless nature of spirit, the rose means purity, death, and life. The rose, is of course, is the sacred flower of the goddess Venus. This is important because the symbol of Venus is the only planetary symbol that when laid over the image of the Tree of Life connects every Sephirot. The rose garden is traditionally the sacred alchemical marriage ground of the sun and moon. This is often referred to as the marriage of opposites or gold and silver.

Without any doubt the Rose Cross is the most powerful healing symbol. There is no symbol that can compare to it, this is why we have shared an in-depth look at this sacred symbol. We have briefly just touched on the symbolism of the Rose Cross. There are entire books written on its mysteries and meaning. Other symbols have their place but if there was only one symbol to use for any kind of healing and especially the sealing of the aura, it is the Rose and Cross. In test situations, Ruach Healers have substituted the Rose Cross for other healing symbols used in Reiki and other traditions, but the result with the Rose Cross is beyond compare. **The Rose Cross is literally the most powerful and effective healing symbol, without a doubt!** Certainly, this does not mean that others symbols too do not have their place, but no matter what kind of healing work you engage in, it is a wise and effective idea to end your work by sealing the aura with the Rose Cross symbol.

### Exercise: Drawing the Rose Cross

Using a closed fist, with your thumb out between your middle and ring finger, draw the cross. This hand position is symbolic of Spirit, within in the center of the elements. Visualize drawing the cross with in bright yellow or gold. Begin drawing the cross at the top, and then from the left to the right. Next, after your cross has been drawn in the air, draw a bright red circle from the 8 o'clock position on the cross clockwise to the right. While drawing the Rose Cross it is appropriate to vibrate **YHShVH**, pronounced *Yeh-heh-shu-ah.* This name comes from the four letters of the Tetragrammaton **YHVH**, pronounced *Yod Heh Vav Heh,* concentrated by the holy letter **Shin**. Shin is the letter of the Holy Spirit. This combination creates the Pentagrammaton.

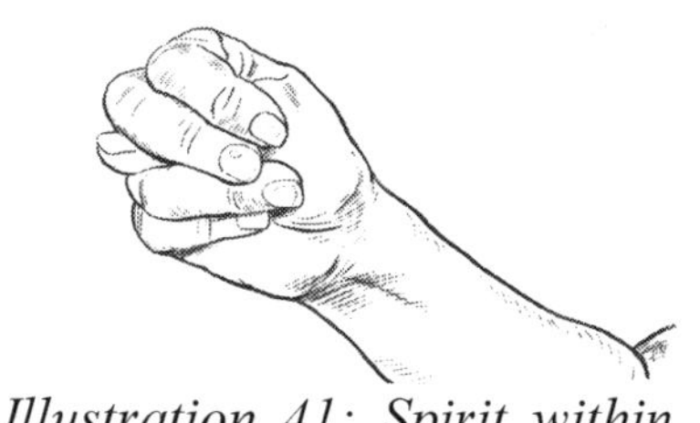

*Illustration 41: Spirit within the Elements*

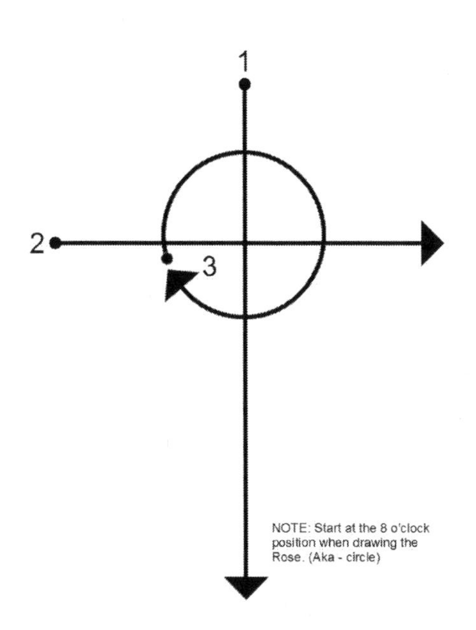


*Illustration 42: Drawing the Rose Cross*

There is a whole secret mystery into this sacred word, YHShVH. In the bibliography found in the back of this book, one of my favorite explanations of this word is found in "Modern Magick" by Donald Michael Kraig. To put it simply, you are vibrating the name of the Pentagrammaton. This spells the name Joshua, which is the root word for the name Jesus. Christians tend to positively enjoy vibrating YHShVH because it is a way of invoking the power of Jesus or Christ to complete the healing work. Pagans and mystic see this as a reference to Christ's consciousness. Another term for Christ consciousness is the perfected man. It should be noted again, that the symbol of the Rose Cross is not a Christian symbol and far out-dates the advent of Christianity. In a great sense, you and I as healers, are perfecting our patient by helping them to return to a state of equilibrium and balance; the perfected man.

*Illustration 43: Tetragrammaton & Pentagrammaton*

## Sealing with the Rose Cross

Now that you know how to draw the Rose Cross, let's look at sealing the Vitality Gates. When you are finished working on each of the seven gates in the human aura, and you know that you will not be returning to it, seal the gate with the Rose Cross. Be aware, that the Rose Cross is not intended to stop the flow of energy in the gate; rather, it is designed to protect your work and insure that the gate does not become clogged or depleted again. Usually, when sealing a Vitality Gate, the Rose Cross is drawn about five inches long and a few inches off the aura itself.

Please note, that when a patient is having deep emotional or psychological problems, it is extremely important to seal the heart center and the back of the head. Since most Ruach Healers are not trained psychiatrists, both are sealed because it is not known if it is an emotional problem or psychological.

Naturally, before drawing the Rose Cross, we have preceded with cleaning and charging. At the end of the entire healing process and after a nice combing of the aura and Vitality Rays, the Ruach Healer will moves about 6 feet away from the patient. From this position hold your hands with fingers apart facing towards the patient. Now pull down the Divine White Brilliance from the top of your head into your hands and project a golden light all around the patient. If possible, walk around the patient to ensure that this golden light is fully surrounding them and infiltrating every area of their energy field. During this process of sealing the patient, it is very important to go inward and connect with Divine Source, giving gratitude and thanksgiving for all of the skills and blessings that you have been given to help this patient in the healing process. End with a silent prayer or a moment of silence. This concludes the basic healing operation.

### Rosicrucian Reiki

This is perhaps is one of the most powerful and well hidden healing techniques available. Simply take your thumb from your right hand and draw a Rose Cross on the palm of your left hand. Next do likewise with the left hand into the right palm. With your palms charged with the symbol of the Rose Cross, you can begin healing and sealing the patient at the same time. This is done by placing your hands on them in a Reiki like style. Stand in back of the patient and place your hands on their shoulders. Allow the energy to flow from your hands through the symbol of the Rose Cross, into the patient. This is a highly sacred symbol and should never be used haphazardly. As a Ruach Healer, I am certain that the depth of power and symbolism in Rose Cross will always be used reverently. For more information on the use of the Rose Cross we recommended "*The Golden Dawn*" by Israel Regardie.

### Exercise: The Rose Cross Breath

As a healer, developing the Rose Cross in your own sphere of sensation, is a powerful exercise. The benefits of this healing will be actualized as the symbol of the Rose Cross is built up within you. You will also build the equilibrium of the physical and spiritual, along with the deep sense of peace, that this symbol expresses.

**Step 1**

Stand in the center of your healing space, facing east, with your arms outstretched forming a cross with your body.

**Step 2**

Empty your lungs and take a deep 7 count breath in through your nose. Visualize a yellow light coming down from the heaven to the ground and coming back up to your heart center. Hold your breath for 7 seconds.

**Step 3**

Exhale through your mouth, seeing the light flow through your outstretched arms forming a golden cross on your body. Keep your lungs empty for 7 seconds.

**Step 4**

Breathe in again for four seconds, while visualizing the rose drawn on the top of your chest. Start at the 8 o'clock position and draw the rose in a clockwise direction. Do not hold your breath. Simply exhale for seven seconds, sealing the Rose Cross in your aura. Allow your lungs to remain empty for 7 seconds and repeat from step one.

**CAUTION: Never use the symbolism of the Rose Cross, or preform the Rose Cross breath if you or the patient have a high grade fever. Remember that this symbol of the Rose Cross seals energy, and in most cases would not harm a fever but in some cases it could raise the fever. Therefore, it is better to avoid the Rose Cross altogether if a fever is present.**

## Sacred Space Rose Cross Ritual

The Rose Cross Ritual is a powerful way to tune your healing space into a higher, cleaner vibrational space void of the influence of outside unwanted forces. The Rose Cross Ritual acts as a veil, as it allows you to create a spiritual healing environment that will not be disturbed by lower forces and energies. One of the things that many healers never take into consideration is that all the Light, Prana, Reiki, Chi, and Ruach, tends to light up the astral plane. Not only do positive energies see this illumination, so do lower, darker, unwanted force (you don't want that). Essentially, you could end up attracting more of what you don't want, or energies that are contrary to healing. The Rose Cross Ritual gives you the unbelievable protection you desire and need as a Ruach Healer by placing six Rose Crosses in your healing space. The Rose Cross Ritual helps, since it creates a protective and meditative environment, both physically and astrally. Moments after performing this ritual you will notice that everything calms down, the energy is smooth, soft and empowering.

It is highly suggested that you as a healer, do this ritual before you begin your healing work. It will aid you in all the ways stated above, but equally important, gives you a clear, clean environment to listen and feel your intuition with greater clarity. The Rose Cross is also a power protection against psychic invasion of others. Often the negative thoughts of other people can be extremely damaging each physically, emotionally and psychically.

You can also perform this ritual with the intention of helping others who are in severe pain or having emotionally difficulty. For this purpose you build up an astral image of the patient. Visualize the patient's presence in the center of the room. Next, invoke the D.W.B. Use the Divine Names of Kether to call down the light, while visualizing the Light surrounding the patient completely. Now, perform the entire Rose Cross Ritual around the image. See the six Rose Crosses around your patient. The patient's astral form should be standing in the Rose Cross space, with the Light completely surrounding him/her. Call the Light to bring about the healing desired. Wait about 20 minutes or so, and then command the astral form to return to the patient. Expect the healing you have invoked.

The Rose Cross Ritual, used in the above fashion, is also used to restore vigor, vitality, a sense of rest, and healing to your patient. The example above is a long distance example, but it can be equally done with someone who is present. Simply have them stand in the center of the room, and proceeding in the same way as above.

One final point, in this book and for Ruach Healing purposes, I have left out what adepts in the Golden Dawn call the analysis of the keyword and the invocation of the Tablet of Union from the Ross Cross Ritual. Neither of them is actually part of the Rose Cross Ritual proper and serves no vital purpose in the healing process.

### Exercise: Sacred Space Rose Cross Ritual

#### Step 1

Light a stick of incense. Go to the Southeast corner of the room. Draw a Rose Cross with the stick of incense. Remember to draw the cross in bright yellow or gold, and the rose in red. Point the incense in the center of the rose, vibrating the Divine Name, **YHShVH**, pronounced *Yeh-heh-shu-ah.*

#### Step 2

With arms outstretched, on a level with the center of the cross, and holding the incense stick, draw a white line from the center of the Rose Cross in the Southeast as you walk to the Southwest corner of the room. Draw the Rose Cross here in the Southwest as you did in step one and vibrate the Divine Name, **YHShVH**, pronounced *Yeh-heh-shu-ah.*

**Step 3**

With arms outstretched, on a level with the center of the cross, and holding the incense stick, draw a white line from the center of the Rose Cross in the Southwest as you walk to the Northwest corner. Draw the Rose Cross as you did in step one and vibrate the Divine Name, **YHShVH**, pronounced *Yeh-heh-shu-ah*.

**Step 4**

As you did before, draw a white line, from the center of the Rose Cross you just made, as you walk to the Northeast corner. Draw the Rose Cross as you did in step one and vibrate the Divine Name, **YHShVH**, pronounced *Yeh-heh-shu-ah*.

**Step 5**

Complete your circle by drawing a white line, as you return to the Southeast corner and bring the point of the incense to the central point of the imagine of the first cross, which you astrally placed there. As you point to the center, vibrate the Divine Name, **YHShVH**, pronounced *Yeh-heh-shu-ah*.

**Step 6**

While holding the incense stick high, draw a white line to the center of the room by walking diagonally across the room towards the Northwest corner. In the center of the room, above your head, draw the Rose Cross and vibrate the Divine Name, **YHShVH**, pronounced *Yeh-heh-shu-ah*.

**Step 7**

Hold the incense stick high, draw a white line from the center of the room to the Northwest Rose Cross, finishing by walking diagonally across the room. Connect the white line in the center of the Rose Cross that was previously made in the Northwest. As you point to the center, vibrate the Divine Name, **YHShVH**, pronounced *Yeh-heh-shu-ah.*

**Step 8**

Next, hold the incense stick low, and draw a white line as you retrace your steps from the Northwest Rose Cross to the floor in the center of the room. You are walking toward the Southeast. In the center of the room, below your feet, draw the Rose Cross and vibrate the Divine Name, **YHShVH**, pronounced *Yeh-heh-shu-ah.*

**Step 9**

As you keep the incense stick low, return to the Southeast by walking diagonally across the room. Again, bring the point of the incense stick to the center of the Rose Cross in the Southeast. Then, move with arms outstretched to Southwest corner of the room.

**Step 10**

Holding the incense stick high, drawing a white line from the Rose Cross in the Southwest to the center of the room, by walking diagonally across the room towards the Northeast corner. In the center of the room, above your head, point to the center of the high Rose Cross that was previously drawn in step 6. It is not necessary to make another cross. As you point to the center, vibrate the Divine Name, **YHShVH**,
pronounced *Yeh-heh-shu-ah.*

**Step 11**

Holding the incense stick high, draw a white line from the center of the room to the Northeast Rose Cross, by finishing walking diagonally across the room. Connect the white line in the center of the Rose Cross that was previously made in the Northeast. As you point to the center, vibrate the Divine Name, **YHShVH**, pronounced *Yeh-heh-shu-ah.*

**Step 12**

Hold the incense stick low, and draw a white line, as you retrace your steps from the Northeast Rose Cross to the floor in the center of the room. You are walking toward the Southwest. In the center of the room, connect the white line in the center of the Rose Cross that was previously made under your feet. As you point to the center of the Rose, vibrate the Divine Name, **YHShVH**, pronounced *Yeh-heh-shu-ah.*

### Step 13

Keep the incense stick low, returning to the Southwest by walking diagonally across the room. Again, bring the point of the incense stick to the center of the Rose Cross in the Southwest.

### Step 14

Hold the incense stick out, and retrace your circle toward the Southeast, from the Southwest connect the white line to the center of the Ross Cross in the Northwest. From the Northwest, connect the white line to the center of the Ross Cross in the Northeast. From the Northeast, connect the white line to the center of the Ross Cross in the Southeast. You are back to where you started this ritual in step one.

### Step 15

Stand in the Southeast, and draw another Rose Cross. This time make it larger, as large as your arm will reach. As you draw the cross vibrate **YHShVH**, pronounced *Yeh-heh-shu-ah,* for the lower half. As you draw the rose vibrate **YHVShH**, pronounced *Yeh-hoh-vah-shah* for the upper half. This cross is the Rose Cross that seals the other six completing the ritual.

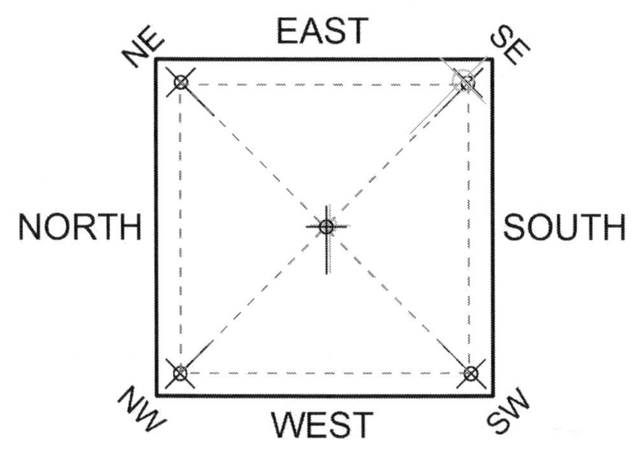


NOTE: The Rose Crosses in the center represents both the cross above the head and below the feet. There are two Rose Crosses in this position.

*Illustration 44: Sacred Space Rose Cross Ritual*

**Step 16**

Return to the center of the room. Visualize the six crosses you made, the four directional crosses and the two in the center of the room. Feel and absorb the new energy in the room.

**Note: This is the primary Rose Cross Ritual for creating your sacred space. There are advanced versions that are taught to adepts of the Golden Dawn and variations, however this version will work in literally every situation. I suggest memorizing this simple ritual and preform it anytime you want to create a safe, sealed healing space.**

## The Symbol of the Rose and Cross Provides Healing Beyond Belief

The powerful uses of the Rose Cross cannot be overstated. Some Ruach Healers claim that performing the traditional work of clearing and charging followed by deep visualization of the Rose Cross into the sickness itself is an effective healing technique. I have personally used this method with the treatment of cancer.

Other healers including myself, light up the symbol of the Rose Cross in our chests. This is the area of Tiphareth on the Tree of Life. Then during the charging the healer not only sends a powerful ray of light from both hands to the specific area or Vitality Gate, but he/she also sends out a healing ray of Light from the center of the Rose and Cross which is glowing in the center of the healer's being. This is a powerful, miracle making technique. The visualization of three rays at one time will take some practice. Also, the ray that comes forth from the Rose and Cross glowing within the center of your being, is virtually always a light pink, while your hands may be charging with an Elemental color, Vitality Gate color, color of the Sephirot or even a Planetary color. This technique is awesome magic and even more awesome healing juice when it's mastered. Practice on plants and trees before you begin doing this with humans. There is no danger, but you will want your skills mastered.

# CHAPTER SEVENTEEN: Elemental Healing Techniques

A few years ago, a good friend of mine, called me for some healing work. He was suffering from bronchitis, otherwise known as "walking pneumonia". He also had a bad cold that had completely stuffed up his sinuses. He was not far from returning to the emergency room, where he usually went, as these conditions flared up. It seemed a chronic occurrence for him.

After I thoroughly scanned his body, as well as, his Vitality Gates, I decided to approach his condition with green, rather than elements of Air and Fire. I first began cleaning his lungs with pale green light. The green light is attributed to the planet Venus. It is a wonderful purifying energy. I added Divine White Brilliance to it to make it pale. With D.W.B. the green vibrates higher and becomes more effective for cleaning. Green is an astonishing energy for cleaning someone's lungs. As a matter of fact, I combed his entire aura, brushing downwards and dumping the negative energy into an Astral Fire Container.

The next step was to charge, using one of the four elemental energies. I began charging with the element of Air. Air is given the color yellow. From an archetypal perspective, and for the purpose of healing, we use a very pale, light yellow, almost clear. Air is literally not any color, but the Ruach Healer projects the light out of the hands and fingers as a pale yellow tint.

I'd like to pause for a moment and clear up some common confusion on the subject. I can almost hear a reader out there wondering, "What is the difference between the yellow of Air and the yellow of Tiphareth?" While the colors are the about the same, the energies are *completely* different. If I were to charge my friend in the chest with the element of Tiphareth, visualizing a yellow color of tinted white light, I would have likely gotten results. However, they wouldn't have been as strong or as quickly received as if I were to have been using an element. The four elements are primal in nature. They are part of the environment which we live in every day. They are the primal forces that comprise our bodies, the food we eat and the water we drink, thus having intense power and energy. Always begin with D.W.B., and then go to the four elements. In many cases this specific charging, along with the charging of the Vitality Gates in their respective colors is enough. EXAMPLE: We have charged the patient with the primary color of air, which is a pale yellow and I now charge the Vitality Gates with their respective colors and see them on top or within the pale yellow. The colors DO NOT mix.

Let me be clear. The Sephirot differ from the elements in that the Sephirot are levels of consciousness. You could say, they are levels of divine consciousness. This consciousness begins in "No-Thing" or "Ain" (refer back to Chapter 3 and the 3 levels of negative existence) and it develops downward through the next two levels of negative existence onward into the Tree of Life. The energy is explored all the way down through the ten states of Divine Consciousness on the Tree of Life and eventually creating the four elements.

Now that this has been clarified, let's return back to my friend with the lung condition. After working on my friend for a few days, the congestion in his lungs began to clear up. He was extremely pleased. In our next session, I began working on his nose and his nasal passages. They were completely clogged. For this, I chose the element of Fire. After thoroughly cleaning his nose area, again with green light, I began clearing the energy from his delicate nasal passages with my pinky fingertips. He began to breathe easier.

Some people take a "no medicine" approach to healing. FYI: Ruach Healers as a whole group are *not* this type of people. Ruach Healers believe the combination of medication, herbs, and oils, along with Ruach Healing, speeds up recovery time. It certainly did for my friend. He had been on decongestants for several days prior to working on him, with little to no results. After working on his nasal system only one time, his system completely cleared up. This elemental healing is astonishing!

I have run into healers and mystics of every type, some of whom reduce elemental healing to something overly simplistic. The goal of Ruach Healing has never been about simplicity or complexity, rather about effectiveness. Using elemental energies in the Ruach Healing process is powerful.

The Ruach Healer will naturally want to invoke all the potency of the elements. The elements, just like the Sephirot, are subject to the four worlds. Each element has its own set of Divine Names. These Divine names traditionally awaken the element within the sphere of sensation of the person vibrating them. To make it simple, when you charge an area of the body using one of the elemental forces, you are first awakening that element within your own sphere of sensation, and next directing it to the area of the body that needs to be charged through your hands and fingers.

The Divine Names awaken a force called **Elementals**. Elementals are not Divine. They are spiritual forces that comprise the very nature of the element. To awaken the element completely, recite the Divine name and the Archangelic Name. Next, begin projecting the healing energy out through your hands, while visualizing the appropriate color.

**Table 8: Hierarchy and Color of Elements**

| ELEMENT | DIVINE NAME | ARCH-ANGEL | ANGEL | COLOR |
|---|---|---|---|---|
| Fire | Elohim | Michael | Aral | Pale Red |
| Water | El | Gabriel | Taliahad | Pale Blue |
| Air | YHVH | Raphael | Chassan | Pale Yellow |
| Earth | Adonai ha-Aretz | Auriel | Phorlak | Pale Green/Earth tones |

## Exploring & Understanding the Elements

The **Element of Air** is warm and moist. Air is projected in the color pale yellow. Air can be used through any part of the breathing system of the body, such as lungs, air passageways, nasal passageways, etc. Air is also effective in the spinal cord and on the nervous system. Air works well in treating mental disorders. It can be used for invoking mental clarity. Air also strengthens the white blood cells in the body, which are used for carrying oxygen. Air is best invoked using the pinky finger, which is the finger of air.

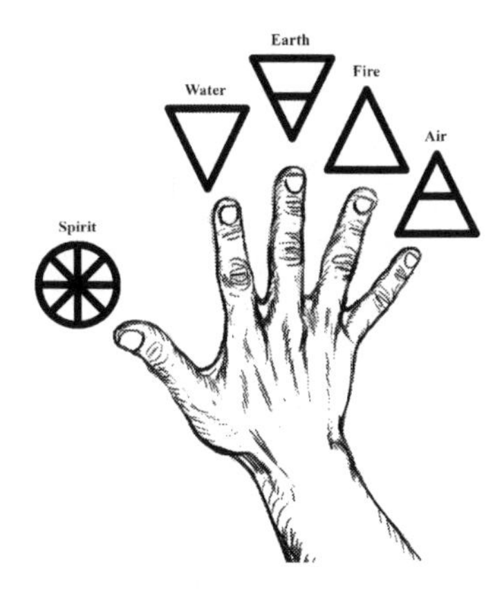


*Illustration 45: Elements on Hand*

The **Element of Water** is cool and moist. Charge your patient with the element of water in a pale bluish color. Water is most effective for treating burns, rashes, bites, blood, eyes and the digestive system, which includes the stomach, large intestines, the small intestine, and kidneys. It can be used for treating fevers. Due to the fact that our bodies are primarily made up of water, using water is an effective form of Ruach Healing. Get into the habit of having a charged pitcher of fresh water for your healing recipients to drink. This charged water literally becomes part of their body. Your index finger is used to send the element of water.

The **Element of Fire** is warm and dry. Charge your recipient with the color red, very pale red light, for red is an extremely powerful energy. It should never be used on certain areas of the body directly; even if you're using the lightest tint of red you're capable of projecting. In particular, the eyes, as well as, any areas that have a mucus membrane are too sensitive to be charged with fire. Fire does speed up the healing process. It is effective in helping to disinfect and aids in the closing of a wound. It aids in the coagulation process of blood as well. Fire is also effective in treating liver disorders, and can also work in the alchemical laboratory called the digestive system. Troubles with digestion, oftentimes can be a fire issue or a water issue. Muscle testing is very helpful in figuring out which element the physical ailment stems from. Fire can also be used to increase will and the desire to fight for life. It can also be used for the treatment of impotence. The finger to use for fire is the fourth finger.

The **Element of Earth** is cool and dry. Charge your recipients with a combination of soft tints of russet, olive, citrine, and/or deep earth tone colors. Use Earth energy colors for the bones of the body, ovaries, uterus, and womb. Earth is also effective for the treatment of shingles and brings about stability. The middle finger is the finger of Earth.

Earth is a very special element because it is not a primary element. Therefore, Earth can be used anytime you want to use one of the three primary elements (air, water, or fire) but believe that the primary element might be too intense for your healing recipient alone. An example of this, let's say a patient has a high fever and a viral infection. Fire can be effective in attacking the virus, but the projection of fire may be too intense for patient's fever. Too much Fire may send his/her fever into the danger zone. Therefore, you would opt to use the element of Earth.

You will notice that all the elements are charged into the aura with a pale color. Let's use the color of Earth, as an example to discuss this reasoning a little bit more. Our experience has shown one would be advised to work with colors that are very light tints of white, such as pale forest green or russet. Even though it is earth, be sure to keep the colors on the pale side by mentally mixing them with white. Many healers use a dark forest green color for Earth. While this is often traditional, it is generally not advisable. Dark colors, in any hue have the power to be destructive. Dark forest green light and some other deeper hues of light can be used safely if the light projected is kept both rigorously contained and willfully directed toward removing illness, which may be too tenacious to eliminate with a lighter tint. Think of this, when you add white to the color you are ensuring that the elemental color is fully and completely infused with the light of Kether. There are those that are able to clairvoyantly see, or otherwise psychically perceive, that the color or colors being projecting are too dark. Some decide to dilute the colors as they are projecting them because they are concerned the subjective internal image of the color might be too dark. The key for projecting colors is to be fully connected to Divine source and the needs of the patient. When in doubt, keep the color light with Divine White Brilliance.

**Table 9: Characteristics of the Elements**

| ELEMENT | CONDITION | SYMBOL | FINGER |
|---|---|---|---|
| Air | Warm & Moist | 🜁 | Pinky |
| Water | Cool & Moist | 🜄 | Index |
| Fire | Warm & Dry | 🜂 | Ring |
| Earth | Cool & Dry | 🜃 | Middle |

# NOTES:

# CHAPTER EIGHTEEN: Planetary Healing

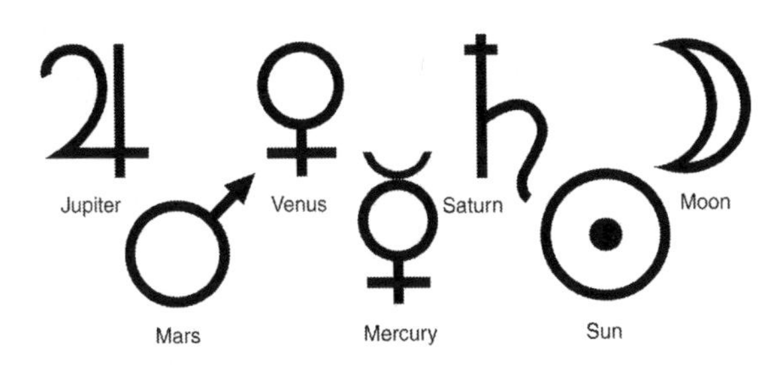


The Ruach Healing Method provides a number of lenses in which to charge the energy field. Certainly, one the most powerful lenses is planetary healing, using the seven ancient planets. In the Golden Dawn, great steps are taken to find out the proper hour of a planet and the best time to invoke that planet for magical purposes. The magical practitioner is also concerned with which day of the week each planet is best invoked. Also, certain times of the month are better than others. For example, when the moon is waxing, or getting bigger, this is an indication that it is a good time for invoking a planetary force and drawing its energy toward you. However, when the moon is waning, or getting smaller, this is the most appropriate time for removing things or keeping unwanted energies away from you. The moon acts as an indicator.

Ancient astrologers and magical practitioners were very simplistic and precise with how they invoked a planet. They simply looked up into the sky and observed the planet in the night sky then projected where it would be in the day sky. The simple rule of thumb was if the planet is above the horizon you can invoke it, but if it is below the horizon being out of sight, the planet cannot be invoked.

In the Ruach Healing Method, planet invocation is kept simple and effective for healing purposes. Ruach Healers are not invoking planets in a ceremonial fashion, rather the healer is awakening the power of the planet that lives within themselves. Remember, everyone is co-creator with the Divine Source. You are a microcosm of the Infinite; therefore, the planets exist within you, as well as, outside you. If you want to learn how to ceremonially invoke a planet there are a number of books in our bibliography that can help you. If you are interested in learning how the Esoteric Golden Dawn invokes the planets and their energies, you can visit: www.esotericgoldendawn.com.

As a magical healer, your focus is on learning the planetary natures as they relate to healing, the colors of the planets, along with an easy to remember hierarchy that awakens the planetary angel. Planetary healing, in the Ruach Healing Method, works through the use of the unique and specific energies of each planet. The planetary energies are extremely powerful, giving the healer a finer focus than the Sephirot or the elements.

Here are a few effective basic guidelines when using planetary energy for healing. First, as covered above, specifically, you need to remember the phases of the moon may have some small influence on planetary healing, but it is not a predominate factor. If moon phases were a predominate factor in the planetary healing process, you could only draw positive energy from a planet during a waxing moon. Then, there would be a two week waiting period to remove negative energy using planetary energy. You can see, that for healing purposes this is ridiculous. The planets are literally a part of the heavenly body in the macrocosmic universe, *and* THEY ARE A PART OF THE MICROCOSMIC UNIVERSE OF THE HEALER. This means that the planets are under the direction of the healer to use. To put it simply, the Ruach healer chooses to govern the planets, rather than succumbing to the belief that the planets govern the healer.

The second guideline is that planetary hours, days, times, etc. play no part in your work; as you the healer are not pulling on the macrocosm, but only invoking the microcosmic reflection governed by your the intention. As stated earlier, planetary times and positions are important to the astrologers and ceremonial magician but have no importance to the Ruach Healer. The reason for this is obvious, when performing healing work on a patient it is ALWAYS NOW. It is not Monday, Tuesday, or Wednesday; it is NOW. The Ruach Healer works in a type of subspace where he or she is aware of the day and time but it has no relevance. The planets that have such powerful influence over our lives, both in a positive and a negative way, that they are always available in the energy field of the Ruach Healer.

The third guideline is that the Ruach Healer invokes the planetary forces by calling on the hierarchy. In many traditions, magicians go through great lengths to recite a hierarchy. The easiest way to invoke the presence and power of the planetary angel is to vibrate the name of the hierarchy given for each planet. Remember, the hierarchy is based on the Four Worlds. If the idea of invoking a hierarchy is new to you, the easiest thing to do is to write them down on a 3x5 card. In this way, you are creating flash cards that can be used until you have the hierarchy memorized.

During the healing process, you can vibrate the hierarchy to yourself or out loud. However, be aware of how comfortable your patient is with vibrating hierarchy names out loud. Vibrating the names should not cause your patient to come out of a relaxed state. Personally, I vibrate the hierarchy silently, unless I know that my patient does not mind it. Some patients like to hear the sound of the angels being invoked, while others get a little uncomfortable. Simply calling on the Divine Name and the angel associated with the planetary energy you are invoking, along with the proper planetary color, is more than sufficient to awaken the planetary power within the energy field of the healer.

We are often amazed at magical types of people who believe that the angels have no ability or power to make a field decision. We believe that they do. The most important thing to keep in mind, as a healer, is to stay in a deep magical state of consciousness. Do not allow the invoking of the angel and the hierarchy to throw you off. Personally, We prefer you focus first on the color, the name of the planet, the Divine name associated with the planet on the Tree of Life and the angel, in that order.

## The Hierarchical Order

Using the hierarchical order simply begins with your name for the highest power that you believe exists within the universe. Personally, I call this highest power "L.O.U.", which stands for Lord of the Universe. You might call this highest power God, Jesus, Allah, Divine Source, Christ Consciousness, Primordial One, Ultimate Source, The Great Unknowable One, *etc*. It is less about the specific name and more about the relationship and energetic connection you have to the name you use. Whatever name you vibrate will be used to invoke the Universe's highest power, sending forth the Archangel of the Sephira.

Invoking planetary energy starts with calling on the highest power of the universe. After having called on the highest power, call upon the Divine Name of the Sephira that the planet is associated with. Next, vibrate or call on the Archangel of the Sephira, followed by calling the Choir of Angels. Finally, invoke the name of the planet and the angel that governs that planet. Remember, even though each planet is associated with a Sephira, the planet has its own governing angel, that may or may not be the same name as the angel of the Sephira.

### Exercise: Invoking Planetary Energy

**Here is a simple outline. We do not want to make this more complex than it needs to be. It is simple. Vibrate, elongating the pronunciation of all names as they are called upon.**

#### Step 1

Invoke the Highest Power

*"In the name of __________ I awaken the Sephira of __________."*

Insert your name for highest power then the name of the Sephira.

**Step 2**

Invoke the hierarchy of the Sephira. See the first chart below.

*"In the Sephira of__________, I invoke the Divine Name __________to be present for this healing operation . With the Divine present, I call to be joined by the Archangel __________ accompanied by the Choir of Angels, __________.*

Insert the name of the Sephira, Divine Name of the Sephira, the Archangel of the Sephira, and the Choir of Angels of the Sephira.

**Step 3**

Invoke the planet and angel of the planet.

*"Under the hierarchy of the Sephira I just united with, I invoke the planet __________ accompanied by the healing Angel__________. May the power of this planetary energy together with this hierarchy manifest wholeness, light and healing. Not unto my name but unto Thy name."*

Insert the name of the planet associated with the Sephira you invoked and then the Angel of that planet.

**Step 4**

Feel the energy of all you invoked. Focus your attention on the Angel and color of the planet. With this Angelic and color connection strong, begin charging and healing your patient with planetary energy.

Here is an example of invocation you have just done. This example invokes the planet Venus. The focus color is pale green.

*"In the name of the Lord of the Universe. I awaken the Sephira of Netzach. In the Sephira of Netzach, I invoke the Divine Name YHVH Tzaboath to be present for this healing operation. With the Divine present, I call to be joined by the Archangel Hanniel accompanied by the Choir of Angels, Elohim. Under the hierarchy of the Sephira I just united with, I invoke the planet Venus accompanied by the healing Angel Anael. May the power of this planetary energy together with this hierarchy manifest wholeness, light and healing. Not unto my name but unto Thy name."*

This chart below shows the hierarchy of the Sephirot on the Tree of Life. Only the Sephira associated with each planet are listed (7 out of 10). The next chart shows the angel and color of each planet.

**Table 10: Hierarchy of the Planetary Sephirot on the Tree of Life**

| Sephira | DIVINE NAME | ARCH-ANGEL | CHOIR OF ANGELS | ASSO-CIATED PLANET |
|---|---|---|---|---|
| Binah | YHVH Elohim | Tzaphqiel | Aralim | Saturn |
| Chesed | El | Tzadqiel | Chashmalim | Jupiter |
| Geburah | Elohim Gabor | Kamael | Seraphim | Mars |
| Tiphareth | YHVH Eloah Ve Da'ath | Raphael | Melekim | Sun |
| Netzach | YHVH Tzaboath | Hanniel | Elohim | Venus |
| Hod | Elohim Tzabaoth | Michael | Beni Elohim | Mercury |
| Yesod | Shaddai el-Chai | Gabriel | Kerubim | Moon |

This chart shows the angel and color of each planet. Remember, the angel of the planet can be the same, or different, from the angels of the Sephira the planet is associated with.

**Table 11: Angel and Color of the Planets**

| PLANET | Sephira | ANGEL | COLOR |
|---|---|---|---|
| Saturn | Binah | Cassiel | Indigo |
| Jupiter | Chesed | Sachiel | Violet |
| Mars | Geburah | Zamael | Red |
| Sun | Tiphareth | Raphael | Orange |
| Venus | Netzach | Anael | Pale Green |
| Mercury | Hod | Michael | Yellow |
| Moon | Yesod | Gabriel | Pale Blue |

*For correct pronunciations, check out free resource at www.ruach healing.com.

## Invoking Only the Angels of the Planets

The method for awakening planetary energy does, at a minimum, require you to know the planetary angels. It is recommended that you memorize each planetary angel. In memorizing the chart above, you will have the background resource to spontaneously pull planetary information to the forefront of your mind during a healing session. If you struggle to memorize information, I suggest putting the planets on a 3x5 card and keeping them with your healing sprays. This way, the names of the planetary angels are always easy to find when you are doing healing work. Simply pull out the 3x5 card for use as a reference.

While it is recommended to invoke the hierarchy of the Sephira before invoking the planet connected to the Sephira, the planet can be invoked with just the angel of the planet and its color. This is done by focusing on the color of the planet, while vibrating quietly the name of the angel of the planet. A rudimentary planetary energy invocation might go something like this:

***"Great angel of the planet _______ I invoke thee to aid me with the manifestation of your planetary energy for the benefit and healing of _______."***

It is a pretty straightforward invocation that can be rewritten anyway you want. Be sure your invocation gives you the feeling that you truly are connected to the angel and the planetary energy you are invoking. As a safe guard, we generally do the full invocation to begin with and then throughout the healing process we simple continue by calling on the angel and using the planetary color.

## Colors and Qualities of the Planets

Charging with planetary energy through the specific planetary color is quite exhilarating, especially after you have called upon the angelic hierarchy of the Sephira. Remember, while the planet may be associated with the Sephira, it is NOT the Sephira; therefore, the color will be slightly different. Both the color of the Sephira and the color of the planet are used in a harmonious dance throughout the healing process. Let's say while scanning, you find a specif area on your patient you feel benefits from both the color of a Sephira and the color of a planet. When you come to the phase of charging the area, start first by sending the color of the Sephira out your hands/fingertips. Fill the area with the color of the Sephira, slowly allowing the color being sent to morph into the color of the planet. In this approach, the planetary energy is a way to extend the energy of the Sephira from the Tree of Life.

Each planet is known for a predominate quality. These qualities can be seen in a patient in a negative or positive way. If the planetary quality is overwhelming the patient in a negative way, the opposite planetary energy can be used to bring the patient into equilibrium. If a patient has too much of the negative quality of a planet this should become obvious to the Ruach Healer through fact-finding, scanning, and mostly applied Kinesiology (muscle testing). To muscle test a planet, simply project the color of the planet onto the patient. If they go weak through muscle testing, two things are possible. First, they are already having an excess amount of this planetary energy affecting them. Secondly, it can be read as a sign that using this planetary energy would not be beneficial to the patient. At this juncture, you are going to want to do additional muscle testing to determine specifically what it is going to be effective. Details of using the planetary qualities follow in the chart below.

**Table 12: Energetic Qualities of the Planets**

| PLANET | COLOR | QUALITY | OPPOSITE ENERGY |
|---|---|---|---|
| Saturn | Indigo | Codifying Energy | Sun |
| Jupiter | Violet | Memory | Mars |
| Mars | Red | Anger | Jupiter |
| Sun | Orange | Vanity | Saturn |
| Venus | Pale Green | Pleasure | Mercury |
| Mercury | Yellow | Imagination | Venus |
| Moon | Pale Blue | Cycles & Wandering thoughts | None-it is harmonious |

**Saturn**

Saturn's color is indigo. Saturn is a codifying energy. Its dark colors tend to slow things down a bit. It is ideal for building and protecting. Saturn helps teeth, bones and anything that is a part of the construction system of the body. Saturn is the opposite of the Sun.

♃

## Jupiter

Jupiter's color is violet. Jupiter relates to memory. This is not simply human memory; this is ancient memory. Ancient memory is the remembrance of life in a perfected state. It is the belief, that on some level, all life remembers how to be balanced and well. This is the ancient memory, within the healer and within the patient, saying, “I know how to be healed”. The knowledge may not be known consciously, but on some level it is known. Jupiter's energy is the opposite of Mars' energy.

## Mars

Mars' color is red. Mars controls anger. Anger manifests itself as a whole host of issues in the energy field and the physical body. During fact-finding, ask questions to see if the patient has emotional problems that cannot be let go, a heart condition, and/or high blood pleasure. All these could be problems indicating too much Mars' energy. On the other hand, if the energy field of the patient is tired, weak and rundown, the red Mars energy could be the most helpful. Mars is the opposite of Jupiter.

**Sun**

Sun's color is orange. Sun governs vanity. Unbalanced solar energy within the personality can lead to a greatly inflated ego. However, lack of solar energy provides a myriad of diseases. The sun truly is the dispenser of light and life into the world. Be careful and aware that anything, growing too fast and too rapidly in the body, such as cancer, can be fed by solar energy. Therefore, it is not advised to use this energy for cancer and tumors. One area solar energy affects almost instantly, is the area of depression. I always advise Ruach Healers and their patients to get fresh air and sunshine. Sometimes it may not be possible so spiritual sunshine is the next best thing. Anything the physical Sun does to help the physical body, the spiritual Sun does to help the astral body. Sun is the opposite of Saturn.

**Venus**

Venus' color is pale green. The primary quality of Venus is pleasure. Initially, you may not know how to take that word and translate it into the healing protocol. What does pleasure have to do with any of this? The state of pleasure is an integrated balance between higher spiritual energy, the ego, and the lower animal self. When these elements are unbalanced in a patient, inner conflict is present and ultimately a lack of pleasure. When every part of the spiritual system of the body is working in harmony and in cooperation with other parts the body, it is said to be in a state of pleasure. The pale green of Venus is used for cleansing infections, and external diseases, that immediately attack the pleasure system of the body. Venus is the opposite of Mercury.

**Mercury**

Mercury's color is yellow. Mercury is particularly powerful in the area of imagination. Mercury is used to awaken the functionality of the nervous system and the brain. You are at your optimum level as a human being when your nervous system, especially your spinal cord and your brain, are functioning to their potential. Quite often, charging the spinal cord with Mercury is amazingly beneficial to the patient. One patient, struggling with college exams, reported he passed his exams after a complete spinal charge of Mercury. Mercury is the opposite of Venus.

**Moon**

Moon's color is pale blue. Moon governs cycles and wandering thoughts. As human beings, life is cyclical. Life is always going through the cycles; the cycles of the year, the cycles of the month, the cycles of the week, and cycles of the day. Humans live within cycles, as they are a part of our being. The life cycle is easily seen in the female body. This makes the pale blue of Moon perfect to heal on any part of the female reproductive system.

In addition, Moon energy can be used to focus patients. This focus allows patients to reach higher goals in their daily life. Human beings are goal oriented. We need goals, no matter how small or how large. It is the challenges of life that keep us moving forward. When a patient's energy field is fluctuating, with an overt amount of wandering thoughts, the invocation of the pale blue Moon can be very effective. Moon works in harmony with all other planets, so there is no opposite energy. Sun is not an opposite energy because Moon is just a different aspect of Sun.

### Final thoughts on Planets

Planets vibrate at extremely high levels of energy, therefore, it is critical that you project only light shades of color, while using planetary energy. When in doubt, lighten it up, keeping the vibration high and healing. There is no time that is inappropriate, or bad, to use planetary energy for healing. Remember, you may choose to use a planetary energy for cleaning the aura, but it is mainly used to charge the aura.

# CHAPTER NINETEEN: Long Distance Healing

Long Distance Healing (L.D.H.) may be one of the most exciting aspects of the Ruach Healing Method. Today, technology gives us more mobility. As people move and travel constantly, families are not confined to the same city of their birth anymore. Mastering the technique of invoking healing light into someone who is a thousand miles away is a powerful skill.

We have been blessed with friends all over the world, so we do a lot of long distant healing. Over the years, we have successfully performed several long distance healing operations with almost identical results as in-person healing. This brings us to explore the whole notion of the space/time continuum.

Many healers and mystics believe the higher up on the Tree Of Life you go, the thinner the space/time continuum is. The highest point on the Tree of Life is Divine Source. Connecting with Divine Source is essential for all healing work, but it is even more important for long distance healing work. This point cannot be emphasized enough. Connecting to Higher Source, literally, removes the distance between you and the patient receiving the healing. The exercise below will greatly help you get centered and perform effective long distance healing. It works very well, for a prelude to your long distance healing work, as it puts you in direct connection with Divine Source.

## Ascending to the Higher

Ascending to the Higher is a simple method for connecting to Divine Source. This exercise is partly based on an ancient magical tradition, along with some Rosicrucian techniques. The old techniques of this exercise have been re-created/re-adapted to make it practical for Ruach Healers. Ascending to the Higher helps you, the Ruach Healer, by developing a genuine powerful connection to Divine Source. This exercise can be used prior to all of your healing work, especially long distance healing. It is another tool for your Ruach Healing toolbox.

In the exercise of Ascending to the Higher, you will be ascending up the Sephirot on the Tree of Life from the lower to the higher. You will be using the pathway of the Middle Pillar on the Tree of Life. To help you understand clearly you will be energetically shooting upward from Malkuth to Kether. You will be using the colors and divine names of Yesod, Tiphareth, and Kether to raise you up, and aid you in making a genuine connection to Divine Source. You will also empower your Long Distance Healing abilities.

### Exercise: Ascending to the Higher

#### Step 1

Breathe, relax, clear and focus your mind on your physical presence in the energy of Malkuth. Strengthen this connection by vibrating the Divine Name **Adonai ha-Aretz.** Remember, you are a physical being with a spiritual core. Now switch your focus to the spiritual core. Visualize the

Divine White Brilliance, or Infinite Light above, as you remain present in Malkuth.

**Step 2**

Breathe and relax, keeping the D.W.B. in your focus, allowing your consciousness to rise to Yesod. Begin to feel yourself surrounded by the purple glowing light of Yesod. Begin vibrating the Divine Name **Shaddai El Chai**. Continue vibrating the divine name until your entire being is surrounded by the purple light and the energy of Yesod.

**Step 3**

Again, breathe and relax, bringing your focus to the D.W.B. above, as you allow your consciousness to rise to Tiphareth. Begin to feel yourself surrounded by the yellow glowing light of Tiphareth. Begin vibrating the Divine Name **YHVH Eloah Ve Da'ath**. Continue vibrating the divine name until your entire being is surrounded by the yellow light and energy of Tiphareth.

**Step 4**

Breathe and relax, bringing your focus to the D.W.B. above, as you allow your consciousness to rise to Kether. Begin to feel yourself surrounded by the white glowing light of Kether. Begin vibrating the Divine Name **Eheieh**. Continue vibrating the divine name until your entire being is surrounded by the white light and energy of Kether.

**Step 5**

Breathe and relax, allowing the white light of Kether to merge with the Divine White Brilliance above you. See the light grow bright and brilliant. Let this light flow through you. Feel this light filling every muscle, bone, and organ in your body. Feel the cells of your body being filled with D.W.B. Notice that you are much bigger and taller now in your astral mind. Your consciousness now fills up the entire galaxy and expands to fill the entire universe. Recite these words, ***"The Divine Spirit is in me and I am in the Divine Spirit. I am co-creator of my reality."*** Now, give thanks to the Lord of The Universe, Divine Source, God or Goddess, etc., in your own personal way, with your own prayer.

**Step 6**

Finally, invoke your Holy Guardian angel in your own personal way, with your own prayer. When you feel ready, open your eyes and continue your healing work, with a new deeper sense of connection to Divine Source.

## Long Distance Scanning

Long distance scanning commences with creating space to connect remotely to the patient. In the exercise above, you created a strong connection to Divine Source. Now, you must create a connection to the patient that is just as strong. Once the connection has been made, the healing process flows effortlessly. You bypass the space-time continuum, providing Ruach Healing as if the patient is present in the room with you.

Begin by turning the lights off. Light a few candles, so the you are healing by natural light, rather than electric light. As with an in-person healing, perform the Lesser Banishing Ritual of the Pentagram, or your preferred method of self-protection. Next, light up your sphere of sensation, using the Middle Pillar exercise. Third, begin to activate your hands and fingers, as if the patient you are healing was in the room with you. These are all the same basic steps as in-person healing.

This next step is specific to the long distance healing, and is essential for making a remote connection to the patient. Each of us has a Divine presence within us; some call it the Spark of Light, others call it the Higher Genius, and many call it the Holy Guardian Angel. Close your eyes, and with a quiet reverence, invoke the presence of the Holy Guardian Angel of the patient whom you are sending healing. In your own words, call upon their Holy Guardian Angel to aid, guide, and direct you in your healing. Here is an example of a simple invocation you might want to use.

### Patient's Holy Guardian Angel Invocation

*Oh Lord of the Universe, I adore Thee and I invoke Thee,*
*Aid me and guide me*
*in this long distant healing work I am about to perform.*
*I call upon the Holy Guardian Angel of _______,*
*to guide my thoughts and my hands*
*as I bring the healing light to _______.*
*Not unto my name, but unto Thy name be the power and glory forever.*
*Amen.*

Visualize the patient in front of you, as if they were present. The clearer and stronger you see the patient in your mind's eye, the easier the patient will absorb the powerful current of healing energy being sent. Remember, their Holy Guardian Angel is present, assisting you. Now, with your eyes closed, begin to scan the patient. It's best to do this work in a quiet place alone, as you don't want to be interrupted during the healing.

As you are scanning, allow yourself to relax, breathe deeply, in through the nose, out through the mouth. Steady breathing helps the Ruach Healer go into a trace-like state, where the long distance connection to the patient is easily maintained. The beautiful nature of long distance healing allows you, the Ruach Healer, to take all the time you want or need to scan. You are not limited by the patient's schedule. You can remain in a hypnotic trance-like state and allow the condition of the patient to be revealed to you. The Ruach Healer seems to know things about patient that could only be shared by the patient's Holy Guardian Angel. Sure, through scanning the healer feels the patient's aura with their hands, but there is also a deeper gnostic-kind of inner certainty of the patient's condition. This is truly working in the Spirit vision. When the healer is working at this level of consciousness, they are operating beyond time and space.

Continue your scan of the healing recipient, throughout their entire energy field, as if they were present. You may find yourself communing with a Holy Guardian Angel. At this level of consciousness, you find that you switch between communing with your Holy Guardian Angel and the patient's angel. The activation and invocation of the patient's Holy Guardian Angel creates a conduit, whereby, their Holy Guardian Angel is communicating with you as the healer through your own personal higher self. Long distance scanning may sound complex, but be assured, it is easier to perform than to describe. After a general scanning of the patient is complete, proceed to scan the gates.

In scanning the gates, the primary difference between long distance scanning and scanning in-person is a kind of gnosis. When you scan someone in person, you have a very tactile feeling in your hands. When you are long-distance scanning, the hands astrally point out the direction, but the feeling is sometimes less intense in the hands, revealing its sensation more in the mind. Find any healer that has done a significant amount of long distance scanning, and you will find a healer that is a thousand percent better at scanning someone in person. There is a certain skill set that develops with long distance scanning. The Neshamah, or intuition, of the healer is strengthened. Intuition is a priceless skill of any Ruach Healer.

## Long Distance Cleaning

Long distance cleaning of the aura is best accomplished with use of a **Ruach Ball of Light**. This healing light is created by the healer and projected to the patient being healed. For general healing purposes, a white ball of light is used, or if the healer feels guided, one of the colors of the Sephirot from the Tree of Life may be use for cleaning. The white light, of course, relates to D.W.B. or Kether on the Tree Of Life. Once made, the Ruach Ball of Light is projected onto the recipient. The ball is then astrally combed through the patient's entire aura, while cleaning ensues. As you are cleaning with the Ruach Ball of Light, focus on the areas that appeared to have congestion during the scanning examination.

Just as if the patient was in front of you, pause for a moment and rescan if necessary.

When doing in-person healing, you create a Ruach Ball of Light, and follow this order of healing: scan the aura, cleanse the aura, and charge the aura. In L.D.H., the Ruach Ball of Light is used to clean the aura. The light ball delivers love and healing energy to the patient as cleansing takes place.

### Making a Ruach Ball of Light

Mastering the technique of how to make the Ruach Ball of Light, or in Eastern tradition they call it a Chi ball, is absolutely essential for long distance healing. Begin by breathing Divine White Brilliance into about a six inch sphere, between your hands. This is most effectively accomplished by first invoking the D.W.B. to light up above your head, vibrating the appropriate divine names of EHEIEH (pronounced *Eh-Heh-Yeh*) and the Archangel Metatron (pronounced *Met-a-tron*). Create the Ruach Ball of Light by breathing the light down into your body,

*Illustration 46: Forming a Ruach Ball of Light*

circulating that light out of your breath and into the sphere for two to ten minutes. As this sphere of light gets heavier and thicker, begin separating your hands, thus allowing the ball to get bigger, until it is about the size of a basketball. Move your hands around the ball from side to side, from top to bottom, feeling the dimensions of the ball of light.

Next, while holding the Ruach Ball of Light, stretch your arms out horizontally in front of you, simultaneously stepping forward with your left foot. As you hold the ball of light at arm's length, slightly tip your head between your arms. (Golden Dawn trained practitioners will know this as the Sign of the Enterer.) Now, project the ball outward from your hands, visualizing the patient in need of the healing. The process of projecting is like turning on a laser pointer, as a beam of energy is sent to a designated location.

*Illustration 47: Releasing the Ruach Ball of Light*

Visualize, as you see clearly in your mind's eye, the Ruach Ball of Light reaching the patient. As the Ruach Ball of Light reaches the patient, see it being absorbed by the patient. Allow the ball to release from your hands, being completely absorbed by the patient, thus accomplishing its healing goal. Seal the Ruach Ball of Light, now

*Illustration 48: Sealing the Ruach Ball of Light*

absorbed by the patient, by stepping back with your left foot, so you are standing straight up. Raise your left hand to your lips. Curl your index finger and place it on your lips. Pause, in a moment of gratitude. Note: Sealing is different than just putting your finger to your lips as if saying "Shhhh"; be sure to curl your finger. (Golden Dawn trained practitioners will know this as the Sign of the Silence.)

As you become proficient with Long Distance Healing, you will come to a point of understanding how to put variation in the ball of light you are creating. Projecting the Ruach Ball of Light can be tinctured with an element, planet, color, or other healing factor.

### Using Elemental Balls in Long Distance Healing

🜁

**Element of Air**

Air can be sent in a pale yellow ball of light. Air is ideal energy to help someone for any type of bronchial, lung, or breathing problem. Air is also a powerful energy to use for thinking difficulties, and difficulties concerning the nervous system. Vibrate the Divine Name **"YHVH"** and the Archangel **"Raphael"**.

▽

## Element of Water

Water is sent in a pale blue ball of light. Water is ideal for dehydration, lowering fever, cleansing the stomach, intestines, and bowels, childbirth and labor. Vibrate the Divine Name **"El"** and the Archangel **"Gabriel"**.

△

## Element of Fire

Fire is sent in a pale red ball of light. Fire is ideal energy for the heart, circulation, liver, immune system, and will to live. Vibrate the Divine Name **"Elohim"** and the Archangel **"Michael"**

🜃

## Element of Earth

Earth can be sent in a dark green, or russet, ball of light. Earth is ideal energy for removal of migraines, healing head injuries, lowering blood pressure, relaxation, calming the nervous system, and helping the patient feel a sense of peace and stability. Vibrate the Divine Name **"Adonai"** and the Archangel **"Auriel"**.

## Using A Photograph For Long Distance Healing

All of the methods mentioned above, regarding the Ruach Ball of Light, can be used with a photograph. It might be old fashioned, but for healing purposes, having a real printed photograph, preferably in a frame and not on a computer screen is ideal. When working on a patient long distance, setting up their picture in your healing space at home helps strengthen the connection to them. It is nice to place a couple of candles on each side of the picture. Use the appropriate color candle for the element, planet, Sephira, or specific healing energy being invoked. Charge the candles and the photograph with Ruach.

The photograph acts as a conduit, or vigil type of a signal, for the patient receiving the healing. The candles act, as they burn alongside the photograph, operating as a type of a battery, constantly recharging the individual as long as they burn. Have a charged picture and candles are a powerful continuation of the healing the Ruach Healer has put into the patient. This is also helpful for Ruach Healers that struggle with visualization.

In conclusion, as a new Ruach Healer, you are urged to begin working with long distance healing. Now, there are controversial aspects of long distance healing, but let your conscience be your guide. Some healers believe it is perfectly acceptable to provide long distance healing, even if the recipient they are performing the healing on is unaware of the healing work being done. Other healers believe this is a violation of the recipient's sovereignty. They believe you must clearly have the patient's permission before sending off any healing energy. Personally, the first position is more practical. Let's say my brother, or sister, is in need of healing, and let's also say it is impossible to contact him or her. Or, perhaps there is a worst case scenario, and they are unconscious in a hospital. Our choices become severely limited if we must receive their permission before sending healing.

There are always ways to find willing patients, for you to develop your healing skills. The newspapers, or online modalities, are filled with people that need healing, as are hospitals. One only has to venture to almost any church in America or Europe, and will discover a list of people that are in need of prayer. Pick someone, and begin developing your Ruach Healing skills.

# NOTES:

# CHAPTER TWENTY: Most Common Illnesses And How To Heal Them

Trends in healing, health, and science are constantly morphing and changing. Scientific studies are just starting to observe how energy affects healing. There have been many finding that are incredible. Healing with energy can really change the body on a scientific level. So, what does cause disease?

There are mountains of books and scientific data purporting to know what causes disease. The most potent antagonist to a healthy body is stress. Research concludes that stress alone is not the cause of disease, but a *constant stream* of stress is the cause of disease. Stress is often caused by negative thoughts and an imbalance in our energy field. This imbalance often shows up as inflammation. Think of the war victims of Okinawa, during WWII. Certainly, they went through outrageous amounts of stress, as they experienced loss of family and home. Yet, many of those who survived WWII lived long and healthy lives. Many lived into their 90's. Stress alone is not the killer. It is the imbalance in the energy field that is the main cause for disease.

When looking for what causes disease, there must also be consideration that our eating habits have greatly changed, due to the toxicity levels of different chemicals in our foods. Diet is also a powerful factor on the causes of disease. Diets too rich in fat and sugar weaken the life force of the body. Experiments completed with scientific muscle testing have proven the body goes weak when exposed to sugar. The disease and illness in the world is also attributed to the ways in which we live our lives. The issues regarding the Earth's environment are main factors causing disease. Recent scientific studies conclude that different parts of the world have different primary diseases.

An environment full of toxins and negative beliefs certainly play a major role on health and vitality. My own father died of Mesothelioma Cancer because of toxins he was exposed to at 16. He got sick and died at 74. Diet, stress and environment all factor into creating health and wellness, or sickness and disease. However, there is one factor that is more devastating than all these combined. **That factor is a serious unbalance of energy, within all or sections of the energy field of the body.**

When illness or chronic disease exists, a combination of healing methods is always recommended. Ruach Healing, along with some sort of physician's medical advice, such as an M.D., chiropractor, or acupuncturist, is the most effective approach. The reason for being in multiple therapies is because every energetic disorder likely has a physical counterpart. The physical counterpart may need regular, or immediate, attention regardless of the energy work. No matter what form of healing work you practice, an energy healer never intends to make a physical diagnosis or replace a physician.

Thoughts have a powerful effect on the condition of the body. The power of the mind deeply influences the condition of the body and vice versa. Positive thoughts of happiness, love, joy and excitement deeply affect the entire energy field, or aura, of the body. Likewise, so can depression, fear, tension, and anxiety. Both sets of thoughts and emotions affect the entire energy field of the body. Thoughts and emotions either raise the body in a spiritual vibration or cause vibrations in the body to become lower with less vitality, thus out of balance.

The following sentence may be tough to accept, but from an energetic perspective it makes perfect sense. Disease and sickness reflect your spiritual state. Our thoughts, desires and actions combine to affect the microcosmic world in which we live. This includes our physical life style, our soul and our body. To put this in an easy to understand manner, let me reiterate; "We are a reflection of our own inner spirit." This "inner spirit" can be seen in the five points of the pentagram as pictured in the Signet Star. The aspects of Spirit, Water, Fire, Earth, and Air must be in balance. When the body and animal-self work in harmony with the ego, and most importantly with our spiritual nature or Neshamah, your own personal temple of vitality and health is created. Does your personal Signet Star have points that are all equal and symmetrical or does your Signet Star have some points that are bigger/smaller than the rest, being a star of asymmetry? Humans are spiritual beings and the lack of attention to our spiritual needs causes disharmony and imbalance.

The Ruach Healing Method is an effective tool, for the restoration and return to natural balance of the body, mind and soul. Sickness, disease, and suffering begin as disruptions of harmonious flows of energy. Eventually, this lack of harmony results in physical ailments, pains and illnesses. Ruach Healing brings balanced communion between all forces that are at war within the human personality and energy field.

Your mission, as a Ruach Healer, is to restore normalcy and balance to the energy field so that disease is no longer manifested within the body. The key is to restore Ruach within a patient's sphere of sensation. Anyone and everyone can benefit from Ruach Healing. Just as the medical field suggests daily vitamins and chiropractors suggest regular spinal adjustments, it is beneficial for everyone to receive regular treatments from a qualified & certified Ruach Healer.

The application of Ruach Healing to the body, more than often, affects the mind as well. Depression and anxiety-filled thoughts weaken the energy field of the body and cause the Vitality Rays to droop, or become tangled. After a period of time, the whole thing becomes like the "Chicken and the Egg." It becomes impossible to determine what came first, the mental imbalance or the physical. At this point, it doesn't matter. Dedicated healing work, by the Ruach Healer, restores balance to the energy field, along with balance to the thoughts.

One of the secrets to the Ruach Healing Method is the utilization of scanning and muscle testing. There is no "one-size-fits-all" formula for any disease or illness. You need to muscle test, scan thoroughly, and use your intuition to determine what Ruach Healing protocol is going to work best for you and your patient. There have been situations where a series of energies and colors of the Sephirot showed up as ineffective with muscle testing. This led to muscle testing elemental energies, which proved to be extremely effective for the patient.

Here is small example. An associate of mine was experiencing a 105 degree temperature, and becoming delirious. What's more, it occurred suddenly, leading me to believe that it could be a magical attack on her energy field. I knew I had to act quickly, as her temperature was still rising. We were prepared to rush her to the hospital, or call 911, if she didn't respond within a few minutes. As you can imagine, I was extremely concerned with her condition and proceeded to work rapidly. When a patient runs an extreme fever, typically it is physically caused by an infection, but when the cause is energetic it is usually caused by congestion of Ruach in the head and most of the gates. I tested the patient with obvious fever reducers, such as elemental water, the Sephira of Chesed, and the planets Saturn and Jupiter. None of these actions proved effective. I then tested her for Mars. The energy of Mars is a fiery hot warming type of energy that seemed almost counter-intuitive to the magical force she needed. Yet, she squeezed my finger with strength and authority when I muscle tested using Mars. I immediately began to clean her Vitality Gates and invoke the red fiery energy of Mars into her sphere of sensation.

Now, I would not recommend this to anybody. I did break a few rules, but the first rule is always test your subject and that is why this worked! Her fever broke in less than 5 minutes, and by the end of the evening it was down to normal. The reason I am sharing this story with you here is because this chapter is about obvious, formulaic processes that greatly save you time, as a healer, and help you to optimize your healing performance.

Ninety-five percent of the time the formula given for an illness listed will be effective. The point is that these are guidelines, but if following these guidelines proves ineffective, it is suggested you test your subject. Don't be locked into one way of healing. Always trust your intuition, first and foremost, and trust your testing.

NOTE: Remember to use the appropriate Divine Names associated with a specific Sephira, Planetary or Elemental energy. If in doubt, use Divine White Brilliance. Please make sure, before using any Ruach Healing, that the patient who would be a recipient for your healing has been treated by a general physician prior to proceeding forward with your healing practice! Healers are not doctors, thus Ruach Healing is not expressly recommended to cure, diagnose, or treat any illness, from a medical standpoint. Familiarizing yourself with anatomy proves very beneficial as a Ruach Healer, but it is not a replacement for a physician. Without further ado, the list of protocol for disease follows.

**Appendicitis:** First take emergency medical action if necessary. A ruptured appendix can be life threatening. Cleanse the Solar Plexus Gate and the Navel Gate with D.W.B. Continue cleaning the actual appendix area using Divine White Brilliance. Recharge the Solar Plexus Gate and the Navel Gate with their respective colors.

**Arthritis:** Perform a generalized cleaning of the entire energy field, with D.W.B. Then, increase your cleansing in the affected areas; scan thoroughly the Solar Plexus Gate, making certain it is not congested in any way. Also, cleanse the Foundation Gate, or base chakra, and charge with the appropriate color of the gate. Charge the affected area of legs, hands or arms with the pale indigo color of Saturn.

**Asthma:** Clean the lungs with the green energy of Netzach. Also, cleanse the Throat Gate and Heart Center Gate. Alternately, you may charge the lungs with the yellow of Tiphareth. Charge the Throat with the color blue, and charge the Heart with the color green. Make sure not to blend the two colors together, using this protocol.

**Backache or Injured Spine:** Clean with D.W.B. Charge the spine with Binah and the color indigo. Be certain to clean thoroughly and charge the Foundation Gate (base) with its appropriate color, red. Recharge the spine with the yellow color of Mercury. Repeat 2X a day; this could take weeks or longer. In cases of complex injuries involving more than one body part, please remember it is always safe to use D.W.B.

**Broken or Fractured Bones:** Light cuts or scrapes, and broken bones, require light charging. Serious fractures require as much Ruach energy as you can direct. Cleansing should be kept to a minimum. It is best to charge breaks with Binah energy, and/or Saturn energy. The best color to use for this is light indigo. Follow this charging up with yellow, the color of Mercury. Mercury will serve to speed up the process. It is not uncommon for bones to heal 25% faster when energized with this combination.

**Cuts, Burns, and Scrapes:** Treat the condition immediately with appropriate first aid remedy. Then, begin charging the affected area with D.W.B. The affected area, essentially, burns through a lot of Ruach energy very quickly, because there is a cut or rip, not only in the physical body but in the energy field as well. It is suggested to clean the affected area quickly with the green light of Venus (don't *charge*, only *clean* with green), and then spend as much time charging as possible. Our preferred energies for charging a burn is the pale blue of Moon or the pale blue of Water. Generally you cannot overcharge a burn. NOTE: When charging/energizing a burn, do not use the colors red, green, or hues of purple. These are considered “hot” colors and are not beneficial for the patient.

**Cirrhosis of the Liver:** Clean the Navel Gate and the Solar Plexus Gate with D.W.B., cleaning out the entire abdomen area, focusing on the liver area. Use the green of Venus/Netzach. Charge the entire abdomen with the appropriate gate color. Yellow for the Solar Plexus and orange for the Navel Gate. Charge a pitcher of water with D.W.B., put the pitcher into your fridge, encourage the patient to drink the whole pitcher over the course of the day.

**Cancer/Tumors:** These can be a very difficult challenge. Part of the problem is that cancer and tumors try to absorb the Ruach energy for their own growth, making it extremely difficult to charge. Clean the affected areas thoroughly. Repeated cleaning two or three times a week is very important. After cleaning with D.W.B., scan the body and re-clean with the green of Netzach or Venus. Through fact-finding discoveries you should know which planetary colors are likely the most effective. Charge the affected organs or bones with the appropriate planetary energy for the infected part of the body. In stage three or four cancer, it is more effective to charge the color of the Sephira that relates to that area of the body (Please refer to Chapter 5: Understanding the Dynamics of the Tree of Life). Then, follow with the appropriate planetary color. Finally, charge each and every gate with either D.W.B., or its appropriate color. For hard tumors, use and focus energy out of "Thoth's Beak" (please refer to Chapter 14: Charging the Aura), charging with the red of Geburah and planet Mars. The whole idea is to destroy the tumor with a focused ray of Mars' energy.

**Diarrhea and Constipation:** Diarrhea and constipation are two different sides of the same coin. In both cases, you will need to scan the Solar Plexus Gate and the Navel Gate. We like to go down and scan the Foundation Gate, as well. With constipation, you should be looking/feeling for congestion in the gate(s). Whereas, with diarrhea, generally the opposite is true. Depletion is usually the problem. Clean the congested gates thoroughly and charge the abdomen area with Divine White Brilliance (D.W.B.) or the orange light of Hod. Naturally, charge the gates in their specific color. In other words, to remove the condition of diarrhea, the entire abdomen area is charged with the color orange from the Solar Plexus downward, and the gates are charged, if needed, in their specific color.

**Epilepsy:** Clean all the gates of the body, especially the Fountain Gate. Also, clean the back of the head and neck, as well as, the spine, with D.W.B. Charge the entire body with the yellow light of Mercury and the orange of Hod. Particularly, charge the spine, head, and back of the neck with Hod/Mercury energy. After the entire energy field is vibrating a brilliant yellow and orange, go back and charge the individual gates with their respective gate colors.

**Eye Infection or Eye Injury:** Thoroughly clean the eyes, including the third eye, using only your fingertips, charging the affected eye with the purple of Yesod or light blue of Moon. Do not charge directly upon the eye. Rather, charge around the eye. The eyes can be particularly sensitive to charging. Another method is to charge with D.W.B, using the Beak of Thoth. This is extremely effective.

**Fever:** Fever is a condition where scanning can be kept to a minimum. It is very difficult to scan the aura when a patient is running a high temperature. It is possible that the heat from the body interferes with accuracy of scanning. If the fever is high, begin cleaning the entire energy field, beginning at the head and ending at the feet. Make certain that every gate is thoroughly clean and that there is no congestion anywhere in the aura. Pay special attention to the Fountain Gate and the Solar Plexus Gate; this is very important because these two gates, in particular, must not be clogged in any way. Scan the back of the lungs for pulmonary infections, as pulmonary infections are often the main cause of high temperatures. Clean the lungs thoroughly. Begin charging the energy field in general, with the cooling blue of elemental Water, and charge each gate with its specific color. So, in other words, over the chest area you charge the Throat Gate with a cooling blue, but the Heart Center Gate would be charged with green. This repeated cleaning and charging should be completed three to four times within a 24 hour period. In addition, it is essential to untangle the Vitality Rays and brush them upward as often as possible.

**Food Poisoning:** Make sure to take the appropriate medical action, such as taking the patient to an emergency room, if necessary. Clean the Navel Gate and the Solar Plexus with D.W.B. Charge with a violet color.

**Frequent Urination/Bed-wetting:** Scan the recipient completely, looking for any signs of erratic energy pouring out of other parts of the body or the gates. Erratic energy that is dull and heavy could be an indication of a more serious problem. Focus on cleaning the Foundation Gate, and alternate charging around the sex organs. Use the light blue color of the Moon and the red color of the Foundation Gate. Do not overcharge!

**Gallstones:** Clean the stomach area thoroughly with the green light of Netzach/Venus. Scan the Navel Gate, making certain that there is no congestion or depletion. Charge the Navel Gate, the bladder, and urinary tract area with the purple of Yesod, and light blue Moon energy.

**Glaucoma:** See eye injury/eye pain.

**Hepatitis:** Hepatitis requires immediate medical attention and can be life-threatening; please ask the patient to advise their spouse or partner to receive immunization and/or treatment as well, if necessary. Hepatitis is generally best treated with a complete cleansing of the solar plexus gate using D.W.B.; apply general cleaning to the liver area. Pause and scan, making sure the liver is not congested, if it is, continue cleaning. To disinfect the liver, energize the liver with the green light of Venus. Follow this up with the violet of Jupiter. Rotate these back and forth, and if the patient is running a fever or suffering from toxins then return back to the green light of Netzach or Venus. It is not uncommon for the body to absorb a tremendous amount of energy when a patient has hepatitis. Continue charging the liver, Solar Plexus Gate, and Navel Gate. Continue to repeat this 2 or 3 times daily.

**Headaches/Migraines:** Headaches are generally a result of severe imbalance and congestion, and commonly occur in the Fountain Gate and Third Eye Gate. Oftentimes, headaches are the result of tension and anxiety as well. Scanning the temples, eyes, and throat are very important. Be sure to clean away any congestion or clogging of these areas. Localized cleaning and downward sweeping of energy near the head with Water energy and the color blue, is extremely effective in reducing and/or removing pain. Another little secret is to have the patient lie down and take off their shoes, and then charge the bottom of their feet with a heavier planetary energy, such as Saturn, or energy of the Sephira, such as Binah. Dark green Earth energy is effective in grounding the patient, thus removing the headache.

**Hardening of Arteries:** Clean the entire energy field with D.W.B., and follow the outline as prescribed for high blood pressure, followed by charging the entire sphere of sensation with Sun energy, particularly the head and back of the head and neck area. Clean and recharge, after cleaning all the gates. Energize them by charging them with their appropriate color.

**Heart Gate, Astral-Spiritual Injuries:** Healing this condition is a very delicate process. Healing must be performed by a Master Ruach Healer, with a minimum of 3 years experience. The Master Ruach Healer uses Rose Cross Ritual healing methods. An extremely light pink-infused white light is used. The color is even lighter than the very pale 'pastel' red tint used for lower body healing. The entire body should be charge with D.W.B. with the specific intention of unclogging arteries and restoring normal blood flow and balance. Also, untangle the Vitality Rays to open the heart and body.

**Heart Condition:** There are various forms of heart conditions; however, the formula given here works on virtually all of them. Clean the Heart Center Gate thoroughly with D.W.B. Charge the gate for about ten seconds with the bright red tinted light of Geburah. Charge with just your fingertips, over the heart and chest area. Pause for a few moments, and then charge the area with the blue tint of Chesed. Finally, charge the chest area with the yellow tinted light of Tiphareth. Never charge too closely, having your hands at least a foot away from the chest. Make sure all congestion is removed from the Heart Center Gate before charging. Follow the color sequence as it has been given.

**Hernia:** Scan the herniated area. Usually with a hernia there is a depletion of energy. Clean the Navel and Solar Plexus Gates, and charge with their appropriate colors of orange and yellow. Charge the herniated area with D.W.B., or the clear tinted violet light of Jupiter.

**Hemorrhoids:** Clean thoroughly the Solar Plexus, Navel, and Foundation Gates with the green energy of Netzach/Venus. Next, apply the violet energy of Jupiter and the blue energy of Chesed to the anal area. Repeat three or four times and the hemorrhoids should dissipate.

**High Blood Pressure:** Clean the energy field (aura) with D.W.B. particularly focusing on the Heart Center and Navel Gate. Oftentimes, high blood is a result of congestion in these two gates and they must be cleaned extensively and repeatedly. Lightly charge using green for the Heart Center Gate and yellow for the Navel Gate. The chest area can be lightly charged with Tiphareth in a yellow golden color. It is important with high blood pressure to not overcharge.

**Insomnia:** Gently clean the entire energy field. Then, use dark elemental Earth colors, such as dark green, as you comb the Vitality Rays downwards over the head and face until the recipient's eyes begin to droop. Make sure the recipient of the healing is in a comfortable resting position and will not be driving any time soon.

**Irregular Menstruation, PMS, Menstrual Difficulties:** Scan the Foundation Gate, and the lower abdomen area, along with the Navel Gate. Apply localized cleaning as needed. In particular, scan the uterus and ovary area. More often than not, these areas will be depleted in energy, although you don't want to rule out congestion. Be certain to clean thoroughly if congested and charge the entire area with the very light purple-tint of Yesod. Upon completion of charging with Yesod, recharge the gates in their specific color. Generally, 3-5 charging treatments will relieve this condition.

**Leukemia:** With leukemia, follow the protocol given under the listing for cancer. The next technique may seem a bit out there, and perhaps risky. After cleaning the energy field, gates and entire body, then, charge the entire body with the color red, for fire or Mars. The entire body must be energized/charged, from head to toe, several times. If the patient begins to heat up, or starts to get sick from the over-charging, pause, for even up to a day, then get right back to it. You need to kill the excessive amount of white blood cells that the body of the recipient is now producing. Clean all of the gates thoroughly and repetitively, and charge them with their appropriate color or D.W.B. This will likely stop the over-production of cells. A patient with leukemia needs to have immediate Ruach Healing and attention, a minimum of twice daily, if possible.

**Lung Infection/Tuberculosis:** Thoroughly clean the Throat Gate, Heart Center Gate, lungs, and Solar Plexus with D.W.B.; making sure there is NO CONGESTION WHATSOEVER. Charge the lungs first with the delicate light blue of Moon, then following up with the bright, light yellow of Tiphareth. Alternate these two colors while charging, and expect to see some results in about a week, provided you are doing daily charging.

**Multiple Sclerosis:** Clean the entire energy field with D.W.B. Proceed to charge the entire energy field with the yellow of elemental Air.

Next, scan and charge the spinal column, the neck and the back of the head, using the orange of Hod and yellow of Mercury. Repeat on a regular basis. In addition, it is important to make sure that the Fountain Gate and the Third Eye are all regularly cleaned and are operating at their maximum potential. If they are in need of charging, do so with the appropriate gate color. Use white for the Fountain Gate, violet for the Third Eye Gate, and blue for the Throat Gate.

**Pancreatitis:** Clean the Solar Plexus and the Navel Gate, removing all congestion. Charge with the appropriate colors: yellow for Solar Plexus, orange for Navel. Next, clean the abdominal area with D.W.B. and charge with the violet of Jupiter, alternating with the red color of Mars. Alternate these two colors back and forth at about a 70%-30% ratio. Repeat this entire process three times a week, if possible.

**Prostate:** Scan the patient completely, looking for any signs of erratic energy pouring out of other parts of the body or the gates. Erratic energy that is dull and heavy could be the indication of a more serious problem. Focus on cleaning the Foundation Gate, and alternate charging around the sex organs. Use the light blue color of Moon and the red color of the Foundation Gate. Do not over-charge!

**Pulled Muscles and Strains:** Clean the affected muscles with D.W.B. Follow up by charging the muscles with the green of Venus, followed by the light blue color of Water. The Venus energy helps the muscle restore itself. The Water energy will help the affected area relax and loosen. Generally speaking, you can decrease recuperation time by 50%.

**Sexual Impotence:** Clean the Heart Center Gate and the Foundation Gate thoroughly. Make certain there is no congestion in either one. Energize the Foundation Gate with its appropriate color, red, and the Heart Center with its appropriate color, green. Energize the groin area with the color of Yesod, purple. The combination of cleaning these two gates, and charging with Yesod, will bring about good results.

**Stomach Ache:** See constipation and diarrhea.

**Snake Bites:** SEEK EMERGENCY MEDICAL ATTENTION! Clean wound with the antiseptic energy of Netzach/Venus, using the color green. Help the patient relax by combing the Vitality Rays downward with light blue color of elemental Water. Alternate back and forth between the actual bite area and calming the recipient of the snake bite.

**Stuffy Nose, Cold, Cough:** Using your fingers, scan the gates of the Third Eye and the Throat. If congestion is also in the lungs, scan the Heart Center Gate as well. Equally scan the lungs. For the most part, this condition is a matter of congestion and there is simply too much Ruach in these areas of the body. Again, sweep with D.W.B. or the green light of Netzach. Clean thoroughly. Rescan, and begin the drying process with the light of the Sun.

**Rotator Cuff Injury:** See pulled muscles and sprains.

**Toothache:** Activate your fingers and scan the jaw area. Generally, where the toothache exists there will be a rip or tear in the aura, indicating a depletion of energy. Clean the affected gate with the color green, the Sephira of Netzach and Venus. The green color of Netzach/Venus is extremely powerful in its antiseptic properties.

**Urinary Infections or Peptic Ulcers:** Complete a thorough cleansing of the Solar Plexus Gate and the Navel Gate. Charge them with their appropriate colors, yellow and orange respectively. Scan and clean the entire abdomen and stomach area. Charge it with the virus fighting energy of Netzach/Venus. Follow this with charging the affected area with the very light blue color of Moon.

# CHAPTER TWENTY-ONE: Putting It All Together

Its four o'clock in the morning and all I could hear on the other end of the phone is a desperate woman crying and screaming. Her husband had just been taken to the ER at one of the major hospitals in San Bernardino, California. He was suffering a major heart attack and she was asking for my help. I told her I would be down there within the hour. Within fifteen minutes, I had a phone tree going and healers all over the country were awake sending incredible healing light. All I could think about on the drive to the hospital was his wife and two little children that depended on this man. He was only thirty-five years old, younger than me at the time, yet his life was being threatened by a coronary attack.

Let's switch gears for one second. A surgeon scrubs up before surgery, walks into the operating room, and begins slicing and dicing away on his patient. If the surgeon has a good set of x-rays, an efficient team keeping track of the patient's vital signs, and a little bit of luck, he will walk out of the operation room 7-8 hours later, never knowing the patient's name. To the surgeon the name does not matter, it's all about technique and applied training.

Now, back to my friend suffering a heart attack. As I was driving to the hospital that night, I realized I wasn't so fortunate. I could not discard who this person was, the fact that he had children and a family. His hopes, dreams, and aspirations, seemingly all dashed away because of a clogged artery. As a matter of fact, there was more going on here than just a clogged artery. There was an entire energy field crying out for the one thing that the physical doctor could not give him, and that one thing was *love*. As I walked down the long hallway of the hospital into a small room, where he was hooked up to monitors and wires of every kind, I realized the one thing that I had going for me in the healing process was I was open to universal, unconditional love. Oh sure, I brought all the techniques taught in this book, but I also brought something else. I brought a deep connection to Spirit and a dogged desire to heal someone whom was in need of healing.

A word of advise to all fellow healers; all the attunements and initiations in the world will not surpass your personal desire to open up and love another human being into perfect health. You don't have to be a Christian to marvel at the story where Jesus raises Lazarus from the dead. In this story, the scriptures state that when Jesus found out that Lazarus had died, he began to cry. Think about this for a moment.

His tears are evidence to us that emotional connection is not a bad thing in the healing process, but a good thing. Although you can scan, clean and charge accurately, without allowing a patients emotions to affect you, there is another side to healing. This other side is you don't have to be scared to allow yourself to feel compassion or empathy, as long as you're able to stay centered, not absorbing the patient's energies into your own aura or Vitality Gates.

When a Ruach Healer sits down to talk with somebody that needs healing, the healer seeks to know everything about the patient. You as a healer will find out about their family, their goals, their dreams, their fears and their doubts. Emotions of love, caring and hope generally express themselves in the energy field as a free flowing energy that is bright, and filled with incredible vitality. Whereas on the other hand, emotions of anger, pain, fear and doubt show up in a patient's energy field as congestion or depletion.

Child abuse is not child abuse, it's person abuse. A child who is abused carries scars on his/her energy field for years. When a patient has such deep emotional pain buried within their sphere of sensation, it often shows up later on in life as a chronic disease or illness. As a healer, you almost have to think about the child within the patient, that little boy or girl, that's lonesome, scared and in pain. You have to be willing to bring them comfort and love.

As I walked into my friend's ER room and saw him hooked to wires and tubes, my eyes began to well up with tears. Some healers would have turned off their emotional nature, yet I knew it was my strongest asset. I walked over to him lying on the bed, placed my hands on his chest, looked into his eyes, and said to him these words, "The Holy Spirit is going to heal you today." As the Divine White Brilliance was pouring out my hands into his body and his heart, I spoke out-loud the words of the Hierophant of the Golden Dawn, ***"I come in the power of Light, I come in the mercy of Light, I come in the wisdom of Light, the Light hath healing in its wings."***

At that moment, I felt the power rushing through my hands, into his depleted energy field, melting away his congested arteries. I continued to do healing work on him in the hospital, until finally, he broke open and began to cry, as he had such deep emotional pain stemming back from childhood. It was all lodged in his heart center gate. The physical result was a heart attack. As I began to leave, he begged me to stay, so I stayed until they kicked me out of the room. Four days later he was at my house excited about his future. I looked into his eyes, at all the hopes and all the dreams. I felt such incredible love for him, as I have for every single patient that I have performed healing work on. I believe love is really where it all begins.

I had a patient coming to my house who was suffering from Parkinson's Disease, but she could have been suffering from any disease or chronic illness. The way that a Ruach Healer puts it all together is essentially the same. The first thing that a Ruach Healer does is get to know the patient. I want to know as much about my patient as possible. I want to build rapport; a connection between the two of us. As a Ruach Healer, this connection is essential. You are a healing being, filled with love, hopes and dreams. Just like everyone else. Somehow the healer finds a way to mesh their hopes and dreams with the patient's dreams, even if for just a moment, to provide a healing experience. If the patient never gets better or improves physically, you want them to feel a moment of true unconditional love and caring. The more the healer knows about their patient, the more the Ruach Healer is able to connect to the Divine White Brilliance that flows through their body and connect the Light into the patient.

After learning about our patient a little bit, healing begins by fact-finding. Fact-finding is different from rapport-building, since now the healer is focused on the patient's pain and any diagnosis previously given to them. In this example, healing work was being preformed on a woman who has Parkinson's disease, but SHE DID NOT HAVE PARKINSON'S DISEASE. NEVER CONFUSE YOUR PATIENT WITH THE DISEASE.

The Ruach Healer continues fact-finding until satisfied and ready to continue. Next, focus on scanning. During the scanning process, there is a type of spiritual intimacy that takes place. Not only is the healer scanning the patient's energy field, but they are tapping into the emotional state of the patient. This intimacy is good. Healers want to feel unconditional love as this too will flow to the patient. As the Ruach Healer is scanning, s/he begins to think about how they are going to treat the patient. In my example of the woman, it was naturally the fact-finding that lead me to Parkinson's disease. Knowing how this disease affects the nervous system showed what energies to use for the healing. I was already more inclined to use the energy of Hod and Mercury in the treatment process.

However, never get hung up on what energy you are using. As a healer, always focus on how to derive these energies and how to draw conclusions. You are a Ruach Healer. You have numerous options available to you. Do you clean the women with Parkinson's with white light, or do you clean her with a colored light? If you choose to use a colored light to clean or charge her, what is the basis for your decision? For the healer, the basis of all decisions is always the intuitive connection to the patient being healed. As a healer, you must to trust your intuition. It is totally plausible that two healers could work on the same patient, with two different approaches, and both achieve positive results. Ruach Healing is as much an art as it is a metaphysical science. This is why, for the Ruach Healer, scanning is so important. It is during this time that you are psychically connecting not only to the patient, but to the incredible love and light of Divine Source that is pouring through you as you heal.

The Ruach Healing Method has given you, the healer, a complete toolbox full of tools. You can use the energy of the Sephirot, the Elements, or the Planets. You may even choose to abstain from using all of them and choose to use the incredible power of D.W.B. The point being made is that as a new Ruach Healer, it is imperative to operate from a position of love and compassion. All the choices you make will likely be smart and intelligent choices. Oftentimes, before actually beginning the charging part of the work, ask your patient to stand up if they can. Tap them in the chest a few times to clear the thymus, then perform a series of energetic muscle testing exams. Remember, don't start with the muscle testing, as muscle testing follows the intuition.

Okay, say that you have decided that light yellow, for example, is going to be the color you will be using for a particular case in healing. So the question is, are you using the yellow of Tiphareth, or the yellow of the element of the Air? In other words, you have limited everything down, and are using your intuition and the muscle testing to confirm what you already know.

One other point to mention before ending this chapter, is that 75% of the time opt for using the planetary energy over the energy of the Sephira, except in the case where it is needed to invoke the meta healing of the Sephirot. Most of the time, planetary energy is going to give a stronger and more focused approach. However, in the Ruach Healing Method, as well as most esoteric teachings, the Sephirot energy must first be awakened to effectively invoke the planetary energy. Think of it like a hierarchy. First, open up the Sephirot consciousness, the Divine Name, the Archangelic Name, the Choir of Angels, and then the Planetary Angel, and color. This is the normal direction Ruach Healers take, 75% of the time. However, let's be clear about this, there are healers that just focus on the planetary color and nothing more. They seem to get surprisingly good results. Personally, I suggest learning the hierarchies of Angels. They are included in charts throughout this book for you. Don't wait until the hierarchies are memorized to begin your healing work. The world is in need of healers. If you only have one thing going for you, and that thing is connection to Infinite Light and unconditional love, I am more than confident that you will be an effective healer. The truth is that you have so much more than love, you have a variety of healing tools available to you. Be a dynamic Ruach Healer, in a world that so badly needs what you have to offer.

One final thought, while the Ruach Healing Method has a certification program with workshops and Spiritual Awakenings, we personally suggest that you begin teaching someone the information you have learned in this book as soon as possible. Our experience is that when you teach something to another person, you learn it on a deeper level. So get started, find someone interested in healing and begin teaching them, or form a local Ruach Healing Circle. The point is, take action and release the magical healer within.

# NOTES:

# CHAPTER TWENTY-TWO: The Law of Attraction and the Ruach Healing Method

The Law of Attraction finds its roots in the ancient teachings of Hermes Trismegistus and the Emerald Tablet. As discussed earlier, this ancient document is the basis from where all magical, metaphysical and spiritual healing takes place. It is the Law of Attraction and the reality that "likes attracts likes", which allow us to create an inner reality of health and wellness that is reflected into the physical plane. Without getting too esoteric, let's make this whole concept easier to understand. Understanding comes from looking at the most simple, yet profound, sentence from the Emerald Tablet. The famous sentence is as follows:

**"As Above so Below."**

As with any text, there are a multitude of interpretations to the Emerald Tablet. A workable and usable interpretation of "As Above, so Below" is that which is created in the higher planes of reality, must manifest in the lower planes of the physical world. This is precisely what you do as a Ruach Healer. You work in the energy field of the patient, thus you are working in the higher planes of reality regarding the patient.

This is a simple concept, but difficult for some to grasp. Some would say that this is just new age mumbo jumbo. Healers would highly disagree. This concept of "As Above, so Below" is directly connected with the Law of Attraction. Law of Attraction is the cornerstone of how the Magic of Light works, Initiation, and/or anything else that has a spiritual/physical counterpart. Naturally, it is the cornerstone of how all forms of esoteric or spiritual healing work. Think of this, if there is no higher reality that expresses itself as the aura or energy field of the body, then all we are doing is playing a mental game with ourselves. On the other hand, if healing a rip in the aura of a patient has a profound effect on a bleeding cut and the bleeding slows down or stops, the very basis of the Law of Attraction has been employed. A healing like the one just mentioned are the *rule*, not the *exception*.

One prolific author who wrote about the Law of Attraction was one of the Chief Adepts in the Golden Dawn Temple in Chicago, during in the 1920's. William Walker Atkinson (1862-1932) was one of the Three Initiates who wrote what has become a kind of bible of modern Hermetics. The book is called the *"Kybalion"*, and after over 50 years it is still in print. The *"Kybalion"* is a must read for anyone interested in the Law of Attraction and Hermetics.

Atkinson coined the phrase *"Thought Vibration and the Law of Attraction."* The idea that William Walker Atkinson and others claim is that, our thoughts have incredible power to create the reality we seek. In other words, if you think about health and vitality, you tend to attract health and vitality and vice versa.

This concept applies to every area of life. The way you think affects your mental state, your physical health and your wealth. It is absolutely critical that a healer, of any healing method, have a basic understanding of the Law of Attraction. It is essential as healers, to never allow yourselves to draw limitations on the universe's ability to heal anyone, of any condition, at anytime.

Another famous Adept of the Golden Dawn tradition is the late Israel Regardie (1907-1985). He is most famous for his book called the

*"Golden Dawn".* Regardie was a proponent of the Law of Attraction and wrote about it in several of his books including, *"The Art of True Healing"* (1932) and *"A Treatise on the Mechanism of Prayer and the Operation of the Law of Nature,"* (1937). In these books he shares with his readers a meditation designed to help the mind heal itself! Regardie claimed the Law of Attraction was not only a valid method for attracting good physical health, but was equally good for empowering other aspects of ones life. I personally agree with Regardie, and simply add that there cannot be any healing if the constructs of the Law of Attraction are not employed by the healer. All good healers invoke the power of the Law of Attraction in their healing, even if they are not aware of it. I guess I am not the only one with a Golden Dawn background that sees how the Law of Attraction and true healing, go hand in hand.

Certainly, there are other great leaders who do not have a magical or Hermetic background that have been active advocates regarding the power of the Law of Attraction. The most revealing things about the Law of Attraction is that its concepts are not limited to one group of people or another. People from every belief system find a way to connect to the concept of the Law of Attraction, especially if healing is involved.

One of these people is Wallace Wattles (1860-1911). Wattles, in his famous book the *"Science of Getting Rich"*, explains to his reader the mere act of simply believing in the object of your desire and focusing on it, leads to that object or goal being realized. Wattles also explains how negative thoughts lead to negative results. If Wattles is correct, and I certainly believe he is, every thought our patients think about themselves, and their physical health, plays a significant role in their disease. In other words, they are attracting into their physical bodies the very sickness they seek to rid themselves of. Taking this a step further, every thought the healer thinks about the patient has a powerful and lasting impact. This is why it is critical that the Ruach Healer learns to control his or her thoughts at all times.

Perhaps the most famous of all the books that have the Law of Attraction as its cornerstone is Napoleon Hill's (1883-1970) book called *"Think and Grow Rich"* (1928). This book continues to be one of the top selling books on the use of the mind in the attraction of wealth. The book has sold over 60 million copies. Hill insisted the importance of controlling one's own thoughts in order to achieve success. Hill also speaks of the energy that thoughts have and their ability to attract other thoughts. The same principles that are employed for attracting wealth can and should be applied to the subject of healing. Napoleon Hill's book *"Think and Grow Rich"* is as much about the subject of healing, as it is about wealth accumulation.

In recent times, we have seen a plethora of books on the subject of attraction. The most well-know examples are the movie and book entitled, *"The Secret"*. Another example are the many writings of Esther Hicks (Weaver Geer 1948-present) and Jerry Hicks ("Abraham" Hicks 1927-2011), including their New York times best seller called, *"Learning to Attract Health, Wealth and Happiness"* (2007). All of these books teach about the power of our thoughts and what we can learn to manifest if we develop control of our thoughts.

## Positive Thoughts get Positive Results

You may be saying to yourself, this is all very interesting but what does this have to do with the Ruach Healing Method. The answer is simple. Your thoughts, as a healer, must be focused on a target. You must hold that target in your mind and it must become crystal clear. When performing healing on a patient, never draw a limitation. Always see the patient in optimum health and vitality. See radiance coming from them; always seeing them in a state of joy and happiness. You need to create this picture in your mind, at times it may become difficult to hold the picture, but nonetheless less this is what you, the Ruach Healer, must do.

Everything you do must align with your overall picture of health and vitality. At times, this may be difficult because your patient may be in pain, sick, hurting, and even more damaging, they may be complaining. Listening to a patient's complaints is vital, as we want to be compassionate, but we must never buy into the the complaint. It is important that you, has a healer, never accept that "this is just the way things are". You ARE a representative of the universe *and* the universe has no limitations.

The picture you create in your mind is *your* picture. Never think it is appropriate to give a patient false hope, but you do want your patient to feel a wonderful sense of positive optimism. This positive thought begins to filter its way into the various steps taken, in the process of using the Ruach Healing Method.

## Scanning

When scanning the patient, stay positive and sensitive to every area of the patient's energy field. As you begin to work, you almost slip into a mild trance. In this trance, begin to feel positive thoughts of gratitude for being given the skills to feel every area of the patient's aura that does not match up with the picture you created of vitality and health. When you have a powerful and positive image in your mind, every detail that does not match begins to stand out. This allows you, as a healer, to be extremely effective.

## Cleaning and Clearing

Some parts of the aura are congested and need to be cleaned. If you have a positive picture of a healthy, happy patient in your mind, you will find the locations to clear with greater ease. Instead of noticing a subtle difference, you will notice areas that need to be cleaned, standing out like the proverbial bull in the china closet.

## Charging the Aura

When you charge the aura, you will know precisely how much energy to provide your patient. You will know because you have an internal picture of that patient in perfect health. As you charge the patient, you will see and feel your patient returning to perfect health. See the patient in your mind, and then see the patient transforming into the picture of health, as you charge their gates and their energy field. Your positive thoughts of what that patient can be and is becoming, provide incredible codification of your work into a wonderful reality. That reality is a healthy patient.

## Training Your Patient in the Law of Attraction

The Ruach Healer works with a patient on several levels. The more the patient understands what you are doing as a healer, the sooner they will experience a recovery. So, as a healer, share a few simple lessons designed to give the patient some powerful tools to facilitate their own healing.

The first lesson shared is visualizing and emotionalizing the outcome the patient wants. If you can get your patient into creating a beautiful picture of themselves in a state of vitality, that picture will become a target for them. I remember doing a workshop in Los Angles and there was a lady who attended who had a leg brace on. She had worn this brace for numerous years. I told her that I believed she could reach a state of inner health, whereby, she would no longer need the brace. She laughed, proceeding to tell me all the things that were wrong with her. I paused her for a moment, asking her to rephrase that in the past tense. In other words, "these are all the things that were wrong with me at one time." She did that, then I did some Ruach Healing work on her leg. I can't remember what color I used, but I believe it was the planetary color of indigo, for Saturn. Anyway, she sat down with the audience, as I continued my class. We paused for lunch, and after lunch, she came back to class and immediately went to the stage where I was standing. She pulled up her pant leg and the brace was gone! Everyone was amazed. She continued attending the class for the next several days and never put the brace on again. The last time we talked was about 5 years ago, and she has resorted back to using the leg brace. She has written me saying her knee was completely healed, not only according to herself, but her medical doctor as well.

What was the reason for this quick and drastic healing? The reason was, perhaps, the work I did on her leg, but I believe it was a combination of the Ruach Healing work and her change in thought pattern. When you, as a healer, teach your patients to think in healing pictures and see issues in the past tense, you will see a dramatic increase in unbelievable healing. Train your patients to visualize.

The second lesson to share, as you perform the Ruach Healing Method, is that from time to time explain to your patient exactly what you are doing. Oh yes, I know many of them like to drift off into trance, but if you can get them to understand they had a depletion in the heart gate for example, but that they do not have a depletion now, their own inner confidence will grow. This will result in their thoughts partnering with you in the healing process. You can often talk, with patients, about sweeping away the negative energy as you are combing the aura, or that you are awaking the Vitality Rays. Talking about these techniques places the suggestion in the patients thoughts that this is making them feel better.

I had a patient who came to me almost weekly. There was really not much wrong with her, except she was always tired. So, after a general cleaning and a light charging with Divine White Brilliance, I would tell her, “I am going to brush your Vitality Rays upward just like a flower grows upward toward the sun." I would go on to say that by sweeping the Vitality Rays upward, she would likely have more energy. I would have her visualize herself swimming, dancing, or doing something active, while combing her Vitality Rays. After about 4 weeks of doing this, she called me and said that she could get her Vitality Rays to go upward just by thinking of the things she wanted enough energy to do. This is a wonderful example of how our thoughts and the Law of Attraction, along with the Ruach Healing Method, work hand in hand to facilitate wellness.

The third lesson to share is having your patient sit down and write out some goals. These goals should be about physical health. For example, how far do they want to walk, how strong do they want to be, how much weight do they want to lose, etc. Patients have made goals on everything from cancer in their body, to simply having more energy. Then, ask your patient what steps might be necessary to reaching these goals. Ask the patient if they are committed to taking the steps necessary to reach their goals, including positive visualization.

## Positive Thoughts about Yourself as a Healer

Sadly, there are some healers who are jaded. They no longer really believe in their art, or their skills. It is hard to say how they got this way, but it is more common than you think. It is essential that you always take time to renew yourself and keep yourself in a state of balance. However even more important, is the inner knowledge that you ARE an instrument of Divine Source. When this thought is in the mind of the healer, everything comes together. It is essential that you know, that you know, that you know, that you are called to play an important role in your patient's life. It does not matter if they or anyone else knows this, but you need to know it and believe it. When you as a Ruach Healer develop confidence and inner power, that confidence will be transferred to the patient in the way of spectacular results. Confidence is a magical power that can only be obtained through thinking the right thoughts about yourself, as a healer, and taking action. Confidence never comes through talking but rather it grows through doing.

There will be times when you surprise yourself. The failing liver of a patient will all of a sudden begin working and healing itself. The doctors will be amazed, but it is important that you do not get attached to the results. While you have created a positive image of the patient and you have inner connection and confidence in yourself, you don't want to lust for results or become too attached to the results. Remember, you are creating the most positive picture possible, but you are only the conduit for the Divine Healing. By the same token, if you are not attached to the results when the patient makes a miraculous recovery, you will not become discouraged or jaded with the patient does not.

## Exercise: Increasing a Healer's Positive Law of Attraction Energy

### Step 1

Visualize a patient you have never seen before coming to you for healing. Notice how the patient is very sick, their color is greenish gray and everything about them expresses illness.

### Step 2

Before you begin to work on the patient, see yourself getting larger and glowing more with radiant light. You should feel as if you are a light bulb and you are glowing.

### Step 3

Begin scanning and cleaning the patient. Feel your energy field growing stronger and stronger as you work on the patient. Repeat the following in your mind, *"I am called to heal because I have surrendered to the power of the Universe and the healing power of the Universe now flows through me."*

### Step 4

Continue your healing, scanning, cleaning, charging and more. See and feel yourself doing it all. As you begin charging the patient, see the patient getting healthier, stronger, and more powerful. Notice that you are making an incredible difference in this patient.

### Step 5

When the patient is healthy looking, simply bow your head and say the following prayer, *"Not unto my name but unto Thy name be the power and the glory forever and ever. Amen."*

You and I have no way of knowing the predominate thoughts in the mind of the patient and the people around the patient. You, as a healer, are responsible for your own thoughts, about your skills and the potential outcome of the patient, but you are not responsible for the outcome. Ultimately, it is a combination of you and the patient. Stay strong in your knowledge and beliefs about yourself as a Ruach Healer, and you will be employing a power tool that will aid you in your healing work, the Law of Attraction.

# APPENDIX A: TWELVE RUACH HEALING IDEAS TO IMPROVE YOUR LIFE

Ruach is life force, and life force is a positive thing to instill in just about anything and everything. The idea is not so much about healing as it is about instilling an object with more D.W.B., so that what the object represents or does is affected in a positive way with life giving healing energy. The whole idea is that by charging something that will be used or consumed, it will have a powerful and positive effect on the person who is using it or consuming it.

As a healer of the Ruach Healing Method, you cannot have too much life force in your energy field. So, if you consume some water that has been charged with Ruach, the water will not only have the properties of the water, but will have the properties of additional life force. The life force given to the water can be just a generally charge for wellness or it can be a charge for a specific intention, like eradicating cancer.

## Charging with Intention

Charging with intention is simple. Simple, invoke the Ruach as if you were about to charge someone's Vitality Gates, or energy field. Spread out your fingers and place your palms over the object you wish to charge, and allow the energy to flow through you. Next, simply state the intention that you want the Ruach energy to be infused with. Allow the energy to flow through your hands until you feel the object has received all the life force, or light, that it can handle, then stop and seal the object with the symbol of the Rose Cross.

Now that your object is engulfed with the Ruach Energy of a specific intention, the life force in it will calibrate the energy of the person using the object. This is done by the object raising the person's vibrations to match the intention of the object. You, as a Ruach Healer, should be doing this important work for objects you use, and also objects others use.

Say you go to a patient's home to perform some Ruach Healing. For example, the patient has a problem with diabetes. After you have done your work, ask the patient if they have a glass pitcher handy. Next, fill it with fresh drinking water. Use filtered pure water if possible, but some clients drink right out of the facet. Whatever they have is what you should use. After filling the pitcher with fresh water, begin clearing yourself with some deep breathing, lay your hands over the water and charge it. After the charging and sealing with the Rose Cross, pour a glass of charged water for the patient. Place the charged water in the refrigerator and suggest that the patient drink one or two glasses of Ruach charged water every day to continue their healing. I can tell, you from many years of personal experience, patient's who have an illness can almost always tell the difference between charged and uncharged water. It is absolutely amazing. Give it a try and prove it to yourself.

## Exercise: Objects to Charge

**1. Water** – See above

**2. Tea** – I like to charge tea, especially natural green tea. Various herbal teas have a variety of healing properties. In general, green tea is always a good choice, but there are a number of herbal teas that you can find that are good for healing everything from blood pressure to arthritis. Pick an herbal tea that has a strong reputation for begin effective for a specific malady. Charge this tea with a well thought out intention. If you are going to a patient's home you can do the research in advance and bring the tea with you. Once there, you can make a pot of tea and charge it with the magical healing intention. I have used this several times and found that people with chronic illnesses do very well with a Ruach charged tea.

**3. Food** – This is a very powerful method of healing. I believe that every Ruach Healer should consider charging their own food before every meal. You really don't need to get elaborate, rather all you need to do is hold both hands over the food and simply give it a few seconds of charging. Most of the time, you will want to give it a general charging and you can even say your favorite blessing while doing this. However, if you have something going on in your own energy field that needs attention and could use some additional healing, then by all means charge with a specific healing intention. Naturally, you can do this for patients too, if you have the opportunity to dine with them. The most effective time to charge food is when it is prepared and cooked. It is not necessary to go digging through the refrigerator, charging everything from the lettuce to the mustard. Just charge the food as you slice, dice, mix and mash during the meal making process.

**4. Pets** – Pets play an important role in many people's lives. Pets can be positively affected with Ruach energy for the specific healing of the pet. First, begin by scanning the pet. You may notice cold spots or spots that seem to be lacking energy. This is depletion. Just like in humans, pets sometimes get depleted in certain areas of their energy field. Next, look for clumps of energy. Clumps of energy will be a signal to you the pet has congested energy in that part of their body. Congestion needs to be cleared out. When I work with pets and animals in general, I for the most part only work with the D.W.B. I use the D.W.B. to do my cleaning and I use it for my charging. Other vibrational colors might be faster in the healing process, but there is too much risk in over charging the animal. It is almost always safe to use D.W.B., as long as your hand is about 12 inches away from the animal and you are scanning the animal on a regular basis. Constant scanning is essential to insure you do not overcharge the sick or injured animal. When it comes to small animals, even dogs and cats, one method you can use is to charge their food and water. This is a safe and easy way to insure they are receiving life giving Ruach energy for their healing needs. One final word of caution is advised, be very careful with tiny animals such as fish. It is almost better to charge the water around the animal, rather than directly charge the animal.

**5. Home** – Charging your entire home is a positive method of insuring that the environment is healthy and energetic. Even if you have a large house, simply go outside and put your hands in the air, palms facing the house and charge it. I like to do this in both the front and the back. I have a friend in California who is in the real estate business, and during the bursting of the real estate bubble in 2008, many of her co-workers were getting out of the real estate business. She, on the other hand, was doing well. She credits the fact that once a week, she would go by every one of her houses that she had on the market and give them a bath, as she called it, in D.W.B. I asked her how long she would do this, and she said about 5 minutes per home. Try this on your home, even if you are not looking to sell it, and you will immediately notice some incredible benefits.

**6. Bed** – Charging your bed, with a blanket of D.W.B., is a wonderful way of increasing the healing benefits of sleep. Simply, hold your hands over your bed and charge the bed for about a minute. You might even want to place an intention with your charge such as, "As I sleep my body and mind are being restored to a wonderful place of health and vitality."

**7. Shoes** – I remember one of my students picking me up from the airport in Los Angeles. I asked if we could stop by a store, so I could buy a pair of sandals. After purchasing my sandals, I pulled them out of the box and was about to put them on my feet. My student immediately asked me if I was going to give my sandals a charge of Ruach energy. I realized, at that moment, that charging your shoes with D.W.B. was essential for a healer, because we are walking a path, and we need life force and light to empower us as we journey down the path. Naturally, I have been charging my shoes ever since.

**8. Gifts** – Why not charge the gifts you give with some Ruach. This is a wonderful way of doing some positive healing for those you care about, while giving them something they will love and use often.

**9. People in the News** – I often hear people say things like, "I wish there was something I could do for that person." Well the good news is that there is something you can do. You can share with them some D.W.B. Focus on the person who is in need of the healing and use their name or picture as a focal point. The rest is simple, follow the instructions given in Chapter 19 on Long Distant Healing.

**10. Pictures and Names** – Here is something that is amazing. You can send healing and support to someone you love simply by focusing on their photo. Naturally, you can do a whole long distant healing with a photo, but you can also send loved ones D.W.B. everyday, by simply holding the palms of you hands over any photo on the wall. It only takes a minute or so and is easy to do.

**11. Crystals** – There is a lot of exciting buzz about healing work done with crystals. I have found that natural crystals, unpolished without too much refinement, work the best. If you can dig them out of the ground yourself, that is ideal. I like to clean the crystal in three different fashions. First, I use sea salt and water to cleanse them. I will, generally, let them soak in it for about an hour or so. Then I look at the crystal, and if it hold any dullness, I place them in sunshine for a day or so. You will be amazed at how sparkly they look after this. Finally, I place them in the center of a circle and do the L.B.R.P. around them. Now, they are ready for some Ruach charging and an intention. As I charge a crystal, I might say something like this; *"I dedicate this crystal to healing and raising the vibrations of anyone who comes in contact with it."*

**12. Plants** – Now, you can impress your friends with the healthiest plants around. Here is something you can do to prove to yourself how powerful the Ruach Healing Method is with plants. Get two identical plants. Charge one plant with Ruach in the morning and evening and the other plant do not charge. Care for the plants with exactly the same amount of water, sunlight, and fertilizer. You will be astonished at how well the plant with the Ruach grows. Likely, you will see results in about 1 week. Naturally you can also charge your garden with Ruach as well. You will be the envy of the garden club.

The Ruach Healing Method is a powerful tool for not only bringing healing to your own life, but empowering the lives of your patients. Be creative, everything in the universe has Ruach life energy, therefore everything can and will benefit from clearing and charging, especially charging. The wonderful thing about charging pictures, food, water etc is that it benefits not only the object being charged, or the person drinking the water or wearing the shoes, it also charges you. Every time you give a bit of yourself, you awaken your own energy field, and thus everything and everyone benefits by the Ruach charging.

## NOTES:

# APPENDIX B: THE EMERALD TABLET OF HERMES

The following is the text of The Emerald Tablet of Hermes, as translated by Sir Isscac Newton. This translation by Isaac Newton is found among his alchemical papers that are currently housed in King's College Library, Cambridge University.

*Tis true without lying, certain & most true.*
*That which is below is like that which is above & that which is above is like that which is below to do the miracles of one only thing*
*And as all things have been & arose from one by the mediation of one: so all things have their birth from this one thing by adaptation.*
*The Sun is its father, the moon its mother, the wind hath carried it in its belly, the earth is its nurse.*
*The father of all perfection in the whole world is here.*
*Its force or power is entire if it be converted into earth.*
*Separate thou the earth from the fire, the subtle from the gross sweetly with great industry.*
*It ascends from the earth to the heaven & again it descends to the earth & receives the force of things superior & inferior.*
*By this means you shall have the glory of the whole world*
*& thereby all obscurity shall fly from you.*
*Its force is above all force. For it vanquishes every subtle thing & penetrates every solid thing.*

*So was the world created.*

*From this are & do come admirable adaptations whereof the means (or process) is here in this. Hence I am called Hermes Trismegistus, having the three parts of the philosophy of the whole world*

*That which I have said of the operation of the Sun is accomplished & ended.*

Source: Isaac Newton. "Keynes MS. 28". The Chymistry of Isaac Newton. Ed. William R. Newman June 2010. Retrieved March 4, 2013

# APPENDIX C: SPIRITUAL AWAKENINGS AND WORKSHOPS

The Ruach Healing Method is a codification of knowledge, techniques, and Awakenings that come together to transform an ordinary person, with positive intention, into an exceptional conduit of the Healing Light. We merely took the Awakenings given to us through mentors and Masters of Esoteric Magic and tabulated it into a workable system. We stripped away the unnecessary adornments that often accompany ceremonial magic and Kabbalistic practice. Thirty years ago, the goal was to create a system that *anyone* could learn and begin using *immediately* without all the trappings of special initiations and attunements.

The memorization of facts in all the foundational academic studies used in the Ruach Healing Method led to an understanding that *every fact* comes with an *energy attached* to it. The Ruach Healing Method is unique from other systems of healing, in that is incorporates so many energetic tools from unique knowledge found in number of healing modalities. When there is a marriage between energy and academic study there is an awakening that takes place. It is for lack or a better term, an "Ah Ha" moment. It is a gnosis that can not be explained to others. Ruach Healing Awakenings are based on the union of academic studies and energy, which mystically transforms the healer from the limitations of the physical world to the limitlessness of the astral and spiritual world.

Some healers in other traditions may claim that an Awakening in the Ruach Healing method is the same thing as an attunement in another tradition. However, it is not. An Awakening in the Ruach Healing Method is based on three things.

1. **Prerequisite Knowledge**

   The healer must have a thorough understanding of the prerequisite knowledge and skills necessary to receive the Awakening. This is significantly different than other systems that provide an initiation or attunement before one receives the knowledge. In the Ruach Healing Method, it is imperative that you know the material and can preform it before you receive an Awakening. The academic study lays the foundation for the energy of the Awakening to flow through.

2. **Classroom Instruction**

   There are a number of ways to communicate, especially in today's world. Communicate is done through books, TV, movies, text, internet, phone, video chat and more. Each form of communication is used for a specific purpose. For example, you would not have a job interview via text or you would not write a book to propose to the one you love. A Ruach Healing class, workshop, or private instruction is a setting of communication with a specific purpose. You will be able to ask questions, be shown all the exercises and try them with an Adept Master Teacher Ruach Healer. He or she will be right by your side providing you the hands on guidance you need. In a Ruach Healing workshop or private class you have a special place to learn both the printed teachings of the system and the subtleties that only an Adept Master Teacher can provide. This is why Awakenings come after you have attended a workshop, class, or private instruction with a Certified Adept Master Teacher

Ruach Healer. Private instruction can be done long-distance if necessary.

3. **Healing Empowerment**

   The Ruach Practitioner when passing through an awakening receives a type of empowerment that allows him or her to operate at a higher and more effective level. The Awakening also allows the healer to have larger capacity receive the increased influx of Healing Light. The increased influx of Light activates the practitioner's aura to act as a healing lantern. This lantern in the Ruach Healer's Spirit causes the practitioner to emanate Healing Light *literally* all the time.

## LEVELS IN THE RUACH HEALING METHOD

### Associate Ruach Healer

awakened to

**"Whirling Air"**

Each level in the Ruach Healing Method is acquired through attending a workshop. A workshop is a two day experience, usually a Saturday and short day on Sunday. During the first level workshop, everything taught in this book is covered with an additional section on emotional healing, and financial healing. At the conclusion of the workshop, you will receive your certification as an Associate Ruach Healer and your first awakening.

The level of Associate Ruach Healer, receives an awakening through the element of Air. This Awakening relates to higher spiritual connection for healing purposes. The Awakening will imprint within your energy field the ability to attune to the patient's aura and heal it from the inside out, as well as, from the outside in. The Angelic Guardian associated with this level of awakening is the Great Archangel Raphael. The name of this awakening is called, **"Whirling Air"**.

**Master Ruach Healer**

awakened to

**"Lustral Waters"**

In this level you will learn more advance methods of applying the Tree of Life including the 22 microcosmic paths within the Tree of Life. These paths relate to various aspects of your patients consciousness. Up until now healing has involved the invocation of the light being brought down to the patient. In this level you will learn how to raise your patient up to the light. Elevating your patient energetically and spiritually will aid them in their own personal healing. Equally important you will be able to apply these techniques to yourself thus gradually raising yourself to your highest spiritual and healing potential.

The level of Master Ruach Healer, receives an awakening through the element of Water. Water is the most potent element for intuition. During this two day workshop you will prepare for a Master's increase in spiritual intuition. The Angelic Guardian associated with this level of awakening is the Great Archangel Gabriel. The name of this awakening is called, **“Lustral Waters”**.

**Adept Master Teacher**

awakened to

**“Holy Fire”**

In this level you will learn how to work with one of the most potent archetypal forces in the universe. These forces are the **Shemhamphorasch**, the 72 Holy Angels of the Kabbalah. Each angel represent 5 degrees of time and space out of the 360 degrees that comprises the Zodiac. Thus at this level not only you will learn how to use Zodiacal energies, you will learn how to do laser like healing with a specific Angel of the Shemhamphorasch.

The level of Adept Master Teacher, receives an awakening through the element of Fire. This special Awaking prepares you to work at an intense level of energy, as well as, gives you the unique ability to teach others, and provide awakenings. The Angelic Guardian associated with this level of awakening is the Great Archangel Michael. The name of this awakening is called, **“Holy Fire”**.

This level takes an additional two days of training, plus a journal of a minimum of 120 patients. The journal shows the illnesses, results of scanning, energies/colors applied during healing and outcomes (where available) of the 120 patients . A Ruach Healer Practitioner must be at the Lustral Water level for a minimum of one year and performed healing on

120 patients at this level. No more than 48 (40%) of these patients can be long-distance patients.

Let us emphasize that the knowledge in this book prepares you to immediately start healing people. However, if you are seriously interested about incorporating the Ruach Healing method in your practice than we encourage you to join us at a workshop. You can also help host a Ruach Healing workshop in your community. To receive more information visit ruachhealing.com.

# APPENDIX D: GLOSSARY

**Applied Kinesiology:** See Kinesiology

**Ain:** The first veil of negative existence; meaning negativity, often called "No-Thing."

**Ain Soph**: The second veil of negative existence; meaning with-out limits, endless, boundless.

**Ain Soph Aur:** The third veil of negative existence; meaning Limitless Light.

**A.R.A.R.I.T.A:** Achad Rosh Achdotho Rosh Ichudo Temurahzo Achad - A notarikon that proposes that the ultimate divinity of God is ONE.

**Archangel:** A higher being than angels. Archangels govern over angels and have free will, whereas angels do not. Archangels are obedient to Source and serve to carry out the WILL of source.

**Atkinson, William Walker:** (December 5, 1862 – November 22, 1932) An attorney, merchant, publisher, and author, as well as, a Chief in the Chicago Lodge of the Golden Dawn. He was an American pioneer of the New Thought movement and Law of Attraction. He coined the phrase "Thought Vibration and the Law of Attraction" in the book titled *"Kybalion"*. He is also known to have been the author of the pseudonymous works attributed to Theron Q. Dumont,Yogi Ramacharaka and Frater Incognito.

**Astral Fire Container:** The canister, created with the pentagram of fire, used to deposit sick or negative energy into. The Astral Fire Container, through the pentagram of fire, serves to transmute the negative energy into neutral energy. Many systems use no astral container for sick or negative energy, while others use salt water.

**Astral Body:** A body made up of light, often called the subtle body found beyond the physical body. There are several layers to the astral body. The Ruach Healing Method primarily focus on the three layers closest the physical body.

**Aura:** The energy field that emanates around a living thing. All living things have an aura. The human aura is in part created by the electromagnetic field produced by the heart beat.

**Auriel:** Archangel of the element of Earth. He dresses in earth tones. He holds a bundle of wheat on a fertile landscape. Stands in the North in the L.B.R.P.

**Awakening:** A shift in consciousness, in which you become aware of your oneness with Divine Source, you absorb new energy and power to use for a higher purpose, like being a healer. A Ruach Healing Method Awakening is a specialized moments of advancement during which there is a transfer of the Divine Energy in a Master Ruach Healer to a inexperienced healer.

**Binah:** The third Sephira on the Tree of Life. It literally means "understanding". The color is black.

**Charging:** The process the healer employs to pass Ruach to the patient. Charging is done with the palm of the hands, fingertips, and Thoth's Beak.

**Chokmah:** The second Sephira on the Tree of Life. It literally means "wisdom". The color is gray.

**Chakra:** The centers of energy and spiritual power in the human body, usually considered to be seven in number. The first chakra is located at the base of the spine with the last chakra on the top of the head. Often seen as a vortex.

**Chesed:** The fourth Sephira on the Tree of Life. It literally means "mercy". The color is blue.

**Crux Ansata:** Another word for ankh. Ankh is a tau cross with a loop on the top often appearing in Ancient Egypt. In Latin, ankh means "cross with a handle". The Crux Ansata is know as the "Key of Life" or "Key of the Nile".

**Da'ath:** The invisible non-Sephira which holds space for knowledge and information to be exchanged between worlds. It is found between Kether and Tiphareth on the Middle Pillar of the Tree of Life.

**Divine White Brilliance. D.W.B:** The infinite Light that emanates from Divine Source, Infinite Spirit or God.

**D.W.B.:** See Divine White Brilliance.

**Divine Source:** The Source from which all creation springs forth, often referred to as God and Goddess.

**Gabriel:** Archangel of the element of Water. He dresses in blue with some orange highlights. The Archangel holds a cup and is surrounded by waterfalls or the ocean. Stands in the West in the L.B.R.P.

**Geburah**: The fifth Sephira on the Tree of Life. It literally means "strength". The color is scarlet.

**Elementals:** The spiritual forces that comprise the very nature of the elements. Elementals are not Divine; they are the energies of the four elements Air, Fire, Water, Earth.

**Esther Hicks:** (Weaver Geer 1948-present) Law of Attraction and empowerment teacher and author. She worked side by side her husband Jerry "Abraham" Hicks until he passed in 2011. Known for the book called, *"Learning to Attract Health, Wealth and Happiness"* (2007).

**Foundation Gate:** The paddle wheel like center located at the base of the spine and the groin area. The color is a light red tint. Responsible for spinal health, prosperity, security and presence.

**Fountain Gate:** The paddle wheel like center located at the crown of the head which moves energy in and out of the body. The color is brilliant white. Responsible for self-knowing and union with the Divine.

**Heart Center Gate:** The paddle wheel like center located at the heart and lung which moves energy in and out of the body. The color is a light green tint. Responsible for the heart, lungs, and entire circulation system.

**Hermes Trismegistus:** Latin: Mercurius ter Maximus. "Thrice-greatest Hermes" is the purported author of the Hermetic Corpus, a series of sacred texts including the Emerald Tablet of Hermes from which long distant healing, long distant initiation and the Law of Attraction find their basis.

**Hill, Napoleon:** (October 26, 1883 – November 8, 1970) An American author in the area of personal success and New Thought movement who was one of the earliest producers of the modern genre of personal-success literature. He is widely considered to be one of the great writers on success. His most famous work, *"Think and Grow Rich"* (1937), is one of the best-selling books of all time (at the time of Hill's death in 1970, *"Think and Grow Rich"* had sold 20 million copies).

**Hod:** The eighth Sephira on the Tree of Life. It literally means "splendor". The color is orange.

**Holy Guardian Angel:** Your main guide and protector in the spiritual realm, other than God or Source, who helps you connect with God/Goddess/Spirit and advance on your spiritual path. This angel also protects you in the physical plane.

**Invocation, Invoking:** A calling to Divine Presence to request that God and/or angels, helper spirits, guides, etc attend the ceremony or healing you're performing to oversee the magic you're bringing to pass.

**Jerry Hicks:** ("Abraham" 1927-2011) Law of Attraction and empowerment teacher and author. He worked side by side his wife Esther Hicks until he passed in 2011. Known for the book called, *"Learning to Attract Health, Wealth and Happiness"* (2007).

**Kabbalah:** A deep esoteric system based on Jewish mysticism. It is the basis for many western religions, magical traditions including the Golden Dawn. It is spelled a number of different ways including,

Qabalah, Cabala, Kabalah etc. Kabbalah provides the basic teachings of the Tree of Life which is used in the Ruach Healing Method.

**Kerubic Symbol:** The fixed signs that govern the middle month of each season. The four Kerubs of the gospel represent the living powers of the Tetragrammaton in each symbol. The Kerubic Symbol operates through the fixed signs of the Zodiac.

| KERUBIC SYMBOL | KERUB | ZODIAC SIGN |
| --- | --- | --- |
| Fire | Lion | Leo |
| Air | Man | Aquarius |
| Earth | Bull | Taurus |
| Water | Eagle | Scorpio |

**Kether:** The highest and first Sephira on the Tree of Life. It literally means “crown”. The color is white.

**Kinesiology:** (Applied Kinesiology) is a muscle testing technique used in the Ruach Healing Method to aid the healer in diagnosing illness or choosing treatment.

**Kundalini:** Energy that flows up the base of the spine. Raising Kundalini is part of Eastern practice, usually under the guidance of a trained instructor, as kundalini activation can be dangerous to the physical body. Kundalini can be used to heal the body and refine the lower body energies so that they are in alignment with the higher spiritual centers. Sometimes raising Kundalini can create illness in those who are not ready to access it, or have a clogged energy field. Kundalini and other forms of yoga are a separate system(s) from Ruach Healing, yet Ruach Healers are sometimes asked to heal those whose spiritual path and/or studies may be quite distinct from their own background.

**L.B.R.P.:** See Lesser Banishing Ritual of the Pentagram.

**L.D.H.:** See Long Distance Healing.

**Lesser Banishing Ritual of the Pentagram, L.B.R.P.:** An effective ritual for blocking out negative energy and unwanted lower vibrational forces. Very powerful for neutralizing a space as well as balancing the person performing the ritual.

**Light:** The creative force in the universe that emanates from Source. It is the primary source of all healing. *"The Light hath healing in its wings."* Golden Dawn Initiation.

**Long Distance Healing, L.D.H:** The process of a healer sending healing to a patient that is not in the same location as the healer.

**Macrocosm:** The entire, whole structure, of a substance contrasted with a small representative part of it. Usually used in reference to the world or universe.

**Malkuth:** The tenth and lowest Sephira on the Tree of Life. It literally means “kingdom”. The color is brown earth-tones. Malkuth can be split quarterly into, specifically citrine, scarlet, olive, and black.

**Mathers, S.L. MacGregor:** (January 1854 – November 1918) A co-founder of the Golden Dawn. Mathers was the guiding light of the Order until revolt and schism took place. The last years of his life were spent working in an ambulance in WWI where he could use his magical skills to help facilitate healing. Perhaps the very first Ruach Healer.

**Michael:** Archangel of the element of Fire. He dresses in a scarlet red robe with green highlights. He is holding a flaming sword. Stands in the South in the L.B.R.P.

**Microcosm:** Something, such as a community, place, or situation that is regarded as a miniature version or something large. The miniature version encapsulates all the characteristic, qualities and features of larger version.

**Middle Pillar:** The center pillar of Sephirot on the Tree of Life. It is called the Pillar of Mildness. Also an exercise to invoke healing light into the sphere of sensation and the physical body.

**Navel Gate:** The paddle wheel like center located about two inches below the belly button. The color is a light orange tint. Responsible for the digestive system of the body.

**Netzach:** The seventh Sephira on the Tree of Life. It literally means "victory". The color is emerald.

**Notarikon:** A method taught in the literal Kabbalah that works with acronyms and abbreviations to create new words that often have a deep esoteric or magical meaning.

**Order of the Golden Dawn, Esoteric; E.O.G.D.:** An esoteric school that thoroughly trains initiates to learn ceremonial magic and advance on their spiritual path. It is mainly connected with Western European and Celtic occult traditions with homage to Egyptian and Grecian mysteries, Hermetics, metaphysics, alchemy, and Rosicrucian magic. The Order of the Golden still is thriving. The Esoteric Order of the Golden Dawn welcomes new members who are sincerely devoted to working with Divine light; if you prefer perhaps you perceive Divinity simply as the forces of goodness in the world. The order welcomes people who are ready to grow in their knowledge, are prepared to use knowledge responsibly, and are committed to having integrity on their path. The reason why most of the secret knowledge and techniques, preserved by the Esoteric Order of the Golden Dawn, have been carefully guarded, and continue to be carefully protected, is because magic in the wrong hands can be dangerous. It should only be used by those who are sincerely committed to serving God, our Divine Creator, to the utmost excellent level of their ability, intelligence and love. If you have found this book, you are likely being Divinely guided to join the order. Talented magicians of integrity are often called to join the Esoteric Order of The Golden Dawn by angels and other helper spirits in higher dimensions. Sometimes those that are seeking are drawn to the E.O.G.D from bonds in the past. Magicians usually share a kindred sense of fellowship and genuine enthusiasm and care about the magical work. If you are a very young person, such as under 18 years old, you may feel that Ruach Healing is the perfect place for you to begin your path before advancing into ceremonial magic and rituals. The irony is that even most people under 21 are far too immature to do magic or seek to join for the wrong reasons. Yet there are people who were magicians or perhaps healers in past lives who are simply 'called' to join. These special souls may be ready to do magic from an extremely young age, such as 12 or 13, even though an example of such an initiate would be quite rare. So, with the permission of the parents, initiation is decided on a case by case basis because the adepts don't want to exclude truly sincere students who are ready and mature enough to do the work. All students are assigned at least one mentor.

**Orgone:** A word invented by Dr. Wilhelm Reich to explain universal life force. Essentially the same as Ruach, Prana, or Chi.

**Pentagram:** A powerful geometric symbol that intertwines the four elements and spirit together in perfect balance and harmony. Used in the pentagram ritual as a blue gas flame.

**Pentagrammaton:** The constructed name of Jesus from Hebrew letters. These letter are the letters of the Tetragrammaton with the letter Shin added. Shin is the letter of the Holy Spirit. This name is YHShVH, pronounced *Yeh-hah-shu-ah*. The name is often written Yeheshua.

**Pillar of Mercy:** When looking at the Tree of Life the right row of Sephirot on the Tree. It is also the masculine pillar.

**Pillar of Mildness:** See Middle Pillar

**Pillar of Severity:** When looking at the Tree of Life the left row of Sephirot on the Tree. It is also the feminine pillar.

**Primum Mobile:** The outermost empty sphere in the Ptolemaic system that was thought to revolve around the earth from east to west in 24 hours carrying with it the inner spheres of the planets, sun, moon, and fixed stars. Also know as the Zodiac. Chokmah is a representation of Primum Mobile.

**Raphael:** Archangel of the element of Air. He dresses in a yellow robe which has purple highlights. He carries a Caduceus Wand (the symbol used by doctors, a wand entwined by serpents, which represents the life force). Stands in the East in the L.B.R.P.

**Regardie, Israel:** (November 17, 1907 – March 10, 1985) Also known as Francis Israel Regardie. He was an occultist, a writer, and Aleister Crowley's personal secretary and transcriber, known for his books and commentaries on the Hermetic Order of the Golden Dawn, he was never actually initiated into the Golden Dawn, but rather an offshoot. He is also the creator of the Middle Pillar exercise which is taught in this book.

**Reiki:** A healing technique based on the principle that the Reiki Practitioner can channel energy into the patient by means of touch, to activate the natural healing processes of the patient's body and restore physical and emotional well-being.

**Rosicrucian:** An adept (magician and healer) who works with the Rose Cross symbols. Most of the work pertains to healing, and magic which heals. Rosicrucian magic, which draws on esoteric Christian beliefs, spiritual methods, healing work, and some Hebrew esoteric knowledge, is powerfully protective. This magic is a very gentle, glowing with exquisitely beautiful energy. Rosicrucians are not surprised when they find that thier work is guided by Jesus Christ Himself. Some healers are able to see and feel His Spirit very strongly while working with Rosicrucian magic.

**Ruach:** Life Force. Explained in detail in Chapter 2 of this book.

**Scanning:** A technique used in the Ruach Healing Method to feel the patients aura or energy field. This allows the healer to detect imbalances in the energy field of the patient and possible illness.

**Sephira (singular), Sephirot (plural):** Levels of consciousness and energy on the Tree of Life, depicted as circles with connecting pathways on the Tree. Also these are ten distinct emanations of the Divine.

**Shekinah:** The glory of the divine presence represented as the feminine principles of Deity.

**Shema:** The Jews' most sacred verse of the Torah that depicts the unity or oneness of Divine Singularity. It reads, *"Here oh Israel the Lord our God the Lord is one"* (Deuteronomy 6:4).

**Shemhamphorasch:** The 72 Holy Angels of the Kabbalah. These Angels are taught to the Adept Master Teacher Ruach Healer. Shemhamphorash is originally a Tannaitic term describing a hidden name of God in Kabbalah.

**Solar Plexus Gate:** The paddle wheel like center located at the solar plexus. The color is a light yellow tint. Responsible for the liver and kidneys.

**Sphere of Sensation:** The aura and energy field of the body that responses to stimuli sending messages to the physical body.

**Tetragrammaton:** The unpronounceable name of God. In Hebrew it is transliterated in four letters as YHWH, pronounced *Yod-Heh-Vav Heh.*

**Third Eye Gate:** The paddle wheel like center located at the spot between your eyes on your forehead which moves energy in and out of the body. The color is a light violet tint. Responsible for physical sight, the Pituitary Gland, and intuition.

**Thoth's Beak:** A Ruach Healing Hand position for charging. The Beak of Thoth gets its name because the hand position looks like the beak of an Ibis, the sacred bird of Thoth to the ancient Egyptians. The beak of Thoth focuses all of the elemental energies under the direction of Spirit into a laser like ray. There is nothing else like it. It is extremely powerful for situations where a small but focused ray of healing energy in required.

**Throat Gate:** The paddle wheel like center located at the throat which moves energy in and out of the body. The color is a light blue tint. Responsible for energy transit from the lower body to the higher mind, represented in sound and speech.

**Tiphareth:** The sixth Sephira on the Tree of Life. It literally means "beauty". The color is yellow.

**Veils of Negative Existence:** A group of three areas above Kether on the Tree of Life that describes the nature of Deity. **Ain** is first veil, **Ain Soph** is second veil and **Ain Soph Aur** is the third veil. These are drawn as three half circles above Kether.

**Vitality Gates:** Seven centers of spiritual power in the human body similar to the chakras. They differ from charkras in that the gate is a paddle wheel moving energy in *and* out of the body rather than a vortex. The first gate is located at the base of the spine with the last gate on the top of the head.

**Vitality Rays:** Rays of light emanating from the aura, or energy field, beginning deep in the core of the being and extending out to the perimeter of the aura.

**Waddles, Wallace:** (1860–1911) An American author. As a New Thought writer, his writings have been an inspiration to many who study the science of the Law of Attraction. His writings have been widely quoted and remain in print to serve the New Thought and self-help movements. Wattles' best known work is a 1910 book called *"The Science of Getting Rich"* in which he explained how to become wealthy.

**Yesod:** The ninth Sephira on the Tree of Life. It literally means "foundation". The color is purple.

**YHVH:** The proper name of the God of Israel. Pronounced *Yod-Heh-Vav-Heh.* Also know as the Tetragrammaton.

## NOTES:

# BIBLIOGRAPHY

Arundale, George S.. *Kundalini: an occult experience*. Adyar, Madras, India: Theosophical Pub. House ;, 1938. Print.

Bartlett, Richard. *Matrix energetics: the science and art of transformation*. New York: Atria Books ;, 2007. Print.

Berg, Philip S.. *The wheels of a soul: reincarnation, your life today--and tomorrow*. Jerusalem: Research Centre of Kabbalah, 1984. Print.

Brennan, Barbara Ann. *Hands of light: a guide to healing through the human energy field : a new paradigm for the human being in health, relationship, and disease*. Toronto: Bantam Books, 19881987. Print.

Butler, W. E.. *How to read the aura and practice psychometry, telepathy, & clairvoyance*. Rochester, Vt.: Destiny Books, 1998. Print.

Byrne, Rhonda. *The secret*. New York: Atria Books ;, 2006. Print.

Byrne, Rhonda. *The secret*. New York: Atria Books ;, 2006. Print.

Emoto, Masaru. *The secret life of water*. New York: Atria Books ;, 2005. Print.

Fuentes, Starr. *Healing with energy: the definitive guide to hands-on technique from a master.* Franklin Lakes, N.J.: New Page Books, 2007. Print.

Hawkins, David R.. *Power versus force: an anatomy of consciousness : the hidden determinants of human behavior.* Sedona, Ariz.: Veritas, 1998. Print.

Hicks, Esther, and Jerry Hicks. *Money, and the law of attraction: learning to attract wealth, health, and happiness*. Carlsbad, Calif.: Hay House, 2008. Print.

Hill, Napoleon. *Think and grow rich original 1937 edition*. S.l.: Duke Classics, 2012. Print.

Kilner, Walter John. *The human aura*. New Hyde Park, N.Y.: University Books, 1965. Print.

Kraig, Donald Michael. *Modern magick: eleven lessons in the high magickal art*. St. Paul, Minn.: Llewellyn Publications, 1988. Print. One of the best books for learning the basics of ceremonial magic.

Leadbeater, C. W.. *The chakras; a monograph.*. Wheaton, Ill.: Theosophical Pub. House, 19721927. Print.

Martin, Barbara Y., and Dimitri Moraitis. *The healing power of your aura: how to use spiritual energy for physical health and well-being*. Sunland, CA: Spiritual Arts Institute, 2006. Print.

PonceÌ$, Charles. *Kabbalah; an introduction and illumination for the world today.*. San Francisco: [Straight Arrow Books; distributed by Quick Fox Inc.], 1973. Print. One of my favorite books for an introduction to Kabbalah.

Powell, Arthur Edward. *The astral body and other astral phenomena,*. Wheaton, Ill.: Theosophical Pub. House, 19731965. Print.

Regardie, Israel. *The art of true healing; a treatise on the mechanism of prayer, and the operation of the law of attraction in nature.*. Toddington, Eng.: [Helios Book Service], 1964. Print.

Regardie, Israel, Cris Monnastre, and Carl Llewellyn Weschcke. *The Golden Dawn: a complete course in practical ceremonial magic : the original account of the teachings, rites, and ceremonies of the Hermetic Order of the Golden Dawn (Stella Matutina)*. 6th ed. St. Paul, Minn., U.S.A.: Llewellyn Publications, 1989. Print.

Regardie, Israel, and Mark Allen. *The art of true healing the unlimited power of prayer and visualization*. Novato, Calif.: New World Library, 1997. Print.

Regardie, Israel, and Mark Allen. *The art of true healing: the unlimited power of prayer and visualization*. Novato, Calif.: New World Library, 1997. Print.

Regardie, Israel, Chic Cicero, and Sandra Tabatha Cicero. *The middle pillar: the balance between mind and magic*. 3rd ed. St. Paul, Minn.: Llewellyn Publications, 1998. Print.

Reich, Wilhelm. *The discovery of the orgone: Vol. 1: The function of the orgasm : sex-economic problems of biological energy*. 2. ed. New York: Orgone Institute Press, 1948. Print.

Reich, Wilhelm. *Character analysis*. 3d, enl. ed. New York: Farrar, Straus and Giroux, 1972. Print.

Samuel, Gabriella. *The Kabbalah handbook: a concise encyclopedia of terms and concepts in Jewish mysticism*. New York: Jeremy P. Tarcher/Penguin, 2007. Print.

Steiner, Rudolf, and Robert A. McDermott. *The essential Steiner: basic writings of Rudolf Steiner*. San Francisco: Harper & Row, 1984. Print.

Sui, Choa Kok. *Pranic healing*. York Beach, Me.: S. Weiser, 1990. Print.

*The Book of formation: Sepher Yetzirah*. London: W. Rider, 1923. Print.

*The Kyballion: a study of the hermetic philosophy of ancient Egypt and Greece*. Chicago: Yogi publication Society, 1908. Print.

*The emerald tablet of Hermes: multiple translations.*. Whitefish, Mont.: Kessinger Pub., 2004. Print.

*The science of breath and the Philosophy of the Tatwas: (translated from the Sanskrit) with fifteen introductory & explanatory essays on Nature's finer forces (eight re-printed from "The Theosophist," with modifications, and seven new)*. London: Theosophical Pub. Society ;, 1890. Print.

Vitale, Joe. *The attractor factor: 5 easy steps for creating wealth (or anything else) from the inside out*. Hoboken, N.J.: J. Wiley, 2005. Print.

Wattles, Wallace Delois. *The science of getting rich*. Waiheke Island: Floating Press, 2008. Print.

Wolfram, E.. *The occult causes of disease: being a compendium of the teachings of Paracelsus*. Whitefish, MT: Kessinger, 2005. Print.

Zalewski, Patrick J., and Joseph Lisiewski. *The secret inner order rituals of the Golden Dawn*. Phoenix, AZ: Falcon Press, 1988. Print.

# ADDITIONAL RESOURCES FROM LAW OF ATTRACTION SOLUTIONS, LLC.

**The Ruach Healing: Rhythms of Light** is specially created by mystical, music Light-workers under the direction of Robert Zink. These musical tools are especially created for Ruach Healers, Reiki and Pranic Healers. You will learn how you can dramatically increase your healing results.

Empower you life with the **Power of Angels**. You will make astonishing contact with angelic beings, receiving powerful aid and incredible life blessings. Angels have almost limitless power to change your life. Discover how easy it is for you to tap into the power of angels.

Experience your full potential – get out of your body with **Astral Fire**! When out of our egos and bodies, our potential is virtually unlimited. Did you know that Einstein traveled astrally on a beam of light to help him create his theory of relativity? Astral Fire is 2-CD set teaches perhaps the most effective method for anyone who wants to astral travel and employ increased mind power during the out-of-body experience.

Several years ago I began healing work on a woman with stage 4 terminal lymphatic cancer. After several months of intensive healing work, her oncologist was shocked to discover that she had no signs of cancer. During this experience I uncovered **Seven Secrets of a Mystical Healer**.

ATTENTION: Light workers **Angels in Your Dreams** is for you. As you sleep, you will receive guidance, blessings and empowerment from these astonishing being of light. Learn how easy it is to uplift every area of your life from the spiritual to the financial. Angels in Your Dreams will have you beginning each morning with light, power, joy, healing and happiness. Why not put your sleeping hours to use by empowering your life with angels in your dreams?

Now you can connect with the four archangels on a level never before imagined outside the walls of a true mystery school. **Invoking the Power & Presence of the Four Archangels** focuses the four Archangels of light and will take you to new heights. Learn how to accomplish incredible connections that are completely your own.

**All of these *incredible* programs and MORE are available at www.lawofattractionsolutions.com as instantly downloadable MP3s.**

Made in the USA
Columbia, SC
24 February 2022